Flash Multiplayer Virtual Worlds

Build immersive, full featured interactive worlds for games, online communities, and more

Makzan

PUBLISHING

BIRMINGHAM - MUMBAI

Flash Multiplayer Virtual Worlds

First published: August 2010

Production Reference: 1100810

Published by Packt Publishing Ltd.
32 Lincoln Road
Olton
Birmingham, B27 6PA, UK

ISBN 978-1-849690-36-2

www.packtpub.com

Cover Image by Vinayak Chittar (vinayak.chittar@gmail.com)

Credits

Author
Makzan

Reviewers
David Crebbin

Prashanth Hirematada

Sergey Suchok

Acquisition Editor
David Barnes

Development Editor
Reshma Sundareshan

Technical Editor
Rukhsana Khambatta

Copy Editor
Sanchari Mukherjee

Indexer
Monica Ajmera Mehta

Editorial Team Leader
Gagandeep Singh

Project Team Leader
Priya Mukherji

Project Coordinator
Ashwin Shetty

Proofreader
Lynda Sliwoski

Graphics Coordinator
Nilesh R. Mohite

Geetanjali Sawant

Production Coordinator
Adline Swetha Jesuthas

Cover Work
Adline Swetha Jesuthas

About the Author

Makzan is a game designer working in Macao and Hong Kong, China.

He started as a web designer and met Flash 4 in 2000. He won a bronze medal in WorldSkills for Web Designing and later became the expert of Macao in this competition.

He has interest in creating games and often explores different ways to implement his game ideas such as making Flash games on Wii, mobile games on iPhone, and social games on Facebook.

Since 2003, Makzan started making multiplayer Flash games with different server solutions. He tried most existing multiplayer game solutions until discovering SmartFoxServer.

I would like to thank the following groups of people for all their efforts. The book would not be possible without the help from the Editors, Reviewers, Proofreaders, and the Project Coordinators. I thank all the reviewers for providing very useful comments from which I have learnt a lot. I thank David, my Acquisition Editor, for inspiring me on the book's ideas. I thank Reshma, my Development Editor, for revising my chapters and helping me in writing them. I thank Ashwin, the Project Coordinator, for the great cooperation while delivering the chapters. I thank Rukhsana, the Technical Editor, for helping me on revising chapters. I thank Kelvin Fong for drawing the graphics of the code examples. I thank again all the people who have worked on this book. Thank you.

About the Reviewers

David Crebbin has spent most of his working life developing and architecting client-side applications, with the vast majority of his projects utilizing ActionScript. He's a firm believer in the technology and what it can offer, along with its amazingly creative developer community. He has used the Flash platform to build both small and large scale applications covering e-learning, gaming, and television.

Prashanth Hirematada is the founder of Gamantra, a game technology company focused on Network engine and server platform. Prior to founding Gamantra in 2006, he was a Chief Architect at Shanda Interactive Entertainment Ltd., where he was responsible for creating a common game development platform for all MMOG initiatives at Shanda. He joined Shanda in 2004 through Shanda's acquisition of Zona, Inc., a MMOG game technology company, headquartered in Santa Clara, U.S.A. At Zona, as a Technical Chief Architect, he was responsible for server-side architecture and implementation of MMOG framework. Prior to joining Zona in 2001, Prashanth worked in various Silicon Valley based technology start-up companies developing software at various levels for well over seven years.

His Master's thesis was a distributed implementation of the Message Passing Library (MPI) on a heterogeneous network of workstations including Solaris, HP-UX, OpenStep, and Windows-NT. He received his M.S. in Computer Science from California State University, Sacramento, California, in 1994 and his B.S. in Computer Science from Bangalore University, Bangalore, India in 1992. He can be contacted at prash@gamantra.com.

Sergey Suchok graduated in 2004 with honors from the Faculty of Cybernetics, Taras Shevchenko National University of Kyiv (Ukraine) and has since then been keen on Information Technology. He is currently working in the banking area and prepares to defend his thesis on the modeling of banking operations. Sergey is the co-author of more than 40 articles and has participated in more than 20 scientific and practical conferences devoted to the economic and mathematical modeling. He is a member of the "New Atlantis" Youth Public Organization (newatlantida.org.ua) and devotes his leisure time to environmental protection issues, the historical and patriotic development and popularization of a grateful attitude toward the Earth. He is also developing a social network for Kombucha's owners called Latusho, and he writes poetry and short stories and makes macramé.

I would like to express gratitude to the author for this opportunity to improve my knowledge of game development, as well as to Packt Publishing for providing such an interesting experience in the review process.

Table of Contents

Preface

Back in the late 1970s, digital virtual world and multiuser adventure games, MUDs, made their debut. At the time Internet reached the masses and got popular in 1990s, **Massively Multiplayer Online Games**, **MMOGs**, became the new market that every game company was eager to get into. Players download or buy discs to install the online virtual world. The world gives players a virtual personality and they can play and interact with each other to finish tasks.

Being a multimedia and interaction platform, Adobe Flash introduced socket connection support to Flash player. The socket connection allows Flash player to connect persistently to a socket server and provide the opportunity for multiple user Flash applications. In other words, socket connection makes it possible to create a Flash online virtual world.

Compared to the traditional multiplayer online games, Flash online virtual worlds are browser-based and do not need any installation (except the Flash player plugin). They allow players to quickly play the virtual world game just like browsing a web page. The convenience fits the nature of Internet and thus can reach a larger variety of potential players.

Thanks to the quick evolution of socket networking service during these years, Flash online virtual worlds are becoming a trend. Every day users log into social networking sites and play with friends on their virtual farms or virtual towns.

With this book, we will have a step-by-step guide to create our own Flash virtual world from scratch. We will discuss several essential parts of creating a Flash virtual world and integrating it into social networking services. At last, we will have a look on how to deploy and operate our virtual world in production and earn money from it.

What this book covers

Chapter 1, Developing Flash Virtual World, discusses the benefit of developing a Flash virtual world. It also discusses different connection methods between Flash clients and compares different server solutions. You will also get introduced to the common features in a Flash virtual world such as avatar, home, items, quests, non-player characters, and others. You will also know about some existing virtual world games such as Club Penguin, Mole, Dofus, and World of Warcraft.

Chapter 2, Installing The Servers, develops and deploys a virtual world environment. You will also install the Java Development Kit and SmartFoxServer, connect it with MySQL server and configure the server settings. You will then load a simple chat application and set up and log in to the administration panel.

Chapter 3, Getting Familiar with SmartFoxServer, configures a Basic SmartFoxServer and discusses how to set up the Flash player to view the Flash trace log without the Flash IDE. You will also see how we can prevent the Flash loading data or connect sockets to other resources that are not in the same domain of the hosting server by using the Flash player's inbuilt security sandbox. You will also create a Flash document to connect the server and finally, create a whiteboard that every connected user can draw on and test it.

Chapter 4, Creating Map and Ground in Isometric View, compares different game views, create an isometric map, and a ground for the virtual worlds. You will then build a Map Editor, which will be used later for development.

Chapter 5, Creating Avatars, designs an avatar and draws the avatar in Flash. You will then customize your avatar with different styles and colors. You will also design and create a customization panel and finally, integrate it to the SmartFoxServer.

Chapter 6, Walking Around the World, covers the different methods to move the avatar in the virtual world. You will code your first server-side extension and create the connectivity between Flash client and the database.

Chapter 7, Creating Buildings and Environments in the Virtual World, teaches you how to place a building on the Map and order the buildings while displaying them. You will also create a map editor for the buildings.

Chapter 8, Creating an Inventory System, classifies items in the virtual world and also discusses about avatars collecting items. You will also learn about defining the data structure of an inventory item and implementing an inventory and an item panel.

Chapter 9, Communicating with Other Players, discusses the various methods for communicating in the virtual world which includes chatting with public messages. You will also learn how to implement a buddy list, add players to it, and finally send messages to these players. You will also see how we can share items between players.

Chapter 10, Interacting With NPC, shows how we can run a virtual world smoothly by introducing non-player characters. You will place your first NPC and control its movements. You will see the different communication methods available for the NPC and how to trade items with the NPC.

Chapter 11, Designing Quests, introduces quests and how they can be triggered in a virtual world. You will set up server environments for quests and design quest panels. You will also see how you can encourage players to participate in quests by placing rewards and improving the quests.

Chapter 12, Social Community, discusses the benefits of having a social networking feature in your virtual world. This chapter will show you how to integrate with the Facebook and the Twitter platforms.

Chapter 13, Deploying and Maintaining Flash Virtual World, shows how you can host the virtual world and operate the virtual world. You will also see some methods to earn money from virtual world. You will also learn to transfer your virtual world to mobile and other platforms such as Apple iOS and .NET and Unity, among others.

What you need for this book

The software that are required for this book are SmartFoxServerPro_1.6.6, Adobe Flash CS4, and MySQL 5.1.

Who this book is for

If you are a Flash or an ActionScript developer who wants to build powerful and immersive multiplayer games, this book is for you. This book assumes that you have some experience with ActionScript 3.0.

Conventions

In this book, you will find a number of styles of text that distinguish between different kinds of information. Here are some examples of these styles, and an explanation of their meaning.

Code words in text are shown as follows: " We have an `npcLoop` function in server-side extension."

A block of code will be set as follows:

```
var javaExt = Packages.it.gotoandplay.smartfoxserver.extensions.
ExtensionHelper;
var helper = javaExt.instance();
var zone = helper.getZone("virtualWorld");
```

When we wish to draw your attention to a particular part of a code block, the relevant lines or items will be shown in bold:

```
res.list = [];
var holder = param.holder;
var sql = "SELECT * FROM quests WHERE holder='" + holder + "'";
var resultCount = getResultArray(sql, res.list);
```

Any command-line input or output is written as follows:

```
javac -version
```

New terms and **important words** are shown in bold. Words that you see on the screen, in menus or dialog boxes for example, appear in our text like this: "If it prompts for login, click on **Skip this Step** to bypass it."

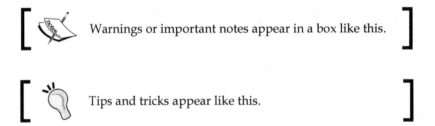

[Warnings or important notes appear in a box like this.]

[Tips and tricks appear like this.]

Reader feedback

Feedback from our readers is always welcome. Let us know what you think about this book—what you liked or may have disliked. Reader feedback is important for us to develop titles that you really get the most out of.

To send us general feedback, simply drop an e-mail to feedback@packtpub.com, and mention the book title in the subject of your message.

If there is a book that you need and would like to see us publish, please send us a note in the **SUGGEST A TITLE** form on www.packtpub.com or e-mail suggest@packtpub.com.

If there is a topic that you have expertise in and you are interested in either writing or contributing to a book, see our author guide on www.packtpub.com/authors.

Customer support

Now that you are the proud owner of a Packt book, we have a number of things to help you to get the most from your purchase.

Downloading the example code for this book

You can download the example code files for all Packt books you have purchased from your account at http://www. PacktPub.com. If you purchased this book elsewhere, you can visit http://www.PacktPub.com/support and register to have the files e-mailed directly to you.

Errata

Although we have taken every care to ensure the accuracy of our contents, mistakes do happen. If you find a mistake in one of our books—maybe a mistake in text or code—we would be grateful if you would report this to us. By doing so, you can save other readers from frustration, and help us to improve subsequent versions of this book. If you find any errata, please report them by visiting http://www.packtpub. com/support, selecting your book, clicking on the **errata submission form** link, and entering the details of your errata. Once your errata are verified, your submission will be accepted and the errata added to any list of existing errata. Any existing errata can be viewed by selecting your title from http://www.packtpub.com/support.

Piracy

Piracy of copyrighted material on the Internet is an ongoing problem across all media. At Packt, we take the protection of our copyright and licenses very seriously. If you come across any illegal copies of our works in any form on the Internet, please provide us with the location address or website name immediately so that we can pursue a remedy.

Please contact us at copyright@packtpub.com with a link to the suspected pirated material.

We appreciate your help in protecting our authors, and our ability to bring you valuable content.

Questions

You can contact us at questions@packtpub.com if you are having a problem with any aspect of the book, and we will do our best to address it.

1
Developing Flash Virtual World

Online game community has been popular for years. Recently many virtual worlds are Flash-based and can run directly in web browser. The latest Flash player 10 and ActionScript 3 gain a performance leap from older Flash player and ActionScript 2. The memory consumption is around 50 percent more and the script performance is around 10 times faster than ActionScript 2.

Thanks to the performance enhancement and the binary socket connectivity support of the latest ActionScript, building Flash virtual world is possible for even independent Flash developers.

In this chapter, we will discuss the benefit of developing Flash virtual world. We will also discuss different connection methods between Flash clients and compare different server solutions.

What is a virtual world?

A virtual world is a digital environment that is similar to real world. Many users can log in to the virtual world and walk around in a virtual city or interact with each other. They can interact with others in different ways such as collaborating, chatting, or playing together.

Let's see how virtual world is used in different areas.

Using virtual world for business

Virtual world connects users in real time so that they can socialize in this virtual environment. They can collaborate with others in an online meeting or virtual workspace. Users can even share their thoughts by Voice-over-IP chatting or whiteboarding.

MPK20 (`http://research.sun.com/projects/mc/mpk20.html`) is one of the virtual workspaces from Oracle, previously Sun. It facilitates several features to target business users. Users in MPK20 can join a briefing with a PDF presenting, join a group meeting or even drag in documents from a computer to share between users for discussion. The following screenshot shows the virtual workspace from MPK20:

Using virtual world for education

Students can play in a simulated reality environment in virtual world. In this environment, students are given some tasks to complete. They can collaborate with other students to complete the tasks assigned by teachers. The students may learn things by immersive learning when solving different missions inside the virtual world.

Using virtual world for game

People can play games with others in virtual world. They can play against other players in real-time battle or team up to play against the missions from the online game. They may also exchange items and establish relationships like in the real world.

The following screenshot is from an online game called Mini Fighter (`http://global.netmarble.com/minifighter/`). It is a virtual world where players can fight against a lot of players at the same time in a 2D horizontal environment.

Background

In the 70s, there was MUD. **MUD** stands for **Multi-User Dungeon** and it is a text-based virtual world that players connect to through Telnet. Players connect to the MUD and interact with others or the world by inputting commands. They get feedback and information from text description. Later in the 80s, some graphical virtual worlds based on MUD were released. They were actually MUD which changed the present method from text to graphic and from command input to GUI input.

Later, Ultima Online (`http://www.uoherald.com/`) and EverQuest (`http://www.everquest.com/`) brought multiplayer virtual worlds to a new level. World of Warcraft (`http://www.worldofwarcraft.com`) and Second Life (`http://secondlife.com/`) followed EverQuest and they all made the trend of online games and virtual worlds.

In recent years, Flash virtual world is becoming more popular. Many new virtual world communities released Flash-based instead of traditional installer-based. In the beginning, Flash virtual world is not mature due to the performance issue of Actionscript 1 and old Flash player. After the introduction of ActionScript 2 and ActionScript 3, the programming language has been enhanced and the performance of Flash player boosts to support better network connections and better graphics. This makes the spring of Flash virtual world.

Benefit of using Flash to build virtual world

Traditional installer-based games require users download an installer or they may even need to buy an installer disk in game shop in order to play the game. And the requirement of installing software means that users may not be able to play it wherever they want. For example, they may not have the privilege to install the software on a friend's computer or public computers.

A Flash player-based virtual world does not require downloading an installer. As long as the web browsers have the Flash player plugin that fulfills the required version, users can log in and play the whole game inside the web browser directly. Traditionally users go to the game website, download the game, install it, log in, and play it. Now with Flash player-based game, users go to the game website, log in, and play it. This simplifies the flow to start playing the game.

Moreover this will attract those first-time players. When someone is landing on the game website and finds the game quiet interesting, they are willing to give it a try. At this time, it will be much better if they can log in through the guest account and try the virtual world immediately instead of downloading a big installer and waiting half an hour before starting the game, as shown in the following screenshot (these are the screenshots of the welcome page of Club Penguin and MMOG):

Another benefit of using Flash is the seamless update of the client application. It is common that updates and patches ship to the existing users after releasing the virtual world. In traditional installer-based virtual worlds, users have to download an update client before launching the virtual world.

On the other hand, updates and patches usually mean a recompile of some SWF files on the web server. When users connect and load the virtual world, the web browser downloads the updated SWF files in the background and even without users' notice. This seamless update advantage lets developers deliver patches more easily and blur the whole update flow in users' view. The following screenshot shows virtual world data update loads automatically when a player logs in:

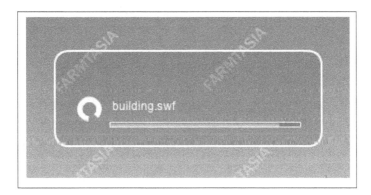

Connecting players in a virtual world

The core of a virtual world is multiplayer. Multiplayer means players need to connect to each other in order to interact in the virtual world. There are two main transport protocols in the Internet—TCP and UDP. We will have a brief discussion on them and then discuss the network model that connects computers.

A brief introduction to transport protocols

There are two main transport protocols that the computers use to deliver data from applications to the network and vice versa. They are **Transmission Control Protocol (TCP)** and **User Datagram Protocol (UDP)**.

There are some main differences between TCP and UDP:

TCP provides reliable communication with error detection and recovery. The data delivered by TCP is in segments that are in order. TCP is used in most applications that require accurate data delivery such as WWW, e-mail, and file transfer. Except the latest Flash Real-Time Media Flow Protocol, all Flash connections used the TCP protocol.

UDP, on the other hand, does not have error recovery and does not guarantee the data is delivered and the order may not be in sequence. However, UDP is so simple that the header size is much smaller than TCP. The small header size and missing error recovery lets UDP give shorter latency and higher throughput. Thus UDP is often used in multimedia broadcasting applications that require faster delivery and allow transfer error.

Peer-to-peer

Peer-to-peer network means every machine connects to the other machine in the same network. In this network, every peer node listens to the requests and provides results to each other.

Recently in the Flash player 10.1, Adobe introduced the **Real-Time Media Flow Protocol (RTMFP)** that supports peer-to-peer connections between Flash clients on top of the UDP protocol. The Flash clients can rely on the Adobe status server, which is in Beta now, to locate and authoricate the peers or directly locate peers in the same local network.

One advantage of peer-to-peer network is that there is not a master computer. Every machine in the network does the same task and thus there is no single point of failure in the network. The network application keeps working when any machine downs.

Another advantage of the peer-to-peer network is that the latency between two computers is half compared to the client-server model of communication. The computers are communicating to each other directly instead of delivering the message by another computer in middle.

Peer-to-peer network is useful for multiplayer applications or games that divide the users into small groups. They can benefit from the peer-to-peer approach that computers in group are communicating directly to their targets and the network bandwidth used in each group will not affect the others.

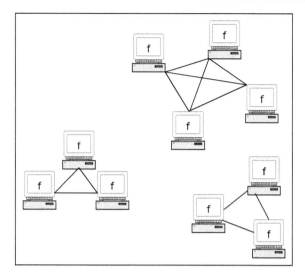

However, there are some disadvantages that make it not suitable to use in a virtual world with massive multiplayer.

As there is not an administrative machine, every machine is the same and they all need to have a copy of all logic and data in local. Users will have access to all critical data and can easily modify the data without validation. Hacked clients can send out altered messages to other peers to cheat them. This raises the security problem that the hacked clients can claim to have unlimited health points or claim that all attacks are missed.

Moreover, every machine establishes connection with each other. This make the number of connections grow quadratically with the increasing number of nodes. There are a total of 5050 connections when there are 100 machines in the network. What if there are 1000 machines and 50,000 connections? Imagine that there are 100 players now in the virtual world and all 100 players are doing different tasks and then broadcasting to each other in every second. The whole network will be overloaded.

Another disadvantage is that the connectionless characteristics of UDP may make peer-to-peer connections fail on computers that are behind a firewall or NAT. The following diagram shows the peer-to-peer architecture:

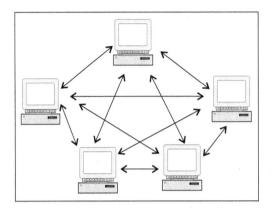

Client-server network

Client-server network means there is a centralized server and every machine connects to this server. The server computes requests from client machines and provides results to client machines that need the results. What clients do is just send a request to the server and display the results. There can be few or even no logic in client side.

This network is usually used in virtual world because there are only N connections between N clients and the security is enhanced as most critical logic and data is in the server so that users cannot modify it themselves.

Take the previous 100 machines in *Peer-to-peer* section as an example. There are 100 players in the virtual world with the server-client machine now. When one player sends a broadcast message to tell others, the message was sent to the server and the server distributes the messages to all other 99 machines. The following diagram shows client-server architecture:

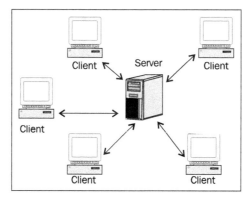

Clients need to keep communicating with the server to keep the whole virtual world synchronized among clients. There are two methods to keep the communication with the server — polling and socket-based.

Polling

Polling refers to the activity wherein the clients keep asking the server for updated status in an interval. It is usually used in multiplayer applications that do not have persistence connections. It could be a PHP chat application or chess game played by two players.

The implementation of this method is easy and thus may be used by developers who are new to multiplayer applications. However, we should not use this approach in Flash. Instead we should use the socket connection from Flash to establish persistent connections to the server.

In the polling approach, clients need to keep asking the server for an update even when there are no updates most of the time. This wastes a lot of bandwidth and greatly increases the server loading. It is a bad practice to use polling in massive multiplayer applications and we should avoid it throughout the development of the virtual world.

Take an example of how a turn-based Tic-Tac-Toe with polling performs poorly.

When two players connect to the server and are ready to start playing tic-tac-toe together, player A is thinking where to put an "X" on the board. When player B is waiting, his machine asks the server if there are any updates from other players per second. After a while, player A put an "X" in the middle of the board. Next when client B is asking the server, the server tells client B that there is an "X" in the middle now. Client B renders the "X" and now it is the turn of player B. The following figure shows polling in Tic-Tac-Toe:

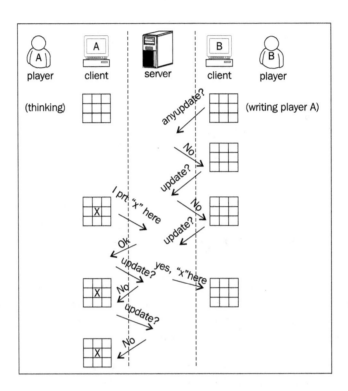

During this process, client B keeps sending messages to the server and the server keeps responding to client B just to tell it that nothing happened. This dramatically increases the network loading and server loading. And this is just a two-players example. What if there are eight other players watching this game as spectators? Every player sends a message to the server and get a response message from the server in every second. Imagine there are 100 rooms and 10 players in each room. Now we are talking about 1000 messages per second just for asking the server if there is any update.

Moreover, there is an update latency problem in polling. When player A updates the board, player B knows the update from player A next time when his machine asks the server. This latency depends on the polling interval. A short interval improves the latency problem while putting more load on the server and network. A long interval with large latency makes it unacceptable for real-time interaction between players.

Another disadvantage of polling is the bad scalability. A server needs to keep responding to the polling clients that use relatively lots of system resources. This results in the server only being capable for a few concurrent connections. Usually a polling server supports up to 300 concurrent connections. I had an experience on creating a Flash multiplayer virtual world with .Net web service backend. Due to the limitation of the server, I had to use the polling approach and it would end up supporting less than 200 concurrent players.

The low concurrent players capacity of a server means it needs many servers to handle massive players' connections at the same time and makes it difficult to manage.

Therefore, polling may be suitable for very small-scale networks and it should be avoided in Flash virtual world.

Socket-based connection

In contrast to polling, a socket-based connection establishes persistent connections to the server. The server sends messages to clients only when it needs and vice versa. There are no more redundant messages such as a client asking the server if there is any update because server will push updates to clients without clients initializing the requests. This is also known as asynchronous socket or event-driven socket.

Take the same Tic-Tac-Toe example with the socket-based implementation. The following diagram illustrates the data flow between player A, B, and the server. There are only three messages in the whole process, player A communicates to the server to put an "X" on the board, player B renders the "X", and a successful acknowledgment of the server to player A. If there are eight spectators in the game, only around 11 messages will be sent to the network in this period instead of 18 messages per second. The following diagram shows event-driven Tic-Tac-Toe:

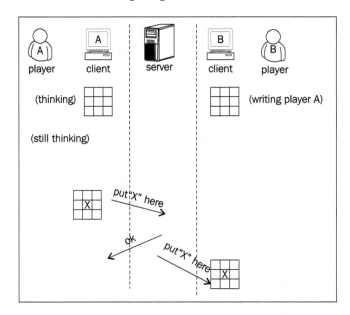

The event-driven socket-based connection eliminates the polling interval latency. The very low server loading enables almost real-time communication between players for which the latency only depends on the client's and server's Internet connections.

It also allows more concurrent players than the polling architecture and is therefore easier to scale. Normally a socket server can handle thousands of concurrent connections.

Socket server

Socket server for virtual world is an event-driven server application that handles clients' connections and manages the communication between clients.

When a user starts up and connects to the virtual world, the machine that the user uses is a client. The place where the client machine connects to is the server. The server can be one single powerful computer or a cluster of networked computers interconnected within a high-speed local network. The purpose of the socket server is to manage all client's connections and provide centralized logic and control to clients. It may also respond to provide and store persistent information for the virtual world such as user profiles or world state.

Unlike developing an offline single player game where all logic and data are placed in a SWF file, logic and data are distributed into different places in a virtual world.

Most critical game logic, such as business logic that handles virtual money transaction, is located in the server to enhance the security. The server is also responsible to handle all users' actions and behavior, and provides each user the information they need.

On the other hand, clients are in-charge to display the virtual world according to the client-side data and latest data that updates from server-side. Client-side data includes terrain, map, UI, and basic logic.

For example, imagine that there is a player standing in front of a fountain and you can see him in the virtual world. It is the client that renders the fountain sight according to your current position. And the client gets an updated message from the server that there is another player standing in front of the fountain and renders this player. The clients also gets the appearance of that player from the server in order to render it.

Available socket servers for Flash

There are several socket servers on the market that fit the development of Flash virtual world. Some are good at media streaming while some are powerful on user management.

SmartFoxServer

SmartFoxServer (`http://smartfoxserver.com/`) was developed by **gotoAndPlay()**. It is a socket server for Flash that provides powerful tools and resource management to enable highly productive development of virtual worlds and multiplayer games.

It was designed for Flash originally and now it also provides a set of API for iPhone, .Net, Java, Silverlight, and even Ajax. It also supports media streaming function by embedded open source Flash media server called Red5.

It also supports clustering through terracotta, an open source clustering software. The logic is distributed into clustered servers and enables the ability to extend the scalability and enhances the failure resiliency. The server comes with fully-documented resources with lots of tutorials for beginners. There is also an active forum to get support.

SmartFoxServer provides different licenses and connection options for developers. It provides Lite, Basic, and Pro options with maximum connections from 100 to unlimited. The Lite version is free with maximum 50 concurrent connections and Basic or Pro version are free for up to 20 concurrent connections. Also the Pro version provides an add-on module called BlueBox (`http://smartfoxserver.com/products/blueBox.php`) to allow connection behind firewalls and proxies via HTTP-tunneling.

However, it will be a little expensive as the server costs $2000 Euros for SmartFoxServer Pro and $400 Euros for the BlueBox add-on with unlimited connections.

ElectroServer

ElectroServer (`http://www.electro-server.com/`) is another mature virtual world server for Flash that was developed by Electrotank in 2001. Similar to SmartFoxServer, ElectroServer provides powerful tools and fits the development of Flash virtual world server.

ElectroServer also provides scalability by load balancing with multiple gateway servers. The gateway servers are used to handle the clients' connections I/O and the logic is kept in one server. ElectroServer also provides media streaming features.

There are two packages with different media connections and concurrent player options available. The costs of ElectroServer can be expensive. Prices start from $700 to $72K depending on the package option. The professional version is free up to 25 concurrent connections.

Flash Media Interactive Server

Flash Media Interactive Server (`http://www.adobe.com/products/flashmediainteractive/`) was developed by Adobe and aims to provide video streaming and real-time communication between different Flash player clients. Flash Media Interactive Server mainly targets real-time streaming and communicating technology that can stream videos with different popular codec and live stream. It supports features such as server-side ActionScript extension and server-side shared objects to make it possible for virtual world development.

This server provides clustering by edge/origin load balancing. Logic is kept in the origin server and clients connect to different edge servers, then edge servers connect to the origin server. It is like the gateway approach from ElectroServer.

However, the lack of game room management and game-related features means that developers have to write their own game management scripts.

Flash Media Interactive Server costs $4500 for unlimited connections.

Red5

Red5 (`http://red5.org/`) is one of the open source Flash socket servers that provides basic server-side features such as real-time protocol and shared memory. It aims to become an open source alternative of Flash Media Interactive Server and thus it is more powerful on video streaming than virtual world resources management.

Red5 uses edge/origin clustering that is similar to the Flash Media Interactive Server while using the open source Terracotta solution.

As an alternative of Flash Media Server, it also lacks server-side game management features. However, as it is open source, you can extend the functionality of Red5 to fit your idea of the virtual world.

Writing your own socket server

Most Flash servers in the market provide extensibility for developers. However, available servers may not fit your budget or design ideas. As an alternative solution, you can program your own socket server to handle Flash connections. The socket server is usually written in C++ or Java. What a virtual world server does is handle all connections and manage all zone, room, and user resources via a predefined protocol. There are some resources from Internet that discuss how to develop a socket server. There is an old article (`http://gotoandplay.it/_articles/2003/12/xmlSocket.php`) from gotoAndPlay() that introduced the basic concept of implementing a socket server that connects Flash. Although the article used an old version of Flash and the XML socket instead of the binary socket, it is a good starting point to learn the concept before developing the socket server. In a real case, two friends of mine implemented a Flash server in Java for one year and now they are working on several multiplayer games in it.

Choosing the right server

	SmartFox Server 1.6	ElectroServer 4	Flash Media Server 3.5	Red5 0.9
Virtual world architecture (Zoon/Room)	Very good	Very good	Bad	Bad
Media Streaming	Good	Good	Very good	Good
Supports Client	Flash, iPhone, JAVA, Unity, .Net	Flash	Flash	Flash
Connections for development	20	25	10	Unlimited
Maximum Connections	Unlimited	200,000	Unlimited	Unlimited
Clustering	Logic distributed without single-point failure clustering	Gateway approach with logic in one server	Gateway approach with logic in one server	Gateway approach with logic in one server
Firewall Traversal	BlueBox HTTP-tunneling	HTTP-tunneling	RTMPT HTTP-tunneling	RTMPT HTTP-tunneling
Cost	Average	Average to expensive	Expensive	Free

Either SmartfoxServer or ElectroServer fits the development of virtual world the most. They all provide solid zone, room, and user managements, and they are ready for extension and can scale big when the virtual world grows.

 Throughout this book, all examples will be based on SmartFoxServer. We choose SmartFoxServer because it supports not only Flash but also iPhone, Unity, Java, and .Net. This keeps the flexibility to extend and spread the virtual world to other platforms with less effort.

Application architecture of a virtual world

There are two fundamental entities at the base of the SmartFoxServer architecture: Zones and Rooms.

SmartFoxServer can run multiple applications at the same time. Each **zone** represents a different application. A developer can configure different zones to host different virtual worlds or games in the same server instance. The activity, messages, and events are totally isolated among zones.

Room can be created within zones to logically group users. Users in the same room can chat, interact, or play games together. For example, I can send a message to all users in Room A when I'm in Room A. And those users in Room B would not receive this message because I'm only interacting with users in the same room. The following diagram shows the Zone, Room, and User relationship:

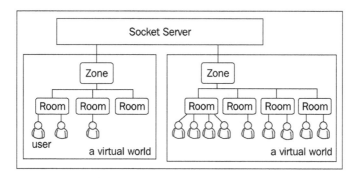

Rooms can also be used as a tool to organize the virtual world's areas into different connected parts. Depending on the virtual world design, a room could represent an entire city, a street, or just a physical room inside a building. These rooms are connected so that when a user walks from one street into another street, he is leaving the old room and joining a new room that represents the street he is walking to.

Most user interactions are limited within a room. Therefore, the resolution of the room that is representing affects how players can interact with others. For instance, users can interact with others within the same street if each street is represented by one room or they can interact with others within the same city if the entire city is represented by one room. The following diagram shows a virtual world in which each city is a room:

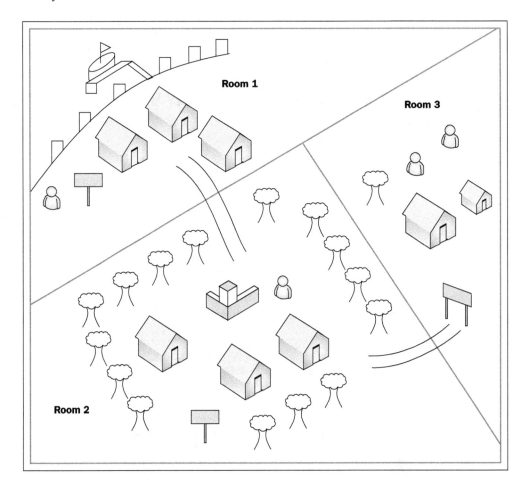

The following diagram shows a virtual world in which several streets compose a room:

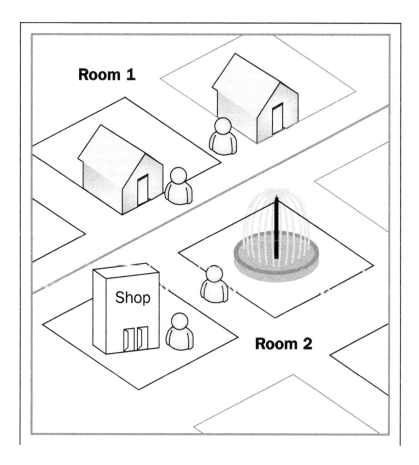

The whole picture of virtual worlds

We have brief ideas on the socket server, client-server concept, and the application architecture now. It is time to put them together to get whole concept of how a virtual world works. The following figure shows the components for a virtual world:

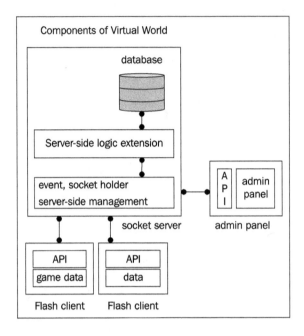

The socket server is the core part. There is a database to store permanent data such as user account info. A server-side extension lets developers program server-side logic, which is related to the virtual world, such as a virtual items exchange or virtual money transaction.

A server-side management component is in charge of following tasks:

- Handles and manages all socket connections
- Manages the memory of zones, rooms, and users
- Dispatches events and messages to appropriate clients, such as send messages when someone left the room
- Calls server-side functions when client requests, such as create room or send public message
- Calls server-side extension by clients requests

Flash client will have some static data of the virtual world, for example, map terrain. It also contains an API for connection to server-side functions.

Usually, there is an admin panel for the virtual world moderator to monitor the whole server. The admin panel can access the server via API and query statistics from the server or perform some admin actions such as server configuration or kick-users.

Common features in virtual world

There are some common features that often appears in a Flash virtual world.

Avatar

An **avatar** is an identity to represent the user when interacting in a virtual world. The avatar often means a character in Flash virtual world. Users can choose different appearances of the avatar and may even be able to customize the color and detail style.

The following screenshot is from the NuYu avatar editor from Data Design Interactive (`http://217.199.176.105/ddigames/`). It allows avatar customization on every part of the face and the players can use these avatars in the games.

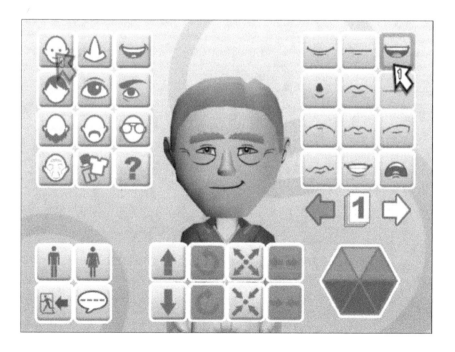

World to explore

In a virtual world, there are different places that users can explore. There is usually a starting city that every new player arrives to. Then players start their own journey in the virtual world by exploring different cities, places, and making game progress or interacting with others in different places in the world.

Home

Players may have their own private place called **home**. They can buy different things to decorate their home. They may invite friends to their home for private group chat.

The following screenshot is a home of a member in Fantage virtual world (http://www.fantage.com/). Players can customize their home with decorations that are available at the game store. They can also create party events that invite others to come and get special party items.

Items

Items are another key feature of a virtual world. Letting players collect items can be a good motivation to make them active in a virtual world. Some players will even put rare items in their home to show off how powerful they are. Items can also be mounted on avatars to enhance appearance and properties such as hats or magic ward.

Quests

Quests are some tasks that players have to accomplish in order to gain rewards. Quests may require players to explore to a certain place, find certain rare items, perform social activity, or combat with some enemy creatures. The rewards are often virtual money, experience, or special items.

Non-player characters

Non-player characters are characters that are controlled by the virtual world instead of by users. They often provide services to users such as selling items, providing quests, and giving introductions to new players. Some enemies or creatures may also be a non-player character.

Social features

It is important to enhance the social features to keep a virtual world live. A successful virtual world let players know what others are doing, discuss the world with each other, and spread the news and progress to others.

Casual game design versus MMOG

Games in virtual worlds can be divided into two types—casual games or massive multiplayer online games. In virtual worlds with casual games, there are many types of mini multiplayer games that players can join from the lobby. Every mini game takes minutes to play with several competitors together. Players may continue to play different types of mini games after each round ends.

In contrast to casual game types, virtual worlds with massive multiplayer game design requires players to play in the same world. It is much like traditional role playing games in which players keep finishing quests in the world to make the story progress.

There can also be a mix between them. Some virtual worlds provide a bunch of light-weight mini games that players can play with each other for fun while at the same time, helping players to keep finishing quests and exploring the world.

Existing virtual world games

There are several existing virtual worlds running successfully. Some of them are Flash-based and some are not. We will introduce them here so that we can give them a try and get some inspiration before starting our virtual world design and development.

Club Penguin

Club penguin (http://www.clubpenguin.com/) is a successful story of Flash multiplayer virtual world with SmartFoxServer as backend. It is a kind of casual game virtual world where players explore in a small town and play multiplayer mini games with each other. It can be a good example of what Flash with socket server can do.

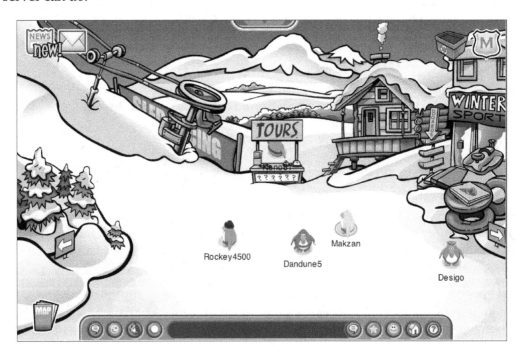

Mole

Mole (`http://www.51mole.com/`) is one of the largest Flash online virtual worlds in China now. It is a casual virtual world game in which players play mini games and some casual quests inside the world. It targets children whose age ranges from 6 to 14. According to a 2010 document, the mole virtual world has a record of 450K peak concurrent players.

Dofus

Dofus (http://www.dofus.com/) is a Flash massive multiplayer online role playing game developed by Ankama from France. Players play against monsters in the virtual world to gain experiences to level up and earn points to buy equipment. Dofus in one of the most successful Flash virtual worlds and has 30 million registered players and 250K peak concurrent connections in 2010.

World of Warcraft

As one of the best-selling virtual world communities, it is worth taking a trial at this game. World of Warcraft (http://www.worldofwarcraft.com/), also referred as WoW, is a kind of serious game play virtual world that contains a huge worldview and complicated story.

Club Penguin, Mole, and Dofus are Flash virtual worlds but World of Warcraft is not. It is developed in LUA, a scripting language, and C++. WoW is a very huge 3D virtual world that contains over 7000 quests and 40,000 non-player characters. The 3D environment with large graphic assets exceeds the limit that Flash player can handle. According to a document from Blizzard, the company behind WoW, in 2009, the World of Warcraft ran on over 13,000 server instances.

Summary

In this chapter, we have a brief introduction to Flash multiplayer virtual world. We also get a rough idea on the architecture and features of a Flash virtual world and some common designs of virtual worlds. In the coming chapters, we will start by installing the socket server and will build a Flash virtual world step-by-step.

2
Installing the Servers

If you have ever played Flash virtual world, such as the club penguin that was mentioned in the previous chapter, you may have had the following experience.

You load the web page in web browser and then log in with your username and password. You may need to fill out some basic information for the first time. Then the Flash player is launched and finally you are connected to the virtual world and can interact with others.

The socket server handles the virtual world after the player is connected to the virtual world. What about those web pages for virtual world information and SWF files? Yes, we need another web server and database server to handle the normal web request that is not the multiplayer part.

In this chapter, we will understand the relationship of the servers and install the needed servers one by one to get them to work with each other.

We will cover the following in this chapter:

- Compare the different features among the SmartFoxServer Lite, Basic, and Pro versions
- Compare the development and deployment environment
- Download and set up a third-party HTTP server and database
- Run an example from SmartFoxServer
- Set up the administration panel

Comparing SmartFoxServer Lite, Basic, and Pro

SmartFoxServer is a commercial product by gotoAndPlay(). There are three package options of SmartFoxServer. They are Lite version, Basic version, and Pro version. The demo license of the SmartFoxServer provides full features with 20 concurrent users maximum without time limitation. We will use the demo license to build the entire virtual world throughout the book.

SmartFoxServer Lite

The Lite version was the original SmartFoxServer since 2004. The maximum concurrent connection is limited to 50. It supports some core features like message passing, server-side user/room variables, and dynamic room creation.

However, the lack of ActionScript 3.0 greatly limits the performance and functionality. Moreover, it is being updated slowly so that many new features from Basic and Pro version are missing in Lite version. When we compare the version number of the three options, we will know that Lite version is developing at a slow pace. The version of SmartFoxServer Pro is 1.6.6 at the time of writing. The Basic version is 1.5.9 and the Lite version is only 0.9.1.

 Because of the slow update, not supporting ActionScript 3 and lack of features, it is not recommended to use Lite version in production.

SmartFoxServer Basic

SmartFoxServer Basic supports ActionScript 3 and a bunch of advanced features such as administration panel, game room spectators, and moderators. The administration panel lets moderators configure the zones, rooms, and users when the server is running. However, the lack of server-side extension support limits the customizability of the socket server. It also means that all logic must reside on the client side. This raises a security issue that the client may alter the logic to cheat.

The Basic version provides enough features to build a Flash virtual world in small scale that does not require high security. If you need a specific server logic and room management or want to put logic in server side to prevent client-side cheating, Pro version is the choice.

SmartFoxServer Pro

There is a long list of features that are supported in Pro version. There are three features amongst all that distinguish the Pro version, they are:

- Server-side extension that modifies the server behavior
- JSON/Raw data protocol message passing
- Direct database connection

Modifying the behavior of server

Server-side extension is some server logic that developers can program to modify the default behavior of the internal event handler and add server-side functions to extend the server for specific usage.

For example, we may want to override the "user lost" event so that we can save the user properties, telling others that someone is disconnected and something else. In this case, we can write a function in server-side extension to handle all these things when the user lost, instead of running the default behavior that was provided by SmartFoxServer.

The SmartFoxServer is written in Java. Therefore the native support language of server-side extension is Java. In order to reduce the development difficulties, SmartFoxServer supports Python and ActionScript as a server-side extension. The support of ActionScript makes it much more convenient for most Flash developers to develop the server-side extension without even knowing Java.

 Please note that the version of ActionScript supported in server-side extension is ActionScript 1, instead of ActionScript 3.

Take a look at the following code snippet on a server-side extension. The functions in server-side extensions are often similar to this one. It comes with arguments to know which user is calling this command at which room. In this snippet there is a command called getSomething and it will use the provided command parameters to get the result and return the result to the corresponding user. Do not worry if this code looks confusing to you, we will learn the extension in more detail in later chapters.

```
function handleRequest(cmd, params, user, fromRoom)
{
    var response = {};
    switch (cmd)
    {
```

```
        case "getSomething":
            var cpu = params['cpuType'];
            response.something = "A Powerful Computer with CPU "+cpu;
            // send the response back to the client.
            _server.sendResponse(response,-1,null,[user]);
        break
    }
}
```

JSON/Raw data protocol

JSON (http://www.json.org) is a light-weight text-based data-interchange format. It is designed for both humans and machines to read and write the data easily. For example, we can format a list of users and their information with the following JSON code.

```
{"users": [
    {
    "name" : "Steve",
    "level" : 12,
    "position" : {
            "x" : 6,
            "y" : 7
    },
    {
    "name" : "John",
    "level" : 5,
    "position" : {
            "x" : 26,
            "y" : 12
    }
}
```

The default data protocol supported by SmartFoxServer Lite and Basic is XML. The Pro version added support of JSON and raw data protocol make it possible to compress the transfer of data between clients and server. The length of messages between clients and server is much shorter and it means the transmission speed is much faster.

Take an example of a client sending data to a server with different protocols.

We are now trying to fetch some data from the server, and this is what it looks like when sending a command to the server via different protocol.

- **XML:**

```
<dataObj><var n='name' t='s'>extension</var><var n='cmd'
t='s'>getSomething</var><obj t='o' o='param'><var n='cpuType'
t='n'>8</var></obj></dataObj>
```

The length of this command is 148 bytes.

- **JSON:**

```
{"b":{"p":{"cpuType":8},"r":1,"c":"getSomething","x":"extension"},
"t":"xt"}
```

The length of this command is 75 bytes.

- **Raw Data:**

```
%xt%extension%getSomething%8%
```

The length of this command is 29 bytes.

When comparing with the bytes used to send a command over the network, XML is two times the JSON and five times the raw protocol. We are talking about several byte differences that may not be considered in a broadband Internet. However, it is a must to consider every byte that was sent to the network because we are not talking about 29 bytes versus 148 bytes in the real applications. Imagine there are 2000 players in the virtual world, sending similar commands every second. We are now talking about 2.4Mbit/s versus 500Kbit/s, and this rough statistic already ignores those commands that fetch a long list of results, for example, a long list of items that are owned by the player.

The raw protocol format takes less bytes to represent the command because it does not contain the field name of the data. All parameters are position-dependent. In the preceding command, the first parameter stands for an extension message and the second stands for the command name. Other command-specific parameters follow these two parameters.

Raw protocol is position-dependent on the passing parameters while JSON is not. It is recommended to use JSON protocol in most case and use the raw data protocol in real-time interaction parts. Also, we should state clearly in comments code what each parameters stands for because others cannot get the field information from the raw data.

Accessing the database directly

Flash does not provide any database access functions. Flash applications always connect to database via server-side technique. The Pro version of SmartFoxServer provides direct database connectivity in server-side extension. The Flash virtual world will call a function in sever-side extension and it will handle the database connection for the Flash.

As the database connectivity is handled in server-side extension, Basic and Lite version does not contain this handy feature. We have to wrap the database access in other server-side technique, such as PHP, to connect database in Basic and Lite version.

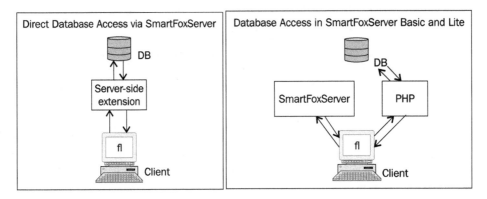

The two graphs compare the architecture of the database access in SmartFoxServer Pro, Basic, and Lite.

Comparing different package options

Core features	Lite	Basic	Pro
Chat message	Support	Support	Support
Server-side variables	Support	Support	Support
ActionScript 2.0	Support	Support	Support
ActionScript 3.0	No	Support	Support
Administration panel	No	Support	Support
Red5 integrated	No	No	Support
Clustering	No	No	Support
Server-side extension	No	No	Support
JSON/Raw protocol	No	No	Support

Core features	Lite	Basic	Pro
Direct database connectivity	No	No	Support
Firewall traversal	No	No	Support by BlueBox plug in

Developing and deploying virtual world environment

SmartFoxServer works excellently as a socket server in connecting clients and provides multiplayer features to virtual world. However, we also need a web server and database set up in practical use.

It may be disorienting at the beginning that we are using three types of servers at the same time. The following graph shows how these servers are responsible for different roles. We need a web server to host the virtual world website and Flash SWF. We also need a database server to store all user information permanently.

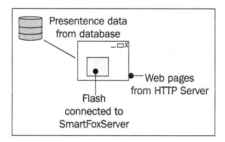

SmartFoxServer comes with an embedded HTTP server (Jetty), which can handle web pages and a light-weight database engine (H2). Using the embedded HTTP server and database can enable a rapid prototype development because we can start coding the Flash prototype of the ideas in mind without handling any server setup issues.

SmartFoxServer is also able to work together with third-party web servers and databases, for example, Apache and MySQL.

There are different situations on setting up the servers of Flash virtual world such as sometimes using SmartFoxServer with its embedded HTTP server and database while sometimes it is more beneficial to use SmartFoxServer with third-party servers.

Setting up a suitable sever environment before coding, on the other hand, enables us to have a plan and design of the whole architecture of the virtual world. It is a good practice to make a detailed plan before developing software, especially big scale software such as Flash virtual world.

We are going to compare the development environment and deployment environment, with different sever settings that may be applied.

Adjusting server setting for the deployment environment

In deployment of the virtual world, we have to choose the SmartFoxServer to fit the platform of the server instead of your own development machine. The SmartFoxServer may be a host in a standalone dedicated machine or a host within the same machine of the web server. There are many different combinations of setting up the servers and we will compare the common solutions.

Hosting SmartFoxServer, web server, and database in one server

For hosting a small-scale or mid-scale virtual world, hosting all severs in the same machine will be a good choice. In this case, there is not much difference between using the embedded web and database server, or using a third-party one. The following figure shows host SmartFoxServer, web server, and database in one machine:

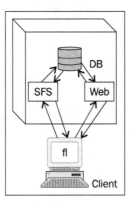

Hosting SmartFoxServer in dedicated standalone server

For hosting a big scale virtual world, it is good to host the SmartFoxServer in a standalone machine. This machine can virtually be a Virtual Private Server or physically a dedicated machine. More SmartFoxServer performance and scaling information can be found in the official SmartFoxServer documentation (`http://www.smartfoxserver.com/whitepapers/performance/index.html`). The following figure shows host SmartFoxServer in standalone:

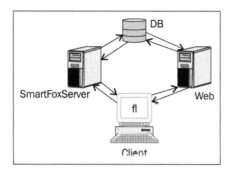

As the web server and database are not in the same machine of the SmartFoxServer, the choice of the web server and database is open. The web server can be Jetty, Apache, or others. The database server can be MySQL, Oracle, or any other available database server.

Benefiting from setting up SmartFoxServer, web server, and database in different machines

These servers are targeting different purposes and tasks. Each of them has a different requirement for server specification. Therefore, they are often put into different machines so that each machine can have the performance tuned to fit each server's purposes best.

Another benefit of putting them into different machines is that it enables centralized managed database storage. It is common in game industry that you log in to different online games or virtual worlds with one user account. After your virtual world has grown, you will probably have more than one server instance running the virtual world server. You may even have grown into to hosting several virtual worlds in several servers. The players will then query and authenticate from a standalone centralized database and then use that information to join different virtual worlds. The following diagram shows a host multi-virtual world server with the same database:

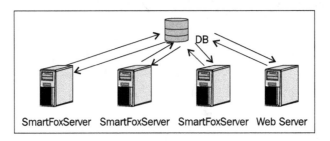

Setting up the development environment

Unlike a deployment environment, it is common to have just once machine acting both as server and client in a development environment. The machine will have SmartFoxServer, web server, and database installed. In this case, there are no noticeable differences between using the embedded or third-party web server and database. However, we will go through both solutions and focus on SmartFoxServer with a third-party web server and database combination.

It is a good habit to simulate the deployment environment as much as possible in development stage. As we are going to use a third-party web server and database, we will set up a development environment that also uses the third-party server instead of the embedded web server and database.

Installing Java Development Kit

The **Java Development Kit** includes the essential development tools (**JDK**) and the **Java Runtime Environment (JRE)**. The development tool compiles the Java source code into byte codes and the JRE is the response to execute the byte codes. We will need several Java compilations in later chapters. SmartFoxServer is build on the Java environment and we need the JRE to start up the server. The JDK and JRE may be pre-installed in some OSs.

Installing JDK On Windows

The steps for installing JDK on Windows are as follows:

1. Go to `http://java.sun.com/javase/downloads/`.

2. Click on the **Download** button of Java. It will lead to the **Java SE Downloads** page.

3. Select **Windows** (or **Windows x64** for 64-bits Windows) in **Platform**.

4. Click on **Download**.

5. If it prompts an optional login request, we can click the **Skip this Step** to bypass it.

6. Launch the installer after the download.

7. Install the Java Development Kit with all default settings.

8. The Java environment is ready after installation completes.

Installing JDK on Mac OSX

The Mac OSX comes with its own set of Java environment. We can check the JDK and JRE version by following steps:

1. Launch terminal from **Applications | Utilities | Terminal**.
2. Type the following and press the *Enter* key:
    ```
    javac -version
    ```
3. The command will output the currently installed version of the Java in the Mac OSX. In my case, it outputs: **javac 1.6.0_17**.

The current version of SmartFoxServer at the time of writing recommends the version 1.6. If the Java is not updated, we can update it via **Apple Menu | Software Update**.

The software update will check for any updates for your existing Mac software, including the Java environment.

Installing JDK on Linux

We can use the general method to download and install the JDK or use the system specific method to install the package. We will show the general method and the Ubuntu method.

Installing for General Linux

1. Go to `http://java.sun.com/javase/downloads/index.jsp` in browser.
2. Click on the **Download** button.
3. The platform **Linux** should be selected automatically. Otherwise, select **Linux** (or **Linux x64** for **64-bit Linux**).

4. Click on **Continue**.

5. If it prompts for login, click on **Skip this Step** to bypass it.

6. For Redhat or Fedora Linux, choose the `rpm-bin` file to download. For other Linux, choose the `.bin` file to download.

7. Launch terminal via **Applications | Accessories | Terminal** after the download completes.

8. Change the directory to the folder that contains the downloaded package. The download destination varies from different profile settings. In my case, it is in `Downloads` folder.

    `cd ~/Downloads/`

9. The version is Java 6 Update 20 at the time of writing and the filename is `jdk-6u20-linux-i586.bin` or `jdk-6u20-linux-i586-rpm.bin`.

10. Then we make it executable and launch the installer by the following commands:

    `chmod a+x jdk-6u20-linux-i586.bin`

    `./jdk-6u20-linux-i586.bin`

11. The installer displays the license agreement. Type *Yes* at the end to agree and continue installation.

12. Press the *Enter* key after the file's extraction to end the installation.

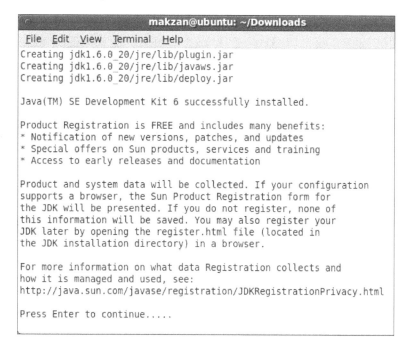

Installing for Ubuntu Linux

Ubuntu users can install the JDK via the `apt-get` command.

1. We will search for the latest package name of the JDK by the following command:

   ```
   apt-cache search --names-only sun-java.*-jdk
   ```

2. The result shows the available JDK packet names. At the time of writing, it is JDK6:

   ```
   sun-java6-jdk - Sun Java(TM) Development Kit (JDK) 6
   ```

3. We use the `apt-get` command to install the JDK:

   ```
   sudo apt-get install sun-java6-jdk
   ```

4. Type in the user password because it requires user's password and the privilege to use `apt-get`.

Downloading SmartFoxServer Pro

We are going to walkthrough the installation of SmartFoxServer Pro and third-party web server and database in all supported platforms.

For Windows, Mac OS, and Linux that have a graphic user interface, you can follow these steps to download the SmartFoxServer Pro:

1. Go to `http://www.smartfoxserver.com/products/pro.php#downloads` in web browser.

2. Select the OS platform. We will use Windows 32-bit as an example here.

3. The download will start after clicking on the **Download** button.

For Linux platform that does not have a graphic user interface, you can follow these steps to download the SmartFoxServer Pro Linux x86-32-bit version:

1. Go to the directory that planned to place the SmartFoxServer.

2. Type the following line in the terminal to download the file:

   ```
   wget http://www.smartfoxserver.com/products/download.php?d=76
   ```

3. The download will start after pressing the *Enter* key.

For a Linux platform that does not have graphic user interface, you can follow these steps to download the SmartFoxServer Pro Linux x86-64-bit version:

1. Go to the directory that planned to place the SmartFoxServer.

2. Type the following line in the terminal to download the file:

   `wget http://www.smartfoxserver.com/products/download.php?d=77`

3. The download will start after pressing the *Enter* key.

Installing SmartFoxServer Pro

The installation process is different from SmartFoxServer for Windows, Linux, and Mac OS.

Installing on Windows

1. Run the installer `SFSPRO_win_1.6.6.exe`.

2. When asked for the installation path we change the install path to any directory under the user folder, such as `C:\Users\username\SmartFoxServerPRO_1.6.6`.

> We change the installation path instead of the default path under Program Files because latest Windows requires administrator privileges to change the files.

Installing on Mac OSX

1. After downloading the SmartFoxServer, it will be automatically mounted.

2. Open the `Applications` folder.

3. Drag the `SmartFoxServer Pro 1.6.6` folder into `Applications`.

Installing on Linux

1. Launch the terminal from **Applications | Accessories | Terminal**.

2. Go to the enclosing folder of the `SFSPRO_linux_1.6.6.tar.gz`.

3. Type following command in the terminal to decompress the `tar`:

   `tar zxf SFSPRO_linux_1.6.6.tar.gz`

Running the SmartFoxServer

There are different ways to run the SmartFoxServer in different platforms.

Starting SmartFoxServer on Windows

The SmartFoxServer can be launched from the start menu. Click on **Start** | **Programs** | **SmartFoxServerPro_1.6.6** | **Start SmartFoxServer**.

```
Start SmartFoxServer                                                _ □ X

          Ranch (inside)      (id: 34, max: 50, pass:N)
          Ranch (outside)     (id: 35, max: 50, pass:N)
          Slopes area         (id: 36, max: 50, pass:N)



    --- [ Server Starting ] ------------------------------------------

Server address: All
Server port   : 9339

18:41:06.106 - [ INFO ] > [TaskScheduler] ... started ::
18:41:06.106 - [ INFO ] > [BlueBoxHandler]... started ::
18:41:06.106 - [ INFO ] > [EventWriter] ..... started :: 1 thread(s)
18:41:06.106 - [ INFO ] > [SystemHandler] ... started :: 1 thread(s)
18:41:06.106 - [ INFO ] > [ExtensionHandler]. started :: 1 thread(s)
18:41:06.106 - [ INFO ] > [DeadChannelsPolicy: strict]
18:41:06.106 - [ INFO ] > Server is up and running!
[dbExtension.as]: Event received: serverReady
[simpleExt.as]: Event received: serverReady
18:41:06.121 - [ INFO ] > [RedBox] Internal event received: serverReady
18:41:06.153 - [ INFO ] > [RedBox] Internal event received: serverReady
18:41:06.153 - [ INFO ] > [RedBox] Internal event received: serverReady
```

A command prompt will then appear and it shows up logs of loading different modules. Error messages may appear if there is any error that fails to start up the server.

Starting SmartFoxServer on Mac OS

The server launcher is located in **Applications** | **SmartFoxServer Pro 1.6.6** | **SmartFoxServer.app**. Double-click to launch it and it will also display the log in a window.

```
  O O O              SmartFoxServer

|:::::::::::::::::::::::::::::::::::::::::::::::::::::::::::|
|                                                         |
|              ...::: SmartFoxServer :::...               |
|                 Multiplayer Socket Server               |
|                      version 1.6.6                      |
|                          ---                            |
|               (c) 2004 - 2009 gotoAndPlay()             |
|                  www.smartfoxserver.com                 |
|                   www.gotoandplay.it                    |
|                                                         |
|:::::::::::::::::::::::::::::::::::::::::::::::::::::::::::|

:::::::::::: { BlueBox INITED } :::::::::::::
:                                          :
: Version 1.0.5 -- (c) 2008 gotoAndPlay() :
:                                          :
::::::::::::::::::::::::::::::::::::::::::::::
03:43:25.040 - [ INFO ] > Starting h2 engine...


--- [ System Info ] -------------------------------------

                                               Cancel
```

Starting SmartFoxServer on Linux

1. Launch terminal from **Applications | Accessories | Terminal**.

2. Go to the SmartFoxServer installation folder | Server.

3. Type the following command in the terminal to launch the server:

    ```
    ./start.sh
    ```

Using embedded web server and database

We are going to play with the embedded web server and database. The embedded web server and database are well-configured and run on startup by default. This lets developers rapidly develop the prototype of the virtual world without worrying about setting up different servers.

Running the embedded web server

By default, the web server is running on port 8080 with same SmartFoxServer location.

After starting up the SmartFoxServer, go to `http://localhost:8080` in the web browser. If a webpage shows up with a message "SmartFoxServer Pro 1.6.6 is installed successfully", it means the server is working with default settings.

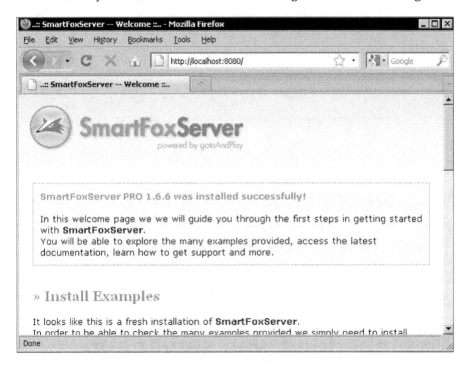

The HTTP documents directory of the embedded server is located in **Installation folder | Server | webserver | webapps | root**. You can modify and store static web pages within this folder to host the virtual world website.

Running the embedded database server

The embedded H2 database server is well-configured upon SmartFoxServer installation.

Windows users can launch the H2 Database Admin Tool by double-clicking the `adminDB.bat`, which is located in `SmartFoxServer installation directory |`
`Server`. Linux and Mac users can launch by executing the following command in the terminal in the `Server` directory:

```
chmod +x adminDB.sh
```

```
./adminDB.sh
```

After executing the `adminDB` script, a web interface of the Admin tool will open in browser.

We will use the default saved settings to connect the H2 database. In Windows and Linux, the default setting is **Generic H2**, while in Mac, the setting is called **Generic H2 (Embedded)**.

If the development is based on H2 Database engine, we can test the database by clicking the **Connect** button with default settings.

After connected to the H2 database engine, the admin panel is divided into three parts. The upper part contains action buttons for operating the database such as the logout or execute commands. The left part lists all available users and tables. The right part is for inputting the SQL commands and viewing the results. H2 database is a light-weight engine that we need to operate the database by typing all the SQL commands ourselves.

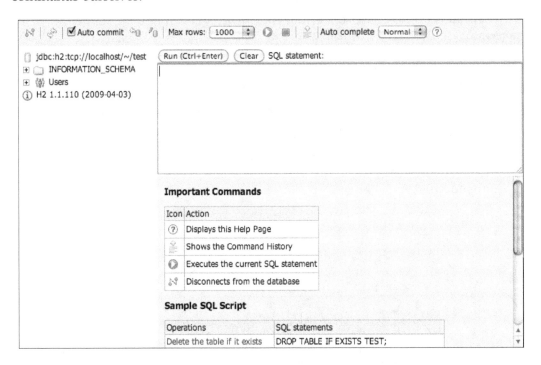

Downloading third-party HTTP and database server package

Using the embedded HTTP and database server can be convenient for development. However, as explained before we will have SmartFoxServer running standalone while putting HTTP and database server in another standalone machine when the virtual world is released to public. We will learn how to set up a third-party HTTP and database server to cooperate with SmartFoxServer.

We are going to download and install Apache and MySQL server package. These kinds of server package features have easy install that auto-configures most of the server settings. It will also install some essential tools for beginners to manage the server easily, such as GUI server administration panel.

Installing WAMP on Windows

WampServer is an open source HTTP and database server solution on Windows. WAMP stands for Windows, Apache, MySQL, and PHP package.

1. Go to `http://www.wampserver.com/en/download.php`.
2. Click on **Download WampServer** to download the installer.
3. Run the installer with all default settings.
4. The server is configured and ready.

The WampServer can run by launching from **Start | Programs | WampServer | Start WampServer**.

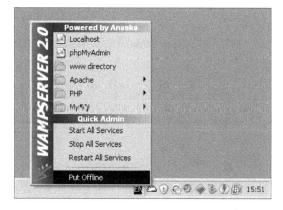

It will be in the task bar and the server management operation can be found by clicking the *WampServer* icon. We can start the server by putting the server online in the menu.

Installing MAMP on Mac OSX

Similar to WampServer, MAMP is the one package web server solution that stands for Mac, Apache, MySQL, and PHP package. The MAMP package can be downloaded at `http://www.mamp.info/`.

1. Download the MAMP package from the official website.
2. Double-click on the downloaded MAMP `dmg` file to mount it.
3. Drag the `MAMP` folder into the `Applications` folder.

To run the MAMP server, go to **Applications | MAMP** and double-click on the `MAMP.app`.

Installing LAMP on Linux

As the same naming convention, the "L" stands for Linux here. Different Linux distributions use different ways to install applications. There may not be a one-click install method on some Linux branch which requires us to install the Apache and MySQL individually. Some Linux may provide graphic user interface to install LAMP by just selecting it in the applications list. We will use Ubuntu to demonstrate the installation of LAMP.

1. Launch terminal from **Applications | Accessories | Terminal**.

2. Type following command to install LAMP.

    ```
    sudo tasksel install lamp-server
    ```

3. The installer will progress and configure different modules.

4. A dialog will prompt several times asking for a new MySQL root password. You can set your own MySQL password, while in the example we will leave the root password blank.

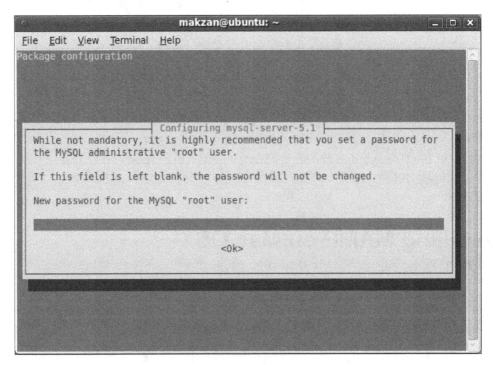

After the completion of the installation, the MySQL server is set up as service in the system. It runs automatically and we do not need to manually launch it to use it.

Connecting SmartFoxServer and MySQL server

SmartFoxServer is a Java application and Java database connection driver is needed to connect from SmartFoxServer to MySQL database.

Downloading JDBC Driver for MySQL

JDBC is a Java database connection driver that we need to establish connections between the Java-based SmartFoxServer and the MySQL server. The JDBC driver for MySQL is called Connector/J. We are going to install it to enable MySQL connection from SmartFoxServer.

1. Go to `http://dev.mysql.com/downloads/connector/j/5.1.html` in web browser.
2. Download the **Platform Independent Zip Archive**.
3. It may ask you to log in to MySQL.com account. Click on **No thanks, just take me to the downloads!** to bypass the login step
4. Choose a mirror to download by clicking on **HTTP**.

Setting up the JDBC driver

The MySQL Java connector comes with a bunch of files. We only need two among them.

1. Extract the `mysql-connector-java-5.1.10.zip` file to a temporary folder.
2. Open the folder and find the `mysql-connector-java-5.1.10-bin.jar` file.
3. Copy that `jar` file into `SmartFoxServer installation directory | jre | lib | ext`.
4. Go into the `src` directory of the extracted directory and copy the `org` directory to **SmartFoxServer installation directory | jre | lib | ext**.

Configuring the server settings

The configuration file of SmartFoxServer is an XML file that allows us to configure many server settings. It can configure the initial zone or room creation, server address, admin authorization, value tuning for performance, and a lot more. We are going to set the database connection for testing our setup in this chapter and we will go through some core settings in next chapter.

The configuration file is called `config.xml` and is located in the SmartFoxServer installation directory under the `Server` directory.

Configuring MySQL server connection in SmartFoxServer

1. Open the `config.xml` in your favorite text editor.

2. Go to line 203 of the `config.xml`. This line should be within the structure of a `Zone` tag with name as `dbZone`.

3. Change the lines 203-218 from the `config.xml`:

    Original code:

```
<DatabaseManager active="false">
        <Driver>sun.jdbc.odbc.JdbcOdbcDriver</Driver>
        <ConnectionString>jdbc:odbc:sfsTest</ConnectionString>

        <!--
        Example connecting to MySQL

        <Driver>org.gjt.mm.mysql.Driver</Driver>
        <ConnectionString>jdbc:mysql://192.168.0.1:3306/sfsTest
                                                </ConnectionString>
        -->

        <UserName>yourname</UserName>
        <Password>yourpassword</Password>

        <TestSQL><![CDATA[SELECT COUNT(*) FROM contacts]]></TestSQL>
```

4. Replace the code in lines 203-218 with the following code:

```
<DatabaseManager active="true">
        <Driver>org.gjt.mm.mysql.Driver</Driver>
        <ConnectionString>jdbc:mysql://127.0.0.1:3306/mysql
                                        </ConnectionString>

        <UserName>root</UserName>
        <Password></Password>

        <TestSQL><![CDATA[SELECT NOW()]]></TestSQL>
```

The new setting activates the `DatabaseManager` and configures the JDBC driver to the MySQL connector that we just downloaded.

We also changed the user name and password of the connection to the database to "root" and empty password.

 We will use the empty password through out the development process but it is strongly recommended to set your own database user password.

There is a `TestSQL` setting where we can write a simple database query so that the SmartFoxServer will try to run it to test if the database connection is correct. As we have not created any new databases for the virtual world, we will test the database connection by querying the current server time.

Restarting the server

We've just set up the connection between SmartFoxServer and third-party database. It is time to test the new setting by restarting the SmartFoxServer.

To stop the SmartFoxServer in Windows and Linux, press *Ctrl* + *C*. To stop it in Mac OS X, click on the **Cancel** button in the SmartFoxServer log window.

 There is a log that appears as usual after we start up the server again. It is important to check the log carefully every time the `config.xml` is changed. The logfile can provide details of any errors that occur when it tries to load the configure file.

For example, if we configure the database connection just now but forget to activate the `DatabaseManager`, the server will start up correctly. Then you may spend a lot of time debugging why the database connection is not working until you find that the `DatabaseManager` is not active at all. This happened to me several times while I was developing my first Flash virtual world.

If the server is running with the new database connection settings, the following lines will be appearing in the log. There can be different database manager settings for each zone. When checking the log, we should be aware which zone the log is referring to. We are configuring the database manager of dbZone zone now.

DB Manager Activated (org.gjt.mm.mysql.Driver)

Zone: dbZone

If we forget to activate the `DatabaseManager`, we will not see the **DB Manager Activated** wording. Instead, the following message may appear in the log:

DB Manager is not active in this Zone!

Moreover, if the SmartFoxServer faces some fatal error on start up, it will terminate itself with more detailed error logs. The following lines are an example for error logs that appear when the MySQL connector file is missing:

Can't load db driver: org.gjt.mm.mysql.Driver

[Servre] > DbManager could not retrive a connection. Java.sql.SQLException: Configuration file not found

DbManagerException: The Test SQL statement failed! Please check your configuration.

These lines state that the testing SQL failed to run, which we just set to test the connection. It also describes what exception has caused this error to help the debugging.

Running examples

The easiest way to run the examples is to browse the examples through the embedded web server.

1. Start the SmartFoxServer if it is not running.
2. Browse to `http://localhost:8080` in the web browser.
3. It will load the default page of the embedded web server with SmartFoxServer logo.
4. Click the **Install Examples** if this is the first time while running the examples.
5. Click the **Browse Examples** after the installed examples.
6. A list of examples appear and you click on them to have some ideas on what SmartFoxServer can basically do.

Loading a simple chat application

Let's test the **Simple Chat** in **Tutorials (AS 3.0)** category.

After loading the simple chat, a progress bar appears with the text **connecting to server**. If the example failed to connect the server, it will freeze at that screen. If it is connected to the server, a login box appears and asks for the login name.

If you failed to see the login box, there is something wrong. It may be a wrong setting in the configuration file, it may be some other issue that failed to start up the SmartFoxServer, or it may be some issue between the testing browser and the server, for example, firewall port blocking.

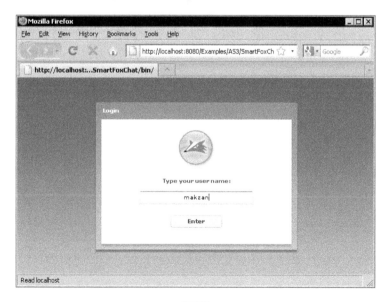

As we are testing a multiuser application, we can actually launch many instances of the chat applications to test the real-time chatting.

1. Open several new browsers.

2. Type in the same address of the chat application in the new browsers. The default URL is `http://localhost:8080/Examples/AS3/ SmartFoxChat/bin/`.

3. Log in to the chat application with different names for different browsers.

4. Test the application by sending messages in different browsers. The messages will all appear (almost) at the same time in all browsers.

Let's take a look on how the messages are sent between different chat application clients.

1. One of the users types in "Hi" in the chat application.

2. The user clicks the **Send** button to send the "Hi" message.

3. The message is sent from the chat application to SmartFoxServer.

4. SmartFoxServer decodes the message and broadcasts this messages to all connected clients in the same room.

5. All clients who receive the "Hi" message display it on the chat application.

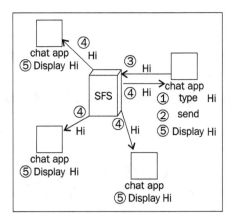

To further understand what SmartFoxServer can do, we may not only test the simple chat example but also test other examples that are provided by SmartFoxServer.

Setting up the administration panel

SmartFoxServer Pro comes with an administration panel to provide a nice graphic interface to monitor and configure the running server. We will often use the administration panel during the whole development process.

The administration panel is located in SmartFoxServer installation directory | Admin | AdminTool.swf. Another way to access it in Windows is to launch from start menu by clicking **Start | Programs | SmartFoxServerPro_1.6.6 | Admin | AdminTool**.

Logging in to administration panel

The default login name is *sfs_admin* and the default password is *sfs_pass*. Leave the server IP address and port unchanged, and log in to the administration panel.

There will be a prompt dialog saying that using the default password is not secure. The password can be changed in the same configuration file that we used to set up the database connection. We are going to change the password in next chapter when we go through the configuration file in detail.

After we are logged in, we have a glance at all server statistics and settings. It will show statistics including data traffic, memory usage, established connections count, and dropped messages count.

It allows many operations for a server moderator to use, for example, a moderator can monitor and manage zones and rooms, send broadcast messages to specific users, kick unusual or idle users, monitor logfiles, or even change the configuration and extension files on the fly when the server is running.

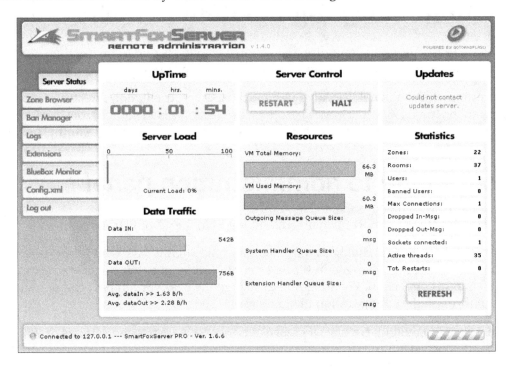

 It is strongly recommended to change the password of the admin panel even in development stage. The default password raises a security issue that someone can log in to the admin panel and retrieve all the server configuration and server extension source code, including all database passwords stored inside.

Locating the Flash Client API

API is **Application Programming Interface** that allows other software to interact with it. Flash Client API for SmartFoxServer is the interface that allows Flash to connect to the SmartFoxServer and interact with it.

The following code snippet shows how Flash uses the client API to interact with SmartFoxServer.

Create an instance of client API object:

```
var client = new SmartFoxClient();
```

Connect the client to the SmartFoxServer with specific IP address and port number:

```
client.connect("127.0.0.1",9339);
```

The connection between the Flash client and the SmartFoxServer is established now. Next, we log in the user to the zone simpleChat with the username *John*.

```
client.login("simpleChat","John","");
```

Send public messages to all users in the same room:

```
client.sendPublicMessage('Hello SmartFoxServer');
```

The Flash Client API is located in **SmartFoxServer installation directory | Flash API**. There are four directories inside it. They are ActionScript 2.0, ActionScript 3.0, RedBoxClient_AS2, and RedBoxClient_AS3. RedBoxClient is the client API for connecting the media streaming **Red5** component that we will not use for the virtual world development now. What we will focus on is the ActionScript 3.0 client that is for SmartFoxServer. We will have a step-by-step example in the next chapter to set up our first Flash application to connect to SmartFoxServer.

Summary

We have discussed how to install the SmartFoxServer and set up a web server and database. We have also understood the whole idea of how a server requirement changed from development stage to deployment stage. Then we ran an example as well as administration panel and began to have some concepts of what SmartFoxServer can basically do.

In the next chapter, we are going to get familiar with the SmartFoxServer by understanding the configuration file. We will also prepare the Flash player for debugging in multiplayer virtual world.

3
Getting Familiar with SmartFoxServer

We have discussed some basic zone room relationship and architecture in previous chapters. We have also set up the development environment and get basic concept on a Flash virtual world. In this chapter, we are going to learn to use the SmartFoxServer by configuring it and making some simple connection applications.

We will discuss the following topics in this chapter:

- Structure of the configuration file for the SmartFoxServer
- Meaning of some important settings variables
- Configuration structure of the zone and room architecture
- Debugging methods without the Flash IDE
- Flash security policy
- Writing a basic cooperative whiteboard application

Configuring a basic SmartFoxServer

As a socket server, there are many settings that can be set up and tuned for the SmartFoxServer. Most of the settings are configured by the `config.xml` file. This `config.xml` is located in the SmartFoxServer installation directory under the `Server` directory.

Overview of the configuration file structure

The configuration file is in XML format. XML is a plain text format that is usually used for describing a data structure and stores data inside.

The `configuration` file is composed of two major parts: **ServerSetup** and **Zones**.

`<ServerSetup>` contains many setting variables to configure and tune the server. `<Zones>` define each application that runs on the SmartFoxServer.

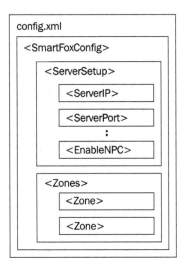

The preceding diagram shows the overview structure of the configuration file visually. The whole configuration file is composed of two blocks: `ServerSetup` and `Zones`. Each of the blocks contain their settings.

Configuring the server

All settings in `<ServerSetup>` describe the behavior of the SmartFoxServer. We will list some commonly used settings in the following sections.

These settings include:

- Automatically binding all available IP addresses to the server
- Listening port for connections
- Setting policy to load data from machines in other domains
- Setting timers for idle user logouts
- Blocking bot connections
- Setting administrator login and password
- Limiting access to the administration panel to specific IP addresses
- Displaying zone information before connecting to the server
- Defining the information separator in raw protocol

Automatically binding all available IP addresses to server

The IP address used by the SmartFoxServer is `<ServerIP>*</ServerIP>`. In the old version of the server, this setting is required to run the server. As of version 1.5.9 of SmartFoxServer, it automatically binds all available IP addresses to the server. Therefore a wildcard "*" value is okay for this setting.

Listening port for connections

The listening port for connections is `<ServerPort>9339</ServerPort>`. If the SmartFoxServer is running behind the firewall, we may need to configure the firewall to allow the port or modify the port number to an port allowed by the firewall.

Setting policy load data from machines in other domains

When `<AutoSendPolicyFile>true</AutoSendPolicyFile>` is true, SmartFoxServer will send the cross-domain policy file to every connected client Cross-domain policy file is an XML file configuration describing how the Flash files are allowed to load data from machines in other domains.

Setting timers for idle user logouts

Max user idle time given by `<MaxUserIdleTime>300</MaxUserIdleTime>` means how long before the server will force users to log out if they are not sending any actions or commands to the server; the unit is in seconds. The duration that the user is allowed to be idle depends on the design of the virtual world. If the virtual world is an online working environment where users may need to read a long text or document, or to observe something for a long time without sending anything out, the setting must allow a longer user idle time. On the other hand, if the server is full of people and often reaches the max of the user collections, then in this case you may want to lower the max user idle time so that non-active users will be kicked out to allow more fresh users in the world and encourage users to keep active.

Blocking bots connections

The interval for how long the socket connection can be idle before the user session is created is given as `<MaxSocketIdleTime>300</MaxSocketIdleTime>` and the unit is in seconds. SmartFoxServer will disconnect any socket connection that stays idle for more than the set interval, still failing to log in and create a user session. This setting is useful to block those bots that aim to scan the port instead of make a connection as a user. This setting will be ignored once the user session is created and the `MaxUserIdleTime` setting will override the idle interval setting.

Setting administrator login and password

Remember how we used the default login and password to log in to the administration panel in last chapter? Here we can set our own set of password with the following format:

```
<AdminLogin>sfs_admin</AdminLogin>
<AdminPassword>sfs_pass</AdminPassword>
```

It is recommended to use a password that is independent from any other system password because this `config.xml` file is in non-encrypted plain text.

Limiting access of the administration panel to specific IP addresses

This setting can limit the access of the administration panel to specific IP addresses to further enhance the security of the administration panel.

After setting an address other than the wildcard — `*.*.*.*`, only the machine from that IP address can load the panel.

The following setting allows connection to administrator panel from all addresses:

```
<AdminAllowedAddresses>
    <AllowedAddress>*.*.*.*</AllowedAddress>
</AdminAllowedAddresses>
```

The following setting allows connection to administrator panel from particular addresses:

```
<AdminAllowedAddresses>
    <AllowedAddress>202.175.123.123</AllowedAddress>
    <AllowedAddress>137.189.123.123</AllowedAddress>
</AdminAllowedAddresses>
```

It is important to protect the administration panel because it allows the panel user to change the zone room architecture, configuration file, or even shut down the SmartFoxServer.

An error message appears when someone tries to access the administration panel from an IP address that is not permitted. In such a case, login fails even with the correct username and password.

Displaying zone information before connecting to the server

If the setting — `<EnableZoneInfo>truc</EnableZoneInfo>` is enabled, the server will respond to a special request by external application, such as PHP, and provide the current connected user number. This is very helpful because we can display the connected number, which often means server loading, before the users connect to the server. This information lets the users choose a faster server to connect to.

By enabling the zone information, we can provide the current server capacity and loading to users before they connect to any of the servers. The preceding image is a screenshot from Club Penguin demonstrating this feature. The server with **FULL** label has reached the maximum simultaneous connected users. The other servers indicate how many users are connected to the server.

Defining the information separator in raw protocol

The setting— `<RawProtocolSeparator><![CDATA[@]]></RawProtocolSeparator>` defines how the SmartFoxServer separates the information in a raw protocol server message to the client. The default value is "%"; this means that when the following message is sent from server with raw protocol, it looks like:

```
%xt%extension%getSomething%1%
```

There is a delimiter "%" between the variables to separate them. We will need to modify this setting when we will send or receive a message that contains this delimiter as meaningful information. If we want to tell the server and client that "% %" is meaningful information in our virtual world, we will need to change this setting to some other characters.

For example, if we change this setting to:

```
<RawProtocolSeparator><![CDATA[!]]></RawProtocolSeparator>
```

The message will become:

```
!xt!extension!getSomething!1!
```

The server configuration file can only be read in the server environment and the client side does not know this raw string separator setting. The setting here only affects the messages sent from server to client. We need to set the raw separator in client side by `rawProtocolSeparator` API property.

 Please note that the raw protocol separator has to be matched between server-side configuration and client-side setting.

Configuring the Zones and Rooms

The other major part of the configuration file is the `<Zones>`. This part defines how many applications, and zones, there are in this server and the initial rooms of these applications. Each of the zones and rooms comes with a set of properties to define their own features. This is useful to create a lobby for the zone and some must-have rooms such as a room for the world environment.

Configuring a zone

A zone is an individual application. Each zone is isolated from the others and no messages or interaction will be passed through the zone. Every zone has its own properties, room list, and server-side logic.

There are some properties to define the behavior of each zone. We will discuss some commonly used properties in following sections.

Naming your zone

The name of the zone which is given as `<Zone name="virtualworld">...</Zone>` is unique within the SmartFoxServer. A zone connection request needs to provide the name in order to connect the zone.

Assigning default names to users

When a login name is empty, given as `<Zone name="virtualworld"` `emptyNames="true">...</Zone>`, the default behavior of the zone is to assign a special name to the user with format like `Guest_1`. The number will be auto incremented. Setting this option to `false` will disable this feature.

Broadcasting the user count

The format for broadcasting the user count is `<Zone name="virtualworld"` `uCountUpdate="true">...</Zone>`. The server will broadcast a message with the user count of all rooms within the zone. The uCountUpdate setting can enable and disable this feature. As it is broadcasting the message to all connected users to the applications, it may draw a lot of traffic bandwidth if the concurrent connection is very large. The pro is that user count update message provides quite useful information to monitor the capacity of each room. When configuring a zone, this setting should be aware of and tuned to the real-world situation.

Limiting the users that can connect to a zone

The format for limiting the users that can connect to a zone is `<Zone` `name="virtualworld" maxUsers="50" >...</Zone>`. The maxUsers sets the maximum number of users that are allowed to connect to the zone simultaneously. This setting is useful when optimizing the bandwidth sharing with other zones within the same server.

Limiting numbers of rooms in a zone

The format for limiting numbers of rooms in a zone is given as `<Zone` `name="virtualworld" maxRooms="100">...</Zone>`. The maxRooms defines the maximum number of rooms that can exist in the zone. By default this value is -1, which means no limit to the maximum rooms.

Limiting the number of rooms a user can create

The format for limiting the number of rooms a user can create is given as `<Zone` `name="virtualworld" maxRoomsPerUser="5">...</Zone>`. This maxRoomsPerUser is the maximum room number that a user can create at once. The default value is 5.

Getting all room variables along with room list requests

The format for getting all room variables along with room list requests is given as `<Zone name="virtualworld" roomListVars="true">...</Zone>`. The `roomListVars` setting indicates whether the room list will include the room variables of each room. Getting all room variables within a room list can be convenient in developing a virtual world application that need the information of the room without joining it. However, putting the whole room variables into a huge list of rooms can make the whole room list very large and use a lot of bandwidth.

Setting moderators for the zone

A list of moderators and their login password can be assigned to a zone. A moderator has a higher access privilege that can kick and ban other users. A moderator list can be like this:

```
<Moderators status="on">
    <Mod name="mod_1" pwd="abc" />
    <Mod name="mod_2" pwd="123" />
</Moderators>
```

Creating rooms

A room is an important concept in SmartFoxServer because all users are contained in a room.

A room can be created when the SmartFoxServer starts up or dynamically created by client-side or server-side commands. Those rooms' settings in the configure file will be created once the SmartFoxServer starts. The following code illustrates how rooms are configured in the configuration file.

```
<Zone name="virtualworld">
    <Rooms>
            <Room name="The Hall" maxUsers="50" isPrivate="false"
isTemp="false" autoJoin="true" uCountUpdate="true" />
            <Room name="The Kitchen" maxUsers="50" isPrivate="false"
isGame="false" isTemp="false" />
            <Room name="The Garden" maxUsers="50" isPrivate="false"
isTemp="false" />
            <Room name="The Bathroom" maxUsers="50" isPrivate="false"
isTemp="false" />
            <Room name="The Garage" maxUsers="50" isPrivate="false"
isTemp="false" />
            <Room name="The Living Room" maxUsers="50" isPrivate="true"
isTemp="false" pwd="test" />
    </Rooms>
</Zone>
```

A user can send messages to others within the same room and receive certain information that is related to the room from the server. This information includes broadcast messages from other users, update of the latest room list, or if someone joins or leaves the room. Sometimes, a room has a certain purpose and thus may not need all information from the server. Therefore, SmartFoxServer provides three types of room for developers to create. Each of them serves different purposes and has different room events availability for optimization.

Regular room

A regular room is the default type of the room. Normal interaction can be performed in this room such as messaging the others, receiving notification messages when someone joins or leaves the room, or even a room list update when a room is created or destroyed.

Game room

A game room contains some special action and events for running a game. It assigns a player ID to every joined user and this player index can be useful for games such as a turn-based board game.

A game room also provides a spectator feature so that user can join the game room as a spectator. The spectator does not receive a player ID and therefore will not be treated as a player of that game logically. The spectator is able to observe all actions from other players but doesn't interact with them within the game. Moreover, a spectator can be switched to player by calling a `switchSpectator` request if there is an empty seat that is awaiting a player.

A user can also join a game room without leaving the previous room. This is called **multi-join room technique** that is useful for playing a game with the avatar still available in the lobby.

The game room will not receive notifications of any room added or destroyed.

Limbo room

A limbo room is a very special type of room. The limbo room is designed to hold a very large number of users so there is a lot of limitation in a limbo room. In order to let a large number of users join without dropping the performance, the limbo room only listens to the notifications of rooms added and destroyed and private message events. Other events or notifications such as when a user joins or leaves room and public messages are disabled.

The advantages of limbo room is that it can handle a lot for users, which is useful for a game lobby that contains all initial connections from users that are connected and have not yet choosen a game room. It is also useful for applications that only need private messages and do not care for any other users that are not in the friend list, such as Instant Messenger.

Properties of a room

There are several properties of a room to indicate its type and features.

Property name	Default value	Optional	Description
Name	guest_X (X is the number of guests)	No	The name of the room has to be unique within a zone. The name will be used when joining the room.
isGame	False	Yes	The room is a game room when isGame is true.
isPrivate	False	Yes	The room is a private room that requires a password in order to join the room.
password		Yes	A password can be applied to a private room so that only specific users can join the room.
limbo	False	Yes	This flag indicates whether this room is a limbo room.
maxUsers	40 (regular rooms) 16 (game rooms)	Yes	This setting is the maximum number of users allowed to join the room simultaneously. The setting of each room should be set carefully because this number will affect the server performance. For example, a regular or game room should not have a large number of maximum user numbers. In this type of room, every chat message will broadcast to all users within the same room. Large maximum number means every message may draw a huge traffic loading. However, this number needs to be large enough for a limbo room because it is often used as a lobby that needs to hold a lot of user connections.
maxSpectators	0	Yes	This sets the maximum number of spectators in a game room.

Property name	Default value	Optional	Description
autoJoin	False	Yes	Usually the room for lobby usage will have this setting set to "true". A user will automatically join this room after successful connection to the server.
uCountUpdate	True (regular rooms) False (game rooms)	Yes	As same as the user count update in zone configuration. This specifies whether the user will receive a message that contains the user count of each room. By default the regular room will receive the uCountUpdate message, and a game room and limbo room will not.

Comparing the available properties of each room type

Different room properties are available in different room types. The following table shows their relationship:

	Regular room	Game room	Limbo room
Name	Yes	Yes	Yes
isGame	No	Yes	No
isPrivate	Yes	Yes	Yes
password	Yes	Yes	Yes
limbo	No	No	Yes
maxUsers	Yes	Yes	Yes
maxSpectators	No	Yes	No
autoJoin	Yes	Yes	Yes
uCountUpdate	Yes	No	No

We have discussed the basic configuration of the SmartFoxServer. The server also comes with more advanced settings. The full list of configuration setting tags and details can be found in the Server configuration in the official SmartFoxServer documentation.

http://smartfoxserver.com/docs/

Introducing the events of rooms

We discussed three types of rooms when configuring the server in the previous section. The regular room, game room, and limbo room come with different purposes. Each type of rooms has its own set of available events. We will go through some common room events and compare the availability of the events in the three types of rooms.

Event name	Description
onUserEnterRoom	This is a notification that a user has joined the room. This is useful to draw a new user's information and his graphics on the Flash virtual world when receiving this notification message.
onUserLeaveRoom	This is a notification telling that a user has left the room. Similar to the onUserEnterRoom, we often clean up that user's information when receiving this notification.
onSpectatorSwitched	This event was fired when a spectator switched to a player in the game room.
onRoomAdded	The notification message comes when any room is added to the zone. It is useful when a player stays in the lobby waiting for a new game room creation.
onRoomDeleted	Similar to the onRoomAdded event, this is an event that a room has just been destroyed.
onPublicMessage	When a public message is sent from a user, everyone within the room will receive this event notification.
onPrivateMessage	This is an event when receiving a private message from other users.

Comparing the available events of each room type

The events are broadcasted to the users depending on which room type they are in. It is important to know which events are available while designing the virtual world.

	Regular room	Game room	Limbo room
onUserEnterRoom	Yes	Yes	No
onUserLeaveRoom	Yes	Yes	No
onSpectatorSwitched	No	Yes	No
onRoomAdded	Yes	No	Yes
onRoomDeleted	Yes	No	Yes
onPublicMessage	Yes	Yes	No
onPrivateMessage	Yes	Yes	Yes

From the preceding table we can see that game room will not receive onRoomAdded/onRoomDeleted messages because while playing a game we are usually not interested whether a new room is created or deleted.

The limbo room as described before only receives onRoomAdded/onRoomDeleted and onPrivateMessage events. Other events that may cause large traffic are all disabled in the limbo room to ensure that the limbo room can handle thousands of concurrent user connections without increasing the traffic bandwidth.

We discussed some basic events in this section. A full list of events and details can be found here:

```
http://smartfoxserver.com/docs/docPages/as3/html/it_gotoandplay_
smartfoxserver_SFSEvent.html
```

Debugging in local machine

It may be difficult to debug in a multiplayer virtual world development. Usually we can test the script by putting "trace" in the logic for debugging purpose and view the trace log in the Flash IDE. To debug a multiplayer virtual world, we often need two or more instances running in parallel. They will most probably be running in standalone Flash player or the web browser locally. We will discuss how to set up the Flash player to view the Flash trace log without the Flash IDE.

There is a method to read the trace log without using the Flash IDE. It requires the following files:

- A debugger version of Flash player
- mm.cfg file
- flashlog.txt

Downloading the latest debugger version of Flash player

The default Flash player installed in OS is a normal version without the debug feature. We need the debugger version of Flash player to output the trace log outside the Flash IDE. We will download and install the debugger version of Flash player by going to the following URL in the browser: `http://www.adobe.com/support/flashplayer/downloads.html`.

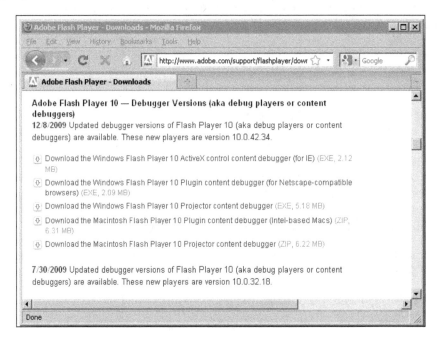

The link to the debugger version is about one page below the Flash player download web page. Scroll down and find the title "**Adobe Flash Player 10 - Debugger Versions (aka debug players or content debuggers)**".

For a Windows user, download the "**Windows Flash Player 10 ActiveX control content debugger (for IE)**" and the "**Windows Flash Player 10 Plugin content debugger (for Netscape-compatible browsers)**".

For a Mac user, download the "**Macintosh Flash Player 10 Plugin content debugger (Intel-based Macs)**" if you are using the Intel-based Macintosh.

If you are using the PowerPC-based Mac, unfortunately the latest Flash player 10 updates dropped the support for PowerPC-based Macs, but you can still download the "**Macintosh Flash Player 9 Plugin content debugger (PowerPC-based Macs)**". All the examples in the book work well on Flash Player 9.

For a Linux user, download the "**Flash Player 10 Linux debugger and standalone players**".

- Double-click the installer and install the Debugger Flash player with default settings.

Creating the mm.cfg file

The `mm.cfg` file configures how the Debugger Flash player behaves.

1. Create a new file in your favorite pure text editor and name it `mm.cfg`.
2. Write these two lines in the file:

```
ErrorReportingEnable=1
TraceOutputFileEnable=1
```

These two lines tell the Flash player debugger to output any error and trace into the logfile.

For Windows XP user, save the file into:

```
C:\Documents and Settings\username\mm.cfg
```

For Windows Vista and Windows 7 user, save the file into:

```
C:\Users\username\mm.cfg
```

For Macintosh user, save the file into:

```
/Library/Application Support/Macromedia/mm.cfg
```

For Linux User, save the file into:

```
/home/username/mm.cfg
```

Testing the debugger log

We will create a simple Flash file to trace something and read it.

1. Launch Adobe Flash.
2. Create a new Flash document—**File | New | Flash File (ActionScritp 3.0)**.
3. Add some trace commands as the action in frame 1 in order to test the logging.

```
trace("Testing Trace without Flash IDE");
```

4. Publish the Flash to make the SWF file and HTML file.

5. Open the newly created HTML file. You may see nothing but the trace should be working and we need to open the trace logfile to confirm it.

Locating the Flash log output file

After setting up the Flash player debugger and running the trace command, a file called `flashlog.txt` is created.

The default location of the `flashlog.txt`:

1. In Windows XP: `C:\Documents and Settings\username\Application Data\Macromedia\Flash Player\Logs\flashlog.txt`.

2. In Windows Vista or Windows 7: `C:\Users\username\AppData\Roaming\Macromedia\Flash Player\Logs\flashlog.txt`.

3. In Mac OSX: `/Users/username/Library/Preferences/Macromedia/Flash Player/Logs/flashlog.txt`.

4. In Linux: `/home/username/Macromedia/Flash_Player/Logs/flashlog.txt`.

Reading the Flash logfile

The simple way to read the Flash logfile is to open the `flashlog.txt` directly. We should see the "Testing Trace without Flash IDE" in the `flashlog.txt` file.

However, it is not convenient to debug because the opened `flashlog.txt` file does not reload automatically when the Flash traces a new output. There are different methods to read the Flash logfile in a better way.

Open the flashlog.txt in web browser

Instead of opening the Flash logfile directly, we can drag the file into a web browser. We can then refresh the browser every time there is an update from trace output.

Using a Firefox add-on to read the Flash logfile

There are some Firefox add-ons that can read the trace file as a sidebar within Firefox.

Reading the log with FlashTracer

FlashTracer can display the trace logfile as a sidebar in Firefox.

1. Go to `http://www.sephiroth.it/firefox/flashtracer/` on the Firefox web browser.

2. Click on **Install now** in the **Install** section of that web page.

3. Click on **Allow** if a yellow bar appear stating that Firefox prevented the site to install the software.

4. Confirm the name as `flashtracer.xpi`.

5. Click on **Install Now**.

6. Click on **Restart Firefox** to restart Firefox and complete the installation.

7. In the Firefox menu, choose **Tools | Flash Tracer** to open the Flash Tracer panel.

8. Click the preference icon to open the preference panel.

9. Click on **Browse** in the **Select output file** section in the **General Settings** tab.

10 Choose the `flashlog.txt` file we just opened.

11. Click on **Yes** if a dialog pops up to ask if you want to replace the `flashlog.txt`.

12. Click on **OK** to confirm and exit the preference panel.

After setting up the Flash Tracer add-on, we can now view the Flash trace output directly in browser while debugging our code.

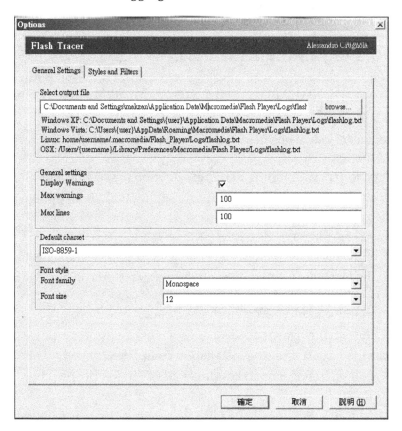

Reading the log with FlashBug

Firebug is a Firefox add-on for web developers to inspect different information from the opened web page. FlashBug is another add-on that adds a Flash Console tab into Firebug to display the Flash trace logfile.

1. Go to the Firebug website `http://getfirebug.com/` in the Firefox web browser.

2. Click on the **Install Firebug For Firefox** button to start the add-on installation.

3. Click on **Allow** if a yellow bar appears stating that Firefox prevented the site to install the software.

4. Click on **Install Now**.

5. Click on **Restart Firefox** to restart Firefox and complete the installation.

6. Go to the Flashbug add-on page after Firefox restarts `https://addons.mozilla.org/en-US/firefox/addon/14465/`.

7. Click on the **Add to Firefox** button to install the add-on.

8. Click on **Install Now** to proceed.

9. Restart the Firefox after the installation completes.

10. Click on the Firebug icon in bottom-right of Firefox to open the Firebug panel.

11. Choose **Flash Console** tab and click the drop-down arrow button.

12. Enable the FlashBug by choosing **Enabled**.

13. The `flashlog.txt` is auto-configured and displayed in the panel.

FlashBug provides some more bonus features than FlashTracer. It cannot only read the trace log but also inspects the list of stored Shared Object data. Shared Object is some data that is stored locally, similar to cookies. The same Flash document can access it and save/load the stored data locally.

"Tail" the trace log file in terminal

In Linux and Mac, we can read the Flashlog file in terminal by executing the following command:

For Mac OSX:

```
tail -f "/Users/{username}/Library/Preferences/Macromedia/Flash Player/
Logs/flashlog.txt"
```

For Linux:

```
tail -f "/home/{username}/Macromedia/Flash_Player/Logs/flashlog.txt"
```

The `tail` command reads the files until the end of the file.

The `-f` parameter lets the `tail` command to keep refreshing for new Flash log output.

This is a convenient way to keep reading the latest trace logfile without Firefox.

Flash Security Sandbox

Flash player comes with a security sandbox to prevent the Flash loading data or connect sockets to other resources that are not in the same domain of the hosting server. It provides a cross-domain policy file for the host to configure the IP addresses of incoming Flash connect requests.

This cross-domain policy is an XML format file placed in the server. We are using the socket connections to establish the connection to SmartFoxServer and thus we will configure the policy file for socket connection. There are two ways to set the socket policy. We can either use the **Master Socket Policy** server or configure the `AutoSendPolicyFile` setting to let SmartFoxServer send out the policy XML.

 Please note that the Flash player security sandbox does not apply to the Flash IDE and Flash projector. It applies only to the Flash player in web browser.

Configuring master socket policy server

Prior to Flash Player 9.0.115, a `crossdomain.xml` policy file served in HTTP could be loaded by socket connection as policy file over port 80. As of version 9.0.115, the socket policy file has to be served on 843 port.

SmartFoxServer provides a Master Socket Policy server to serve the policy file on 843 port.

1. Go to `http://www.smartfoxserver.com/products/download. php?d=42` in web browser. It will start the download process of the `SocketPolicyServer.zip` file.

2. Extract the ZIP file to the SmartFoxServer installation directory.

3. Open `policy.xml` with any text editor.

4. Configure the policy file. The following setting accepts from all addresses:

```
<?xml version="1.0"?>
<!DOCTYPE cross-domain-policy
    SYSTEM "http://www.macromedia.com/xml/dtds/cross-domain-policy.
                                                 dtd">
<cross-domain-policy>
        <site-control permitted-cross-domain-policies="all" />
        <allow-access-from domain='*' to-ports='9339' />
</cross-domain-policy>
```

5. Launch the policy server.

For Windows platform: Run the `policy-server.bat` in command prompt.

For Linux/Mac platform: Execute following command in the terminal to run the server. It will require administrator access to run the Master Socket Policy server.

```
chmod a+x policy-server.sh
sudo ./policy-server.sh
```

Configuring SmartFoxServer to send socket policy

Without the Master Socket Policy server set up, the Flash player will look for the policy file from the port of SmartFoxServer. We can configure the SmartFoxServer to send out the policy by setting `AutoSendPolicyFile` to true in the configuration file.

An example of a wildcard policy file to default port of SmartFoxServer looks like:

```
<cross-domain-policy>
    <allow-access-from domain='*' to-ports='9339' />
</cross-domain-policy>
```

We can further set the allow domain by using the `PolicyAllowedDomains`:

```
<PolicyAllowedDomains>
    <AllowedDomain>*.something.com</AllowedDomain>
</PolicyAllowedDomains>
```

Loading policy file from Flash client

If neither the policy server nor SmartFoxServer serve the policy file, we need to load the socket policy manually in Flash by calling a `loadPolicyFile` request before establishing the connection.

The following line will load the policy file from the specific server address and port of SmartFoxServer.

```
Security.loadPolicyFile("xmlsocket://server_address:9339");
```

This will force the Flash player to load the policy file that was created by the SmartFoxServer to ensure the cross-domain access issues.

Enabling the network access for the Flash document

There are two sandboxes of the local playback security provided by Flash. The Flash file that is opened locally is limited to access either a local file or network. In a normal case the Flash document cannot access both a local file and network.

As we will be testing the SmartFoxServer connection with the opened Flash document, all the examples will be set to "Access network only" by default.

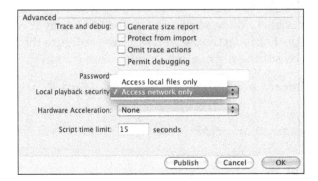

Keeping updates to Flash player security policy

The security policy of Flash player is often updated with new restrictions and rules along with Flash player version updates. We can check the latest security policy in the **Resources for developers** section from the official Adobe web page: http://www.adobe.com/products/flashplayer/security/.

The document of SmartFoxServer — http://www.smartfoxserver.com/ whitepapers/fp_security/ — will also update and summarize how the latest Flash player security policy affects the connections.

Creating a Flash document to connect to the server

Let's try to connect to the SmartFoxServer that we've set up and play around some basic connection functions.

1. Create a new Flash document with ActionScript 3.0 supports and save it to the disk.
2. We need to set the class path for the API client of the SmartFoxServer.
3. Click on **File** | **Publish Setting** | **Flash** | **Script: ActionScript 3.0** | **Settings....**
4. Click on the "+" and input the path of the Flash API client. It is located in the SmartFoxServer installation directory | **Flash API** | **ActionScript 3.0**.

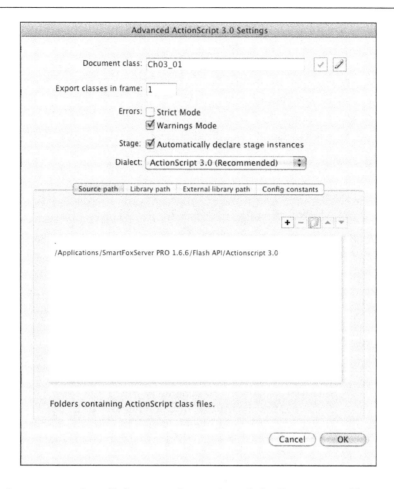

5. In the same setting dialog, we also assigned the Document Class to Ch03_01 for our first example in Chapter 3.

6. Save the file in a new directory.

Next, let's create the document class file:

1. In Adobe Flash, click on **File** | **New** | **ActionScript** file to create an empty class file.

2. Save the file, and naming it as Ch03_01.as, to the same directory of the Flash document that was created in the previously mentioned steps.

3. Put the following code into the document class and save again:

```
package {

import it.gotoandplay.smartfoxserver.SmartFoxClient;
import it.gotoandplay.smartfoxserver.SFSEvent;
import it.gotoandplay.smartfoxserver.data.Room;
import it.gotoandplay.smartfoxserver.data.User;

import flash.display.*;

public class Ch03_01 extends MovieClip{

        private var _sfs:SmartFoxClient;

        public function Ch03_01()
        {
            _sfs = new SmartFoxClient(true);
            _sfs.connect("127.0.0.1",9339);
        }

    }

}
```

 Please make sure the class name is public class Ch03_01, the constructor function name is public function Ch03_01, the filename Ch03_01.as, and the Document Class set in the Flash document is identical.

Take a look at our first code. To make the SmartFoxServer Client API available for this class, we need to import the required Client API classes.

```
import it.gotoandplay.smartfoxserver.SmartFoxClient;
import it.gotoandplay.smartfoxserver.SFSEvent;
import it.gotoandplay.smartfoxserver.data.Room;
import it.gotoandplay.smartfoxserver.data.User;
```

We will have an instance of the client of SmartFoxServer so we need the client instance to be an instance variable.

```
private var _sfs:SmartFoxClient;
```

Next we have a constructor. As this is the document class of the Flash file, this constructor is the entry point of the Flash document and will be run immediately after the Flash runs.

```
public function Ch03_01()
{

}
```

We need to create an instance of the Client API before performing any action on the SmartFoxServer. There is one Boolean parameter when creating it. This parameter indicates whether the client API outputs debugging messages to log. The default value is false. We are in testing phase now so we need to set the debug option to true to view the connection message between the client API and the SmartFoxServer.

```
_sfs = new SmartFoxClient(true);
```

After the SmartFox client is ready, we can connect to the SmartFoxServer. The server is in the same machine with default port setting. Therefore we connect to 127.0.0.1 and the default 9339 port.

```
_sfs.connect("127.0.0.1",9339);
```

When we test the Flash movie, we will have some debug message from the Client API indicating the 'conversation' between the Client and the SmartFoxServer. The "Sending" message means the Flash client is trying to send the message to the server and the "RECEIVED" message is the message that the Flash client received from the server. We have both Send and Receive messages now, because we have succeeded to connect to the server and the server is responding to us.

[Sending]: <msg t='sys'><body action='verChk' r='0'><ver v='158' /></body></msg>

[RECEIVED]: <cross-domain-policy><allow-access-from domain='*' to-ports='9339' /></cross-domain-policy>, (len: 91)

[RECEIVED]: <msg t='sys'><body action='apiOK' r='0'></body></msg>, (len: 53)

Logging into a zone

After connecting to the SmartFoxServer, we are now going to log in to the zone that we just configured.

```
package {

    import it.gotoandplay.smartfoxserver.SmartFoxClient;
    import it.gotoandplay.smartfoxserver.SFSEvent;
    import it.gotoandplay.smartfoxserver.data.Room;
    import it.gotoandplay.smartfoxserver.data.User;

    import flash.display.*;

    public class Ch03_02 extends MovieClip{
```

```
        private var _sfs:SmartFoxClient;

        public function Ch03_02()
        {
                _sfs = new SmartFoxClient(true);

                _sfs.addEventListener(SFSEvent.
                                        onConnection,onConnection);
                _sfs.addEventListener(SFSEvent.onRoomListUpdate,
                onRoomListUpdate);

                _sfs.connect("127.0.0.1",9339);
        }

        private function onConnection(e:SFSEvent):void
        {
                var ok:Boolean = e.params.success;
                if (ok){
                        _sfs.login("simpleChat","myname","");
                }
        }
        private function onRoomListUpdate(e:SFSEvent):void
        {
                _sfs.autoJoin();
        }
    }
}
```

Let's take a look at the code in more detail. Compare it to the first example; we added two event listeners and two corresponding event handlers to the class.

In the constructor we added the event listeners before connecting to the server.

This line of code tells the SmartFoxClient that we need to handle the logic when the connection is established, and it will call the "onConnection" function when we try to log in to a zone.

```
_sfs.addEventListener(SFSEvent.onConnection,onConnection);
```

We also need to know when we got the latest room list and join the room. So we also register the onRoomListUpdate event to the event listeners.

```
_sfs.addEventListener(SFSEvent.onRoomListUpdate,onRoomListUpdate);
```

In the first example, we only connected to the server and we didn't perform anything, whether it was a successful connection or whether it failed. Here we define what happens when a connection is established or fails. After the connection successes, we log in to the `simpleChat` zone with a predefined name.

```
private function onConnection(e:SFSEvent):void
{
    var ok:Boolean = e.params.success;
    if (ok){
        _sfs.login("simpleChat","myname","");
    }
}
```

The client will receive a room list from the server once the client logs in to a zone successfully. This room list is retrieved automatically and it will fire an event `onRoomListUpdate`. The client needs this room list to know which room it can join. Therefore, we have the auto-join room command inside the `onRoomListUpdate` event handler.

```
private function onRoomListUpdate(e:SFSEvent):void
{
    _sfs.autoJoin();
}
```

When running the Flash, we have a lot of debugging message output to the Flash logfile by the SmartFoxClient API. It is important to understand at least some basic meaning of those debug messages because it helps us a lot when debugging the virtual world and knowing what is going on between the Flash client and the SmartFoxServer.

The debugger message often comes with pairs for [Sending] and [Received] messages. A pair of these messages means the client sent a request to the server and received a response from server. If there is a send out message without receiving any corresponding message, most probably something went wrong in-between.

Creating a cooperative drawing whiteboard

We have created a basic example to log in to the SmartFoxServer. Now we are going to create a whiteboard so every connected user can draw on the same whiteboard.

The concept is to add mouse listeners to handle the event when mouse is down, mouse moves, and mouse is up. When the mouse is down and moves, the application broadcasts the mouse coordination to all users within the room and all users then draw the lines according to the received coordination.

We will have a glance of the full code and explain it part by part in detail.

```
package {
    import it.gotoandplay.smartfoxserver.SmartFoxClient;
    import it.gotoandplay.smartfoxserver.SFSEvent;
    import it.gotoandplay.smartfoxserver.data.Room;
    import it.gotoandplay.smartfoxserver.data.User;

    import flash.display.*;
    import flash.events.MouseEvent;
    public class Ch03_03 extends MovieClip{

        private var _sfs:SmartFoxClient;

        private var _drawing:Boolean = false;

        //---------------------------------------
        // CONSTRUCTOR
        //---------------------------------------
        public function Ch03_03()
        {
            _sfs = new SmartFoxClient(true);

            _sfs.addEventListener(SFSEvent.
                        onConnection,onConnection);
            _sfs.addEventListener(SFSEvent.onRoomListUpdate,
                            onRoomListUpdate);
            _sfs.addEventListener(SFSEvent.onPublicMessage,
                            onPublicMessage);

            _sfs.connect("127.0.0.1",9339);

            stage.addEventListener(MouseEvent.MOUSE_DOWN,
                            startDrawing);
            stage.addEventListener(MouseEvent.MOUSE_
                            MOVE,drawing);
            stage.addEventListener(MouseEvent.MOUSE_UP,
                            stopDraw);
        }
```

```
private function onConnection(e:SFSEvent):void
{
        var ok:Boolean = e.params.success;
        if (ok){
                /* Login to the zone 'simpleChat' with empty
                   name and empty password */
                _sfs.login("simpleChat","","");
        }
}


private function onRoomListUpdate(e:SFSEvent):void
{
        /* Auto-join the default room of the zone */
        _sfs.autoJoin();
}


private function onPublicMessage(e:SFSEvent):void
{
        /* Get the message from the onPublicMessage Event*/
        var message = e.params.message;

        // Split the Array into three parts by the comma ','
        var splitArray = message.split(',');

        /* The starting indicates that the coordinatation
         * is a starting point or drawing point */
        var starting = Number(splitArray[0]);

        /* The coordination of the drawing point */
        var pointX = Number(splitArray[1]);
        var pointY = Number(splitArray[2]);

        /* Move the starting point if it is the first point
           of the line*/
        if (starting == 1){
                this.graphics.moveTo(pointX,pointY);
        }else{
                /* Draw the line accroding to the received
                   cooredination */
                this.graphics.lineStyle(5,0x000000);
                this.graphics.lineTo(pointX,pointY);
        }
}
```

```
private function startDrawing(e:MouseEvent):void
{
        /* Send a public message with coordination as message
            text */
        _sfs.sendPublicMessage('1,'+mouseX+','+mouseY);

        _drawing = true;
}

private function drawing(e:MouseEvent):void
{
        if (_drawing){
                _sfs.sendPublicMessage('0,'+mouseX+','+mouseY);
        }
}

private function stopDraw(e:MouseEvent):void
{
        _drawing = false;
}
    }
}
```

Let's get in to detail of the code part by part. We are using mouse as input so we need to import MouseEvent to the class.

```
package {
    import it.gotoandplay.smartfoxserver.SmartFoxClient;
    import it.gotoandplay.smartfoxserver.SFSEvent;
    import it.gotoandplay.smartfoxserver.data.Room;
    import it.gotoandplay.smartfoxserver.data.User;

    import flash.display.*;
    import flash.events.MouseEvent;

    ...
```

Except for the SmartFoxClient instance variable, we need a Boolean flag to know whether the user is drawing.

```
private var _drawing:Boolean = false;
```

In the constructor, we add three more event listeners to listen to the mouse up, mouse down, and mouse move event. Also we will add an onPublicMessage event to receive the drawing coordination from other users.

```
public function Ch03_03()
{
    _sfs = new SmartFoxClient(true);

    _sfs.addEventListener(SFSEvent.onConnection,onConnection);
            _sfs.addEventListener(SFSEvent.
                            onRoomListUpdate,onRoomListUpdate);


    _sfs.connect("127.0.0.1",9339);
        _sfs.addEventListener(SFSEvent.onPublicMessage,
                            onPublicMessage);
    stage.addEventListener(MouseEvent.MOUSE_DOWN,startDrawing);
    stage.addEventListener(MouseEvent.MOUSE_MOVE,drawing);
    stage.addEventListener(MouseEvent.MOUSE_UP, stopDraw);
}
```

In the previous examples, we used "myname" as the login name. In this example we are going to test the Flash with multiple instances, therefore we need to log in with different names. However, we have not made the name input feature yet, so we will assign an empty name when joining the application. SmartFoxServer will make the name look like "Guest_1" when joining the zone with an empty name.

```
private function onConnection(e:SFSEvent):void
{
    var ok:Boolean = e.params.success;
    if (ok){
            _sfs.login("simpleChat","","");
    }
}
```

This is a drawing application so we will add logic to the mouse interactivity.

When the mouse is down, it will call the startDrawing function. This function will send a public message with the mouse coordination as the message text.

```
private function startDrawing(e:MouseEvent):void
{
    _sfs.sendPublicMessage('1,'+mouseX+','+mouseY);
    _drawing = true;
}
```

If the mouse is moving with the left button pressed, it means the user is drawing on the canvas. We will send out the drawing coordination in a public message too.

```
private function drawing(e:MouseEvent):void
{
    if (_drawing){
        _sfs.sendPublicMessage('0,'+mouseX+','+mouseY);
    }
}
```

When the mouse is up, we need to reset the _drawing flag to false so that any mouse moving after mouse up will not be wrongly treated as drawing.

```
private function stopDraw(e:MouseEvent):void
{
    _drawing = false;
}
```

We have added an onPublicMessage event listener. This event handler will be called when there is an incoming public message. We will draw the lines in the onPublicMessage handler.

```
private function onPublicMessage(e:SFSEvent):void
{
    var message = e.params.message;
    var splitArray = message.split(',');
    var starting = Number(splitArray[0]);
    var pointX = Number(splitArray[1]);
    var pointY = Number(splitArray[2]);
    if (starting == 1){
        this.graphics.moveTo(pointX,pointY);
    }else{
        this.graphics.lineStyle(5,0x000000);
        this.graphics.lineTo(pointX,pointY);
    }
}
```

Let's take a detailed look at this handler.

We first retrieve the content of the public message.

```
var message = e.params.message;
```

The message is something like 0,{mouseX},{mouseY} and the three pieces of information are separated by a comma (","). The first number is either 0 or 1 to indicate that this is the start drawing point or a mouse moving point. The second and third numbers are the mouse coordination of the user who is drawing.

We split the received message into an array to retrieve those three numbers.

```
var splitArray = message.split(',');
var starting = Number(splitArray[0]);
var pointX = Number(splitArray[1]);
var pointY = Number(splitArray[2]);
```

If it is a starting point, we will move the point to the coordination and be ready for drawing the line. If it is a moving point, we draw the line with a five-pixels width black line.

```
if (starting == 1){
this.graphics.moveTo(pointX,pointY);
}else{
    this.graphics.lineStyle(5,0x000000);
    this.graphics.lineTo(pointX,pointY);
}
```

That is how the `onPublicMessage` handler draws the lines. Please note that a public message is sent to all users including the sender of that public message. Therefore, the sender also receives the `onPublicMesasge` event with the same message that is sent out.

To test the synchronization drawing effect, we have to publish the Flash file into HTML and SWF by **File | Publish** in Flash IDE.

Testing the cooperative whiteboard

Open the newly published HTML file in the web browser. If you read the Flash logfile, it will show the trace and debug messages from this Flash document.

We need another instance of Flash to test the synchronization effect. To open another instance, copy the URL of the opened web browser and paste in another web browser window. Then we will have two same Flash documents connected to the SmartFoxServer to simulate two users logging in to the same server.

Draw something in one of the Flash document and you will see every instance draws the same line magically. This is our first multiuser application with SmartFoxServer.

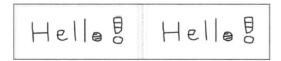

These are two web browsers opening the whiteboard application with one drawing the "Hello" text and the other drawing the shading.

Summary

We have learned how the configuration file set the behaviors of the SmartFoxServer. We also know the security sandbox and the method to configure it. We also tried some experimental examples to test the server and learned basic debugging method with multiple Flash documents running at the same time. At the end of the chapter, we've created a simple whiteboard application so that every connected user can cooperate and draw in the same canvas. In the next chapter, we are going to start the development of our virtual world.

4
Creating Map and Ground in Isometric View

Isometric Projection is a common game view that has been widely used for almost 30 years since the 1980s. Thanks to the good-looking 3D depth presentation in 2D coordinate, isometric projection is being used in many games in different platforms. It provides some kinds of 3D depth feeling to the game without handling full 3D coordinates and manipulations. This is an important technique in making Flash game and Flash virtual world because Flash does not support full 3D in mature way yet and isometric game view is one of the best solutions in Flash to provide 3D-like representation.

In this chapter, we are going to learn basic isometric techniques in Flash. The following topics will be discussed:

- The concept of isometric projection
- Drawing an isometric tile in Flash
- Drawing the bitmap graphic textures for isometric map
- Loading external map data
- Converting the coordination between isometric and screen
- Building a map editor

This chapter mainly focuses on the basic techniques of applying isometric map. There are some advanced techniques such as sorting objects to make correct depth in isometric projection which will be discussed in *Chapter 7, Creating Buildings and Environments in the Virtual World*.

Comparing different game views

There are different game views in presenting a Flash virtual world. Top-down, side-scrolling, 3D, and isometric view are four common views. It is important to decide which game view is being used for the whole virtual world because they require totally different graphic drawing techniques implementation. We will compare the advantages and disadvantages for each game view.

Top-down perspective

This is a game view where the camera hangs in the sky looking downwards to the player. The camera can be perpendicular to the ground or it can view the ground from some angles.

As the angle and rotation of the camera is fixed in top-down perspective, all static objects in the world need to be drawn only once.

One disadvantage of the top-down perspective is that the graphic detail cannot be viewed if it is not facing the player.

The following screenshot from Pokemon in Game Boy uses top-down perspective. We can only see the front wall of the house that faces the player and we cannot see any side walls.

Side-scrolling view

In this type of game view, the game is viewed by the side-view camera. Game objects are placed side-by-side and the characters usually move towards left and right.

The advantage of the graphic implementation is that the rich graphics can be drawn in lesser time compared to other views because almost all graphics only need to be drawn in one-angle view, and the left and right view can be duplicated.

The disadvantage is that there is not much depth and 3D effect in the side-scrolling view.

The following screenshot shows one of the most representative works of side-scrolling games, Super Mario Brothers:

3D view

In a full 3D game view, the camera is not fixed into one angle. Instead, the camera can be placed and rotated freely.

There are some 3D engines for Flash. Papervision3D and Away3D are two famous 3D engines for Flash that can import and manipulate 3D mesh objects that are created from 3D software. Game developers can pan and rotate the camera view freely without drawing a lot of artwork because they are be rendered from the same mesh object.

The following graph shows a mesh rendering by Away3D. Different texture can apply to the same mesh and the mesh can be rotated and panned freely.

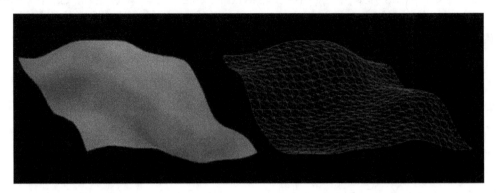

The disadvantage of using 3D view in Flash is that displaying complex 3D mesh in Flash may result in slow performance, and programming 3D world requires much more advanced programming and graphic techniques than other game views.

Isometric game view

Isometric projection is a method to display 3D objects in 2D. It is sometimes called "2.5D" because it can give a good effect on 3D depth in 2D coordinate. Isometric has been widely used in the game industry for almost 30 years.

The advantage of using isometric game view is that it gives some basic 3D features without dealing with 3D coordinates and complicated 3D mesh objects.

The following screenshot shows the game that uses isometric projection to add depth and details in the city view of a virtual world (screenshot from the Flash game hosted on www.seasonlao.com).

There are some disadvantages of using isometric game view. One is that extra coordination conversion and calculation is needed because the isometric world is displayed in a diamond form instead of a square form.

Another disadvantage is that every movable element requires more then one graphic to display in isometric projection because there are different angle views. An object may face North, East, South, West or even NW, NE, SW, SE. When comparing isometric projection to other game views, it requires much more artwork production time.

Many virtual worlds and games are in isometric projection because the 2.5D game view can present the game world better while preventing the much more difficult full 3D programming.

The virtual world we are going to build will also be based on isometric projection.

Getting an isometric projection view

We have emphasized that the isometric projection gives a 2.5D- or 3D-like feeling. So what are the differences between a full 3D camera view and isometric view? It is often a good option to demonstrate isometric projection with a perfect cube.

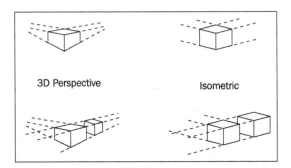

In 3D perspective projection, objects have vanishing points and while they are moving, the lines and shapes keep changing.

In isometric projection, objects do not have vanishing points. The shapes and lines of the objects do not change while they are moving.

Isometric coordination

The world map is divided into a set of small pieces in games with tile-based geometry. These pieces are called **tiles**. The tiles align adjacent to each other into a grid. Each tile represents a graphic asset and the whole tile set forms the virtual world. When the tiles are rectangles, they align on traditional X/Y coordination.

The geometry of an isometric ground can be mapped to the traditional tile-based geometry. It is actually a rotated tile-based coordination. The following graphs show a common mapping between traditional tile-based geometry and isometric geometry:

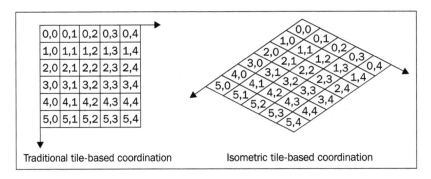

Making an isometric map

Isometric map means the graphics of the ground of the virtual world.

There are several techniques to make the graphics of the isometric map in Flash.

Creating the base tile of an isometric map

It will be convenient to draw a base grid with isometric perspective and this will be a reference of all other isometric graphics.

1. Draw a square.
2. Rotate the rectangle right by 45 degrees.
3. Open the **Transform** panel in Flash by choosing **Window | Transform**.
4. Set the **Scale Height** value from **100%** to **50%.**
5. Draw the inner lines.

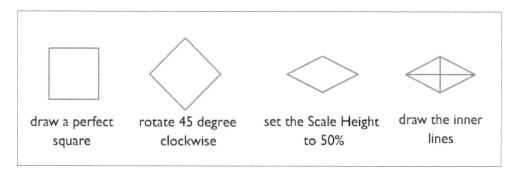

draw a perfect square   rotate 45 degree clockwise   set the Scale Height to 50%   draw the inner lines

After drawing the basic grid, we can resize the grid to a specific width and height. This dimension can be treated as the basic unit of the whole isometric map.

For example, we will use 48 pixels width and 24 pixels height here.

To make it easier for further use, we will make this isometric shape as a movie clip symbol and name it IsoTile.

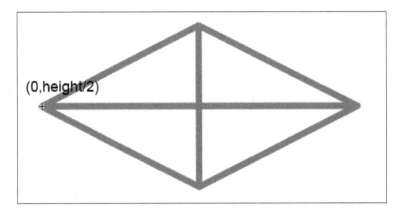

Furthermore, we need to modify the IsoTile movie clip so that the original point is placed in the (0, height/2) point instead of the default (0,0) point. This setting enables future depth sorting much more easily. We will discuss the depth sorting later but all tile graphic examples in this chapter will follow this original point setting.

Creating a basic isometric tile map

In traditional tile map, we often use a map coordination to represent each tile inside the map. This is like accessing a 2D array that the `array[0][0]` is the tile in the first row and first column, and `array[3][2]` is the tile in the fourth row and third column.

Isometric tile map is a rotated traditional tile map so that the same coordination system can apply to isometric tile map. However, it is not like a traditional tile map in which all tiles are placed regularly as a big square. Isometric tiles are placed in a diamond shape so that the tiles are not placed along with the screen X/Y coordinate. A more complex formula is needed to place the tiles properly.

Let h be the height of the tile and w be the width.

For a tile with coordinate (i, j), its screen position is:

x = (j-i) * w / 2;

y = (i+j) * h / 2;

We will demonstrate the positioning formula in the following example:

1. Create a new Flash document in Adobe Flash.

2. Copy the previously created IsoTile movie clip to the library.

3. Configure the IsoTile to export as ActionScript with class name `IsoTile` in the **Symbol Properties** panel.

4. Configure the document class of the Flash document as `IsometricTile`.

5. Create a new ActionScript file and save it as `IsometricTile.as`.

We will have an overview on the complete class and explain how it works.

```
package {
    import flash.display.*;
    import flash.events.*;
    public class IsometricTile extends MovieClip{

        private var _map:Array;
        private var _gridWidth:Number = 48;
        private var _gridHeight:Number = 24;
        private var _mapHolder:MovieClip = new MovieClip();

        public function IsometricTile() {
            addEventListener(Event.ADDED_TO_STAGE,init);
        }

        private function init(e:Event):void {
            _map = new Array();
            for(var i:int=0;i<4;i++){
                _map[i] = new Array();
                for(var j:int=0;j<4;j++){
                    _map[i][j] = new IsoTile();
                    _mapHolder.addChild(_map[i][j]);
                    _map[i][j].x = (j-i) * _gridWidth / 2;
                    _map[i][j].y = (i+j) * _gridHeight / 2;
                }
            }

            addChild(_mapHolder);
            _mapHolder.x = (stage.stageWidth - _gridWidth)/2;
            _mapHolder.y = (stage.stageHeight - _mapHolder.
                                                height) /2;

        }
    }
}
```

Let's take a look on the instance variables of the document class.

```
private var _map:Array;
private var _mapHolder:MovieClip = new MovieClip();
private var _gridWidth:Number = 48;
private var _gridHeight:Number = 24;
```

The `_map` array is the data structure of the isometric map. Every grid in the array stored a copy of the IsoTile.

`_mapHolder` is the container of the map. Instead of putting all tiles on the stage directly, we would create a movie clip on stage to contain all the tiles. This setting allows us to move the whole tile map by just changing the position of this map container.

`_gridWidth` and `_gridHeight` defines the dimension of each tile. These numbers are useful when calculating the position of each tile.

We are going to place the tiles as soon as the Flash loads. One way is to place all codes in the constructor. However, it is always better to initialize the code that is related to stage and display list after the class is added to stage.

> Placing code that is related to stage and display list after `ADDED_TO_STAGE` event can prevent it from accessing other display objects, or stage before it is added to the display list. Otherwise null pointer access exception may occur.
>
> The other advantage of putting code in another function instead of constructor is the performance issue. After Flash Player 9, all code other than constructor is just-in-time compilation that gives a performance boost from the traditional interpreter.

We added an event listener in constructor to handle the initialization after the `ADDED_TO_STAGE` event fired.

```
public function IsometricTile() {
    addEventListener(Event.ADDED_TO_STAGE, init);
}
```

The `init` function will do all initialization that needs to access the stage and display list.

```
private function init(e:Event):void {
    ...
}
```

There are two steps to instantiate the 2D map array in ActionScript:

1. Create a 1D array with map height as length.
2. For every tile in the 1D array, create another 1D array with map width as length.

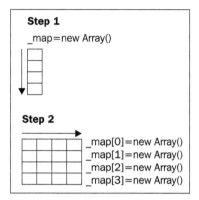

In this example, the map will be 4x4. The nested loop creates the 2D map array

```
_map = new Array();
for(var i:int=0;i<4;i++){
    _map[i] = new Array();
    for(var j:int=0;j<4;j++){


    }
}
```

Inside the nested loop, we instantiate an IsoTile on every row and column, and add it to the display list of the map holder. IsoTile is the basic isometric tile that we have created:

```
_map[i][j] = new IsoTile();
_mapHolder.addChild(_map[i][j]);
```

Then we place the IsoTile according to the formula:

```
_map[i][j].x = (j-i) * _gridWidth / 2;
_map[i][j].y = (i+j) * _gridHeight / 2;
```

Finally, we add the map holder to the stage and place it in the middle of the stage:

```
addChild(_mapHolder);
_mapHolder.x = (stage.stageWidth - _ gridWidth)/2;
_mapHolder.y = (stage.stageHeight - _mapHolder.height) /2;
```

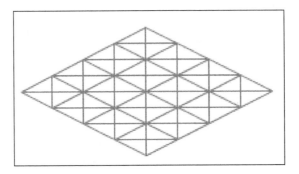

The result of the code places 4x4 tiles in isometric projection.

Drawing seamless shore border

Drawing the graphic precisely in isometric projection is not easy sometimes. We will create a shore and island graphic in Photoshop for isometric projection. We use Photoshop to demonstrate the technique but it can also be done in most other graphic applications.

The principle is to create a graphic in top-down view and then cut every tile and convert it to isometric projection by rotating it 45 degree and scale down the y-axis by 50 percent. The following graph illustrates the steps:

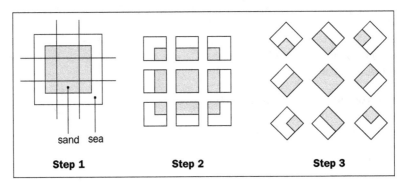

We are using 48 pixels width and 24 pixels height isometric tile as an example and now we need to know the dimension of the square before converting to the final isometric dimension.

Let *W1* be the width of the square and *W2* be the width of the isometric tile.

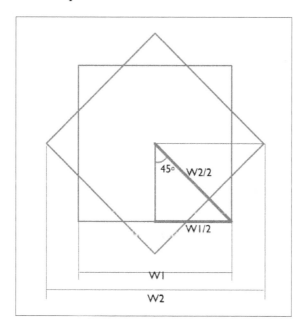

The graph shows the relationship between the square and the 45-degree rotated square.

Sin(45) = a/b = W1/W2

Therefore, W1 = W2 * Sin(45)

We have W2 = 48 in the example so the width of the square is 33.94, which is 48*Sin(45).

As rotating a bitmap graphic is not as perfect as rotating a vector graphic, we usually give one or two more pixels to the square. This can prevent white gap between tiles due to the bitmap rotation. Therefore, the dimension of the square for the 48x24 isometric tile will be 35x35.

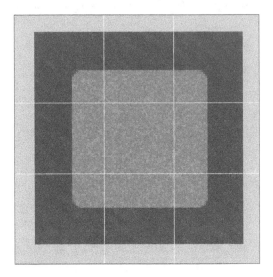

According to our principle, we will draw 3x3 tiles for the shore and island. The dimension of the Photoshop document is set to 105x105.

For easier selection later, we create four guidelines on the document. They are placed at 35px and 70px, in both vertical and horizontal positions.

Then we draw a blue background as the sea and a rounded square in the middle as the island.

After creating the island graphic, we need to cut and convert into isometric tiles one by one.

1. Select and copy every single tile and paste it into a new 35x35 pixels document with transparent background.
2. Rotate the image 45 degree clockwise by **Image** | **Image Rotation** | **Arbitrary**.
3. Finally scale the y-axis to 50 percent by editing the image size.

The dimension of the final isometric tile graphic is 50x25, which is slightly bigger than the defined tile size. If the bitmap size is exactly the defined tile size, some white gaps may appear when tiling them because the edge of the bitmap graphic may not be perfect for seamless connection. Therefore adding one or two more pixels to let the edges slightly overlap can fix this problem.

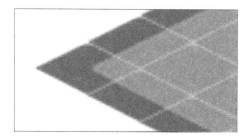

Texturing an isometric map

The whole map is composed tile by tile. Therefore, one way is to draw different pieces of graphics that can be seamlessly aligned together. For example, there may be 15 pieces of graphics for grass, sand, sea, and the shore. We can use these pieces to compose an island map with some grass and sand on it. Graphics on every grid are chosen from the predefined 15 pieces of graphics.

A simple way to implement this in Flash is to place all predefined pieces of graphics frame by frame in the timeline of the grid movie clip. We are not going to animate this timeline, therefore we put a stop command in the first frame. When all graphics are stored in this structure, we can easily control the graphic of this grid movie clip by calling gotoAndStop to the frame with the graphics.

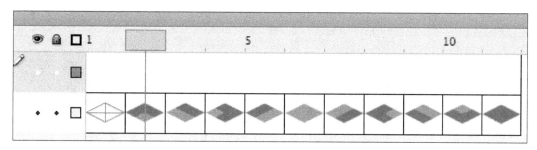

For example, we can add the tile to stage and fill the map with different textures by the following function:

```
private function init(e:Event):void {
    ...
    _map[0][0].gotoAndStop(2);
    _map[0][1].gotoAndStop(3);
    _map[0][2].gotoAndStop(3);
    _map[0][3].gotoAndStop(4);
    _map[1][0].gotoAndStop(5);
    _map[1][1].gotoAndStop(6);
    _map[1][2].gotoAndStop(6);
```

```
_map[1][3].gotoAndStop(7);
_map[2][0].gotoAndStop(5);
_map[2][1].gotoAndStop(6);
_map[2][2].gotoAndStop(6);
_map[2][3].gotoAndStop(7);
_map[3][0].gotoAndStop(8);
_map[3][1].gotoAndStop(9);
_map[3][2].gotoAndStop(9);
_map[3][3].gotoAndStop(10);

}
```

These lines set the 4x4 isometric tile map with textures that form an island using the pieces of bitmap graphics that were created in the previous example.

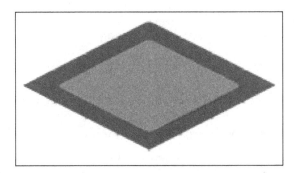

Texturing a big map

It is difficult to set every tile texture line by line in a big map. We may sometimes even want to display different combinations of the map to represent different places. We need a more dynamic way for displaying the isometric tile map. In this chapter, we will modify the previous example code to enable the class to read the map data from an external file and texture the isometric map according to the map data.

The map data is defined in the following structure of XML in this example:

```
<map>
    <name> Sample Map  (Map Name)</name>
    <width>10 (The amount of tiles in width side)</width>
    <height>10 (The amount of tiles in height side)</height>
    <terrain>
        <![CDATA[
        11,11,11,11,11,11,11,11,11,11
        11, 2, 3, 4, 2, 3, 3, 3, 4,11
        11, 5, 6, 7, 5, 6, 6, 6, 7,11
```

```
11,  5,  6,  7,  5,  6,  6,  6,  7,11
11,  5,  6,  7,  5,  6,  6,  6,  7,11
11,  8,  9,10,  5,  6,  6,  6,  7,11
11,11,11,11,  5,  6,  6,  6,  7,11
11,11,11,11,  5,  6,  6,  6,  7,11
11,11,11,11,  8,  9,  9,  9,10,11
11,11,11,11,11,11,11,11,11,11
(Tile texture information separated by commas)
]]>
```
```
    </terrain>
</map>
```

The XML structure here is the map format that we will be using for the whole book. However, it may not fit to other virtual world projects and it is the virtual world designer's job to figure out a custom map format or XML structure that fits to a different virtual world.

The main flow of the Flash program is slightly changed. In the previous examples, we draw the isometric tile map in the initial stage. However, loading an external file is an I/O operation that needs some time to load the full text. The drawing process has to wait till the external map data is completely loaded. The following diagram shows the flow of loading map data:

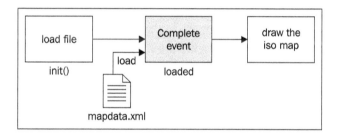

In this example, we need to import the `flash.net` package to load the external data.

```
import flash.net.*;
```

We need to load the external map data before drawing the isometric map on the stage. Therefore we put the loader codes in the `init` function now instead of drawing the map.

```
private function init(e:Event):void {
    // An URLLoader is needed to load an external text file.
    var loader:URLLoader = new URLLoader();
```

```
    /* In order to know when the external text file is loaded, we need
to listen to the COMPLETE event and handle it in the onMapDataLoaded
function.*/
    loader.addEventListener(Event.COMPLETE,onMapDataLoaded);

    /* After setting up the loader, we will actually load the file.
The filename is defined as mapdata.xml in this example. The filename
can be dynamically set in the future to load different map data
according to the needs. */
    loader.load(new URLRequest('mapdata.xml'));
}
```

The map drawing code is now placed in the onMapDataLoaded function which is called after the map data is loaded.

```
private function onMapDataLoaded(e:Event):void {
    /* The loaded XML data is stored in the loader.data. The e.target
is the target of the COMPLETE event which refer to the loader we used
to load the map data. We create an XML object to parse the map data. */
    var _xml:XML = new XML(e.target.data);

    /* The width and height as children under root node so we can
directly access them and type casting it into integer. */
    var mapWidth:int = int(_xml.width);
    var mapHeight:int = int(_xml.height);

    /* For the terrain data, they are stored as comma separated number
with line break for every row. We can prepare the terrain data by
trimming the white space and break it into rows. */
    var terrainString:String = _xml.terrain;
    terrainString = terrainString.split("\t").join('');
    var terrainData:Array = terrainString.split("\n");

    // parse the terrain data
    addChild(_mapHolder);
    _map = new Array();
    for(var i:int=0;i<mapHeight;i++){
        _map[i] = new Array();
        var mapRowData:Array = terrainData[i+1].split(",");
        for(var j:int=0;j<mapWidth;j++){
            _map[i][j] = new IsoTile();
            _mapHolder.addChild(_map[i][j]);
            _map[i][j].x = (j-i) * _gridWidth / 2;
            _map[i][j].y = (i+j) * _gridHeight / 2;
            _map[i][j].gotoAndStop(mapRowData[j]);
        }
    }
```

```
        _mapHolder.x = (stage.stageWidth - _gridWidth)/2;
        _mapHolder.y = (stage.stageHeight - _mapHolder.height) /2;
    }
```

For every row of the map, we split the line into column data by splitting the comma. The line looks like "**11**, **2**, **3**, **4**, **2**, **3**, **3**, **3**, **4,11**" which means use the number 11 texture for the first column, number 2 texture for the second column, number 3 texture for the third column, and so on. The following graph shows how a row of data represents in the map:

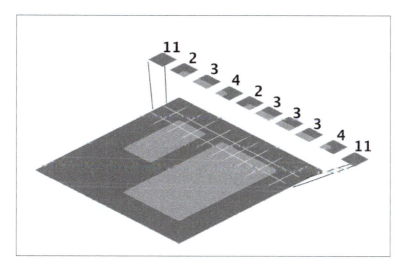

In the column for loop, every column on that row is set to its designed texture by gotoAndStop at the designed frame number.

```
    _map = new Array();
    for(var i:int=0;i<mapHeight;i++){
        _map[i] = new Array();
        var mapRowData:Array = terrainData[i+1].split(",");
        for(var j:int=0;j<mapWidth;j++){
            _map[i][j] = new IsoTile();
            _mapHolder.addChild(_map[i][j]);
            _map[i][j].x = (j-i) * _gridWidth / 2;
            _map[i][j].y = (i+j) * _gridHeight / 2;
            _map[i][j].gotoAndStop(mapRowData[j]);
        }
    }
```

Converting between screen coordination and isometric map coordination

The game consists of two coordination systems after applying the isometric map. One is the isometric map coordination and the other is the screen coordination. We often need to convert the coordination of a point between two systems when dealing with more than one coordination system.

For example, we may need to drag-and-drop some objects in the isometric map. When we press the object, we need to convert the screen position of the mouse to the isometric coordination. Then we will drag the object. The object follows the mouse position in screen coordination during the drag. After we drop the object, it is converted back from screen to isometric coordination so that it can align into the new position of the isometric map.

Let sx and sy be the screen x and y coordinate.

Let ix and iy be the isometric x and y coordinate.

We have already placed the isometric tiles properly, which means we are not far away from the isometric-to-screen coordination conversion function. The following isometric-to-screen function uses the same formula that we used to place the IsoTiles onscreen in the previous example.

```
function i2s(ix:Number, iy:Number):Point{
    var sx:Number = (ix-iy) * _gridWidth / 2;
    var sy:Number = (ix+iy) * _gridHeight / 2;
    return _mapHolder.localToGlobal(new Point(sx,sy));
}
```

We put all tiles into a map container named _mapHolder. We need to add a localToGlobal function to convert the local screen coordinate of _mapHolder to the global stage screen coordinate.

```
return _mapHolder.localToGlobal(new Point(sx,sy));
```

For screen-to-isometric convert function, we need to reverse the isometric-to-screen function, including the formula.

```
function s2i(sx:Number, sy:Number):Point{
    var localPoint:Point = _mapHolder.globalToLocal(new
                                          Point(sx,sy));
    sx:Number = localPoint.x;
    sy:Number = localPoint.y;
```

```
        var ix:Number = Math.floor((sy*_gridWidth+sx*_gridHeight)/(_
                                gridHeight*_gridWidth));
        var iy:Number = Math.floor((sy*_gridWidth-sx*_gridHeight)/(_
                                gridHeight*_gridWidth)) + 1;
        return new Point(ix,iy);
    }
```

In contrast to the isometric-to-screen conversion, the point is converted into the local point of the map container before applying the formula.

```
var localPoint:Point = _mapHolder.globalToLocal(new Point(sx,sy));
sx:Number = localPoint.x;
sy:Number = localPoint.y;
```

The isometric coordinate formula is a reverse of the isometric-to-screen formula. Please note that we added 1 to the *iy*. It is because the original of a tile is not at (0,0) point. The calculated isometric coordinate starts from (0,-1) instead of (0,0) because of the irregular original point of the tile.

```
var ix:Number = Math.floor((sy*_gridWidth+sx*_gridHeight)/(_
                            gridHeight*_gridWidth)),
var iy:Number = Math.floor((sy*_gridWidth-sx*_gridHeight)/(_
                            gridHeight*_gridWidth)) + 1;
```

At last, we return the calculated isometric coordinate as a Point.

```
return new Point(ix,iy);
```

Building a map editor

As we are building a tile-based isometric map, the whole map is composed grid-by-grid. Every grid is set to a number which represents the graphic of that grid.

When the map dimension is getting larger and when the amount of maps is getting bigger, inputting the texture information into the external map data file can be time-consuming. We usually build a map editor for fast development on the huge amount of map data. Like Warcraft has its own map editor, we will have our own editor for the Flash virtual world.

Building a map editor here can also be a good summarized example for the whole chapter. We will make use of different techniques that we learned in this chapter including tile texturing and coordination conversion.

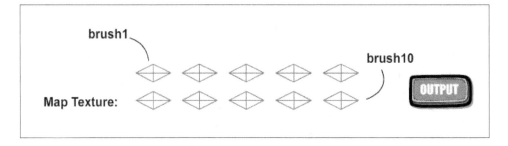

1. Create a new Flash document.
2. Copy the previously created IsoTile movie clip into the library.
3. Drag the 10 instances of IsoTile movie clip on stage from the library.
4. Name the 10 IsoTile instances as brush1 to brush10.
5. Create a button on stage and name it btnOutput.

The 10 IsoTiles placed on the stage act as the brush texture selector. It is like selecting the color of the brushes in paint application. The button is for us to ask the map editor to output the map drawing into our own map data format.

Let's take a look at the document class of the map editor.

Compared to the previous examples, we added four instance variables to the map editor. _mapWidth and _mapHeight is the dimension of the map. Here we set a 10x10 tiles map. _currentBrush stores the current brush type for painting in the map. The brush type is actually the current frame of the IsoTile because every frame in the IsoTile represents different graphic texture of the tile. The _drawing Boolean variable determines when to paint the map.

```
private var _mapWidth:Number = 10;
private var _mapHeight:Number = 10;
private var _currentBrush:Number = 1;
private var _drawing:Boolean = false;
```

The initialize function is similar to the previous example while newly added code is highlighted.

```
private function init(e:Event):void
{
```

```
    // For each IsoTile brush, we display one texture by gotoAndStop
function. We also add a mouse click event listener to change the
brush.
    for(var i:int=1;i<=10;i++){
        this['brush'+i].gotoAndStop(i+1);
        this['brush'+i].addEventListener(MouseEvent.
                            CLICK,onBrushClick);
    }

    addChild(_mapHolder);
    _map = new Array();
    for(i=0;i<_mapHeight;i++){
        _map[i] = new Array();
        for(var j:int=0;j<_mapWidth;j++){
            _map[i][j] = new IsoTile();
            _mapHolder.addChild(_map[i][j]);
            _map[i][j].x = (j-i) * _gridWidth / 2;
            _map[i][j].y = (i+j) * _gridHeight / 2;
        }
    }

    _mapHolder.x = (stage.stageWidth - _gridWidth)/2;
    _mapHolder.y = (stage.stageHeight - _mapHolder.height) /2;

        /* We need to keep track of the mouse movement and the mouse
pressed and released. When the mouse is pressed, we will prepare the
drawing and painting. When the mouse is moving, we paint the map. When
the mouse is released, we stop the painting action. */
    stage.addEventListener(MouseEvent.MOUSE_DOWN,startDraw);
    stage.addEventListener(MouseEvent.MOUSE_MOVE,drawing);
    stage.addEventListener(MouseEvent.MOUSE_UP,stopDraw);

    /* We somewhere need to tell the map editor to output the map data
and this button will call the map data output logic */
    btnOutput.addEventListener(MouseEvent.CLICK,onOutputClick);
}
```

When the map editor is in painting mode, we will keep painting on the tile by calling following function.

```
private function drawTile(sx:Number,sy:Number):void {
    /* In the drawTile function, we will make use of the screen-to-
isometric coordinate conversion function. When painting, we need
to select the IsoTile, which is in isometric coordinate, from mouse
screen position. */
    var isoCoord:Point = s2i(sx,sy);
    /* The coordinate conversion function calculates the result from
formula so we need to ensure we have a valid tile there. */
    if (isoCoord.x >=0 && isoCoord.x < _mapWidth
```

```
        && isoCoord.y >=0 && isoCoord.y < _mapHeight
    ) {
        /* We will then paint the tile if it is valid. Painting the tile
means set the tile to display the frame number as same as the selected
brush. */
            var isoTile:IsoTile = _map[isoCoord.y][isoCoord.x];
            isoTile.gotoAndStop(_currentBrush);
        }
    }
```

When one of the ten brushes IsoTile is clicked, we set the brush texture to the frame number of the latest selected IsoTile.

```
    private function onBrushClick(e:MouseEvent):void {
        _currentBrush = e.currentTarget.currentFrame;
    }
```

When the mouse is pressed, we start drawing by setting the _drawing flag to true and try to draw the tile under the current mouse position.

```
    private function startDraw(e:MouseEvent):void {
        _drawing = true;
        drawTile(stage.mouseX,stage.mouseY);
    }
```

When the mouse is moving, we need to check if the _drawing flag is true. The _drawing flag as true means the mouse is moving while being pressed. Then we draw all tiles that the mouse moves over.

```
    private function drawing(e:MouseEvent):void {
        if (_drawing){
            drawTile(stage.mouseX,stage.mouseY);
        }
    }
```

The _drawing flag is set to false when the mouse is up so that a normal mouse move will not trigger the tile painting.

```
    private function stopDraw(e:MouseEvent):void {
        _drawing = false;
    }
```

The map editor outputs the map data when the output button is clicked. As Flash cannot write files directly, we use trace, the simplest way, to output the map data. We will output the map data according to our XML structure and map format that was defined previously.

```
    private function onOutputClick(e:MouseEvent):void
    {
```

```
trace("<map>");
trace("\t<name>Map Name</name>");
trace("\t<width>"+_mapWidth+"</width>");
trace("\t<height>"+_mapHeight+"</height>");
trace("\t<terrain>");
trace("\t\t<![CDATA[");

/* output the map terrain data. The tile textures are separated by
commas and line breaks. */
for(var i=0;i<_mapHeight;i++){
        var rowData = "";
        for(var j=0;j<_mapWidth;j++){
                rowData += _map[i][j].currentFrame+",";
        }
        trace("\t\t"+rowData);
}
trace("\t\t]]>");
trace("\t</terrain>");
trace("</map>");
}
```

The following screenshot shows a very basic feature of our map editor:

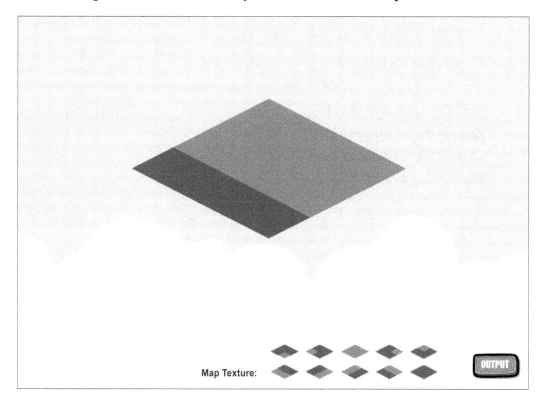

The map data is traced into the output window in Flash IDE and the `flashlog`. `txt`. We need to copy the text from the output window to the map data file to use it. Using trace output method of map data is convenient for a small or medium amount of maps. If there are huge amounts of map data that need to be edited and stored, it is better to save the files from the map editor instead of tracing the output.

There are several ways to save the map data into files from the map editor. We only list the methods here instead of implementing them because that is beyond the scope of this book.

One method is sending the data to server-side HTTP server and saving the data into files with server-side logic such as PHP and JSP.

Another method is building the map editor into AIR runtime and using the `FileStream` class to save the data into files.

One more solution is to use third-party SWF plugins that can convert the SWF into EXE with the extra permission of writing files.

The main purpose of building a map editor is to speed up the map data editing process during development. The map editor is mostly used by the developing team of the virtual world, so it is recommended to modify and add features to the map editor to make it as handy as possible for the developing team.

The map editor that we built has only very basic core features. In order to make it more handy and powerful, the following features can be considered:

- Save/load any map data file
- Change the map dimension
- Change the name of the map
- Multi/mass map editing

Summary

In this chapter, we have discussed some important techniques to create the map and ground of the virtual world. We also built a basic map editor for future development use. We have created ten graphics for an island and the shore; ten pieces of graphics are a very small amount in the real production of a virtual world. It is recommended to create more tile graphics such as rocks, grasses, different types of roads, and different shapes of shore to create a graphic-rich virtual world.

What we have not discussed yet is how the buildings and objects are placed in the isometric map. We tried to first focus on basic concept and texturing the ground of the isometric map. In the *Chapter 7, Creating Buildings and Environments in the Virtual World*, we will discuss more advanced techniques of using isometric view.

In the next chapter, we will focus on making avatars in isometric view. We are going to extend the isometric world from a basic one to a complete virtual world in the coming chapters.

5
Creating Avatars

In a virtual world, there is always a character or symbol to represent the user. This visual representation is called creating **avatars**. It can be a 2D image of the player or a 3D character of the player. Every avatar has different styles and colors, and thus gives personality to the players.

Avatar is very important in a virtual world because most of the features are designed around avatars. Users interact with each other via their avatars, they explore the virtual world via avatars, and they complete challenges to level up their avatars.

In this chapter, we will discuss several important techniques for creating avatars in virtual world. For example, we will discuss how to make an avatar unique by customization, and how to decide the rendering methods and reduce the graphic workload optimally.

We will also integrate avatars with the SmartFoxServer and begin building our virtual world.

Designing an avatar

An avatar is composited by graphics and animation.

The avatar graphics are its looks. It is not a static image but a collection of images to display the directions and appearance. There are different approaches of drawing the avatar graphics depending on the render methods and how many directions and animations the avatar needs.

Animations represent different actions of the avatar. The most basic animation is walking. Other animations such as hand waving and throwing objects are also common. There will be different animation sets for different virtual world designs. A fighting topic virtual world will probably contain a collection of fighting animation sets. A hunting topic virtual world will contain animations of collection items and using hunting tools.

Determining the direction numbers of avatars' views

Isometric tile is composed by diamond shapes with four-edge connection to the other tiles. It is not hard to imagine that every avatar in the isometric view may face towards four directions. They are the north east, south east, south west, and north west.

However, sometimes using only these four directions may not be enough; some game designs may require the avatar to face the user or walk to the other isometric tile a cross the diamond corner. In this case, eight directions are required.

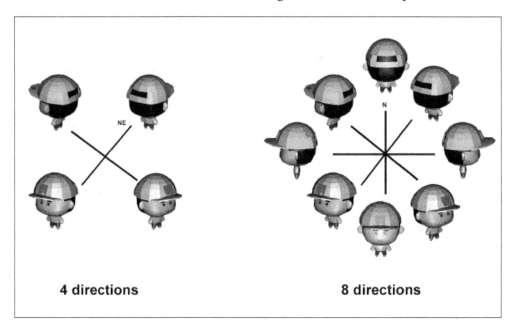

4 directions   **8 directions**

The direction number of the avatars affects the artwork drawing directly. Just imagine that we are building a virtual world where players can fight with each other. How many animations are there for an avatar to fight? Say, five sets of animations. How many directions can the avatar faces? 4? 8? Or even 12? For example, we are now talking about five sets of animations with 8 directions of each avatar. That's already 40 animations for only one avatar. We may design the virtual world to have 12 kinds of avatars and each avatar to have different clothes for customization. The graphics workload keeps increasing when only one of these aspects increases.

That's why I often consider different approaches that reduce the graphic workload of the avatars. Take four directions as an example. In most cases, we have very similar animations when the avatar is facing south-east and south-west. And the animation of north-east and north-west are similar too. Therefore, it is a common technique that mirrors the animation of west side into east side. It can be easily done in Flash by just changing the x-axis of the scaling property to between -1 and 1. This property results in the avatar flipping from one side to another side. For a 4-directions animation set, only 2 directions need to be drawn. In an 8-directions animation set, only 5 directions need to be drawn.

Next, we will discuss the rendering methods that will conclude how the amount of directions, animations, and customization affect the graphic workload.

Rendering avatars in Flash virtual world

There are different approaches to render avatars in Flash virtual world. Each rendered method comes with both advantages and disadvantages. Some methods take more time to draw with fancy outlook while others may take more time to program.

 It is important to decide which rendering methods of the avatar are required in predevelopment stage. It will be much more difficult to change the rendering method after the project is in development.

We will discuss different rendering methods and the pros and cons of them.

Drawing an avatar using vector animation

It is convenient to use the Flash native vector drawing for avatar because every drawing can be done within the Flash. The output can be cute and cartoon style.

One advantage of using vector is that color customization is easy to implement by using the native ActionScript color transform. We can easily assign different colors to different parts of the avatar without extra graphic drawing.

Another advantage of using vector animation is that we can scale up and down the avatars whenever needed. It is useful when we need to zoom in or out of the map and the avatars in the virtual world. The following graph shows the comparison of scaling up a vector and bitmap graphic:

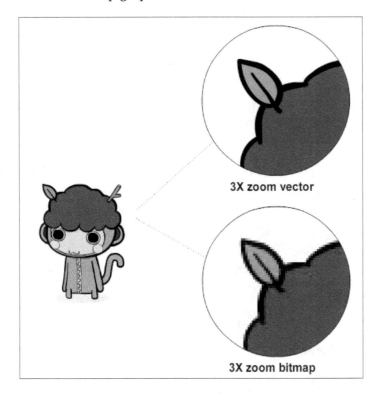

The disadvantage is that we need to draw the animation of every part of the avatar in every direction frame by frame. Flash tweening can help but the workload is heavier than other methods. We can prerender the animations or control them by ActionScript in methods discussed later. In vector animation, every animation is hand-drawn and thus any late modification on the avatar design can cost quite a lot of workload. There may not be too many directions of the avatars meaning the rotation of the avatars will not be very smooth.

Rendering avatars using bitmap sprite sheet

Sprite sheet is a graphics technique that is used in almost all game platforms. **Sprite sheet** is a large bitmap file that contains every frame of animation. Bitmap data from each frame is masked and rendered to the screen. A Flash developer may think that there is a timeline with frame one on the top left and counting the frame from left to right in each row from top to bottom.

This technique is useful when the avatar graphic designer has experience in other game platforms. Another advantage of using bitmap data is faster rendering than vector in Flash player.

The other advantage is the sprite sheet can be rendered from 3D software. For example, we can make an avatar model in Maya (http://autodesk.com/maya) or 3Ds Max (http://autodesk.com/3dsmax) with animations set up. Then we set up eight cameras with orthographic perspective. The orthographic perspective ensures the rendered image fits the isometric world. After setting up the scene, just render the whole animation with eight different cameras and we will get all the bitmap files of the avatar. The benefit is that the rendering process is automatic so that we can reduce the workload a lot. Later if we want to modify the character, we only need to modify it in the 3D software and render it again.

One big disadvantage of using sprite sheet is the file size. The sprite sheets are in bitmap format and one set of animation can cost up to several hundred kilobytes. The file size can be very large when there are many animations and many more bitmaps for switching styles of the avatar.

The other disadvantage is that changing color is quite difficult. Unlike vector rendering where color replacement can be done by ActionScript, we need to replace another bitmap data to change the color. That means every available color doubles the file size.

Rendering avatars using real-time 3D engine

We described how to use 3D software to prerender graphics of the avatars in the previous section. Instead of prerendering the graphics into 2D bitmap, we can integrate a Flash 3D engine to render the 3D model into isometric view in real time.

Real-time 3D rendering is the next trend of Flash. There are several 3D engines available in the market that support rendering complex 3D models with animations. Papervision3D (`http://blog.papervision3d.org/`) and Away3D (`http://away3d.com/`) are two examples among them.

The advantage of using 3D rendering in isometric is that the rotation of avatars can be very smooth. Also different textures can share the same model and different models can share the same animation skeleton. Thanks to this great graphic reusability, 3D rendering virtual world can create different combinations of avatar appearance and animations without adding extra graphic workload in development.

However, one disadvantage of using 3D rendering is the Flash player performance. The latest version of Flash player is 10.1 at the time of writing. The following screenshots from Cafeworld (`http://apps.facebook.com/cafeworld/`) show that the CPU resources usage is very high when rendering the isometric 3D environment with three avatars on screen:

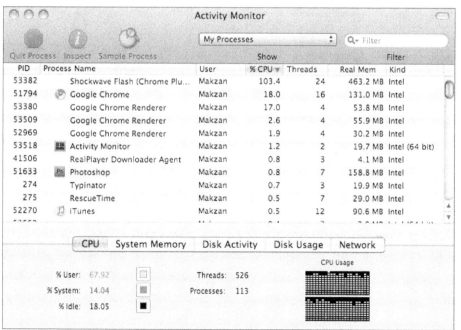

Rendering avatars using 2D bone skeleton

Bone skeleton used to be an uncommon method to render avatar. What it does is creates an animated skeleton and then glues different parts of body together onto the skeleton. It is somehow similar to the skeleton and mesh relationship in 3-D software but in two dimensions instead. A lot of mathematics is needed to calculate the position and rotation of each part of the body and make the implementation difficult.

Thanks to the introduction of bone tool and inverse kinematics in Flash CS4, this technique is becoming more mature and easier to be used in the Flash world. Adobe has posted a tutorial about using bone tool to create a 2D character (`http://www.adobe.com/devnet/flash/articles/character_animation_ik.html`).

The following screenshot shows another bone skeleton example from gotoAndPlay demonstrating how to glue the parts into a walking animation. The post can be found in this link: `http://www.gotoandplay.it/_articles/2007/04/skeletal_animation.php`

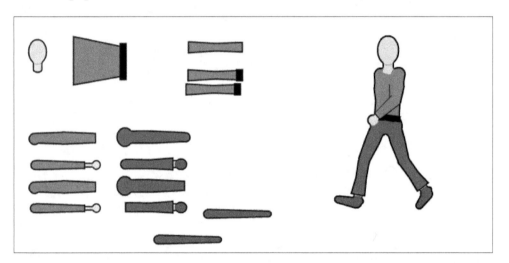

The advantage of using 2D bone skeleton is that animations are controlled by ActionScript. The reusing of animations means this technique fits those game designs that require many animations. A dancing virtual world that requires a lot of different unique animations is one example that may need this technique.

One disadvantage is that the large amount of mathematic calculation for the animations makes it difficult to implement.

Every rendering methods has its own advantages and disadvantages and not one of the methods fits all type of games. It is the game designer's job to decide a suitable rendering method for a game or virtual world project. Therefore, it is important to know their limitations and consider thoughtfully before getting started with development.

 We can take a look at how other Flash virtual worlds render avatars by checking the showcase of the SmartFoxServer (`http://www.smartfoxserver.com/showcase/`).

Drawing an avatar in Flash

We are going to draw the avatar now. In this example, we use the vector animation as the rendering method. Our avatar graphic is divided into six parts—head, body, two hands, and two feet. We will use 4-direction representation in our virtual world.

A 4-direction avatar faces four directions and therefore needs four sets of graphics and animations for each part. However, we only need to draw two directions and then mirror them along the x-axis.

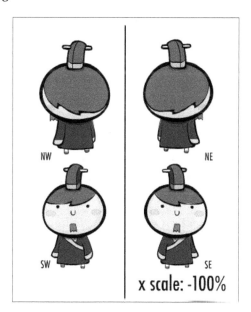

In order to make the avatar graphics flexible for different directions and different animations, we need to put each part into different layers. Each layer has its own animation timeline for each part of the avatar. And each direction of the graphics is placed into one movie clip.

All four directions are placed into the same place with overlap shown in the following graph. Then we display each direction by hiding the others using ActionScript. This setup makes the direction switch as simple as turning on and off the visibility instead of replacing graphics. The following screenshot shows how the four directions of movie clip overlap together in four layers within a parent movie clip:

Drawing the idle and walking animation

We need to draw the animation for all available directions. As NW and NE direction is the same movie clip and SE and SW is another same one, we need to draw the animation two times for all four directions. We have to make sure the animation length matches among all directions so that the animation is smooth when we rotate the avatar in the virtual world.

We will use the south-west direction as an example here. The walking is a two-frame animation loop. The interval of the walking animation needs some fine-tuning to make it look like really walking on the ground. Too long or too short of the interval will affect the realistic walking.

Idling an avatar does not mean putting it into static stopped frame. Users often watch avatars idling in the virtual world and this animation becomes important. The avatar gives a live and organic feeling to the player via a good idling animation. We will make the avatar breathe when idling in this example. Some other virtual worlds will play some different animations when the avatar is idle, such as looking around or sitting down.

To make the breathing effect realistic, we extend the timeline to around two seconds. We will set the frame rate per second to 30 and it takes 60 frames for two seconds. The duration is around the normal breathing time of human.

 Typically, we would set the frame rate at 24 or 30. Setting the frame rate too high may result in performance issue and lagging in old machines when the Flash virtual world requires intensive CPU resources.

In the first and last frame of the animation duration, we created two copies of the key frame and named the first frame as idle. In the middle point of the duration, we created one key frame for the head, body, and two hands. When a human breathes, the whole body moves slightly up and down periodically. Therefore, in this key frame we move the head, body, and two hands slightly up by several pixels.

Finish the animation by applying classic tween between the key frames and putting a gotoAndPlay('idle') script in the last frame to loop the animation.

There is one trick of making the breathing animation more organic. When we breathe, the moving up motion is slightly slower then the moving down motion. Therefore, we usually make the moving up animation last longer then the moving down animation. The following graph shows how the idle animation is composited:

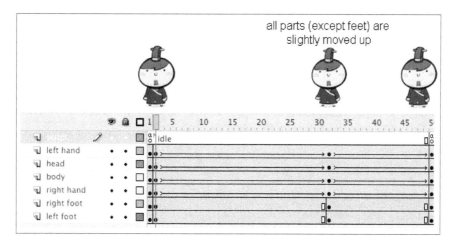

Creating an avatar class

We will now embed a class to the avatar graphics. This class controls the directions and other avatar helper functions.

There are two instance variables in the class. One array is used to reference the movie clips of the four directions. Another one is to reference the current direction.

```
private var _directionArray:Array = new Array();
private var _activeDirection:MovieClip;
```

The initial function sets default direction and idle animation. The dir_nw, dir_ne, dir_sw, and dir_se are the names of the four directions of movie clip set in the Flash document file. We put them into an array for easier access later.

```
private function init(e:Event):void {
    _directionArray[0] = this.dir_nw;
    _directionArray[1] = this.dir_ne;
    _directionArray[2] = this.dir_sw;
    _directionArray[3] = this.dir_se;

    showDirection("se");
    playAnimation("idle");
}
```

The showDirection function displays the movie clip with the new direction and hides others.

```
public function showDirection(dir:String = "se"):void {
    for each(var avatar:MovieClip in _directionArray){
        avatar.visible = false;
    }
    this['dir_'+dir].visible = true;
    _activeDirection = this['dir_'+dir];
}
```

As different animations are placed in the timeline of the movie clip in each direction, we can simply tell the movie clip with current direction play that specify timeline.

```
public function playAnimation(animation:String = 'idle'):void {
    _activeDirection.gotoAndPlay(animation);
}
```

Logging in SmartFoxServer with avatar

We have discussed a basic SmartFoxServer connection example in *Chapter 3, Getting Familiar with SmartFoxServer*. We will keep applying new techniques into the SmartFoxServer during the book to create our virtual world. It is now time to try to give every user an avatar.

When users login to the virtual world, all existing users and their avatars will be drawn. We also need to draw a new avatar when another user joins the world and remove it when someone leaves.

When we integrate the avatars into SmartFoxServer, we will separate the logic into different server event handlers. It is very important to know when and which event is called during the connection so that we can place correct code in correct event handlers.

The implementation of onConnection and onRoomListUpdate event will be the same as in *Chapter 3, Getting Familiar with SmartFoxServer*. We now add three more events to our document class.

When we successfully join a room in the virtual world, the onJoinRoom event will be called. How about when someone logs in or leaves the room? SmartFoxServer provides the onUserEnterRoom and onUserLeaveRoom event.

We need one instance variable to keep all the avatar movie clips with existing users so that we can reference them later.

```
private var _avatarList:Array = new Array();
```

The SmartFoxServer events are registered in the constructor.

```
public function Ch05_02() {
    _sfs = new SmartFoxClient(true);
    _sfs.addEventListener(SFSEvent.onConnection,onConnection);
    _sfs.addEventListener(SFSEvent.onRoomListUpdate,onRoomListUpdate);
    _sfs.addEventListener(SFSEvent.onJoinRoom,onJoinRoom);
    _sfs.addEventListener(SFSEvent.onUserEnterRoom,onUserEnterRoom);
    _sfs.addEventListener(SFSEvent.onUserLeaveRoom,onUserLeaveRoom);

    _sfs.connect("127.0.0.1",9339);
}
```

Before handling the events, we prepare a function to draw an avatar at a random position on the stage. This function is placed in the document class. The avatar movie clip reference is returned after executing this function for other logic to access it. The username is also passed into this function so that we can display the name later but now we just focus on the position.

```
private function drawAvatarAtRandomPlace(username:String):Avatar {
var avatar:Avatar = new Avatar();
addChild(avatar);

/* random position with 50 pixels margin to the border */
avatar.x = Math.random()*(stage.stageWidth-100)+50;
avatar.y = Math.random()*(stage.stageHeight-100)+50;
return avatar;
}
```

When the user successfully logs in and joins the default room of the virtual world, we will get a user list from the event parameters and draw avatars of all existing users. Please note that the newly joined user is already included in the user list.

 The SmartFoxServer event parameters are useful and handy to quickly access the target information such as user and room instance. Every event has its own set of parameters and the detail usage is listed in a document of the SmartFoxServer Flash API (`http://smartfoxserver.com/docs/docPages/as3/html/index.html`).

```
private function onJoinRoom(e:SFSEvent):void {
    /* get current room data */
    var room:Room = e.params.room;

    /* load all users and draw, including myself */
    var userList:Array = room.getUserList();
    for each(var user:User in userList){
        var avatar:Avatar = drawAvatarAtRandomPlace(user.getName());

    /* Remember which avatar movieclip is from which user*/
        _avatarList[user.getName()] = avatar;
    }
}
```

We need to draw some new avatars when some other users join our current room.

```
private function onUserEnterRoom(e:SFSEvent):void {
    /* get the username of the new user*/
    var username:String = e.params.user.getName();

    /* draw the avatar */
    var avatar:Avatar = drawAvatarAtRandomPlace(username);

    /* Remember which avatar movieclip is from which user*/
    _avatarList[username] = avatar;
}
```

We have an avatar list to map all users in the room to the avatar movie clips on stage. This allows us to remove the user's avatar graphics when the user leaves the room.

```
private function onUserLeaveRoom(e:SFSEvent):void {
    /* know which user is leaving the room */
    var username:String = e.params.userName;
    removeChild(_avatarList[username]);
}
```

We need to test the Flash movies with several instances. Open the Flash movies in several web browsers to test and we will see that the avatars are coming in and out when we are increasing or reducing the Flash movie instances.

However, the position of the avatars is not synchronized among the Flash movies. It is because we are now using random position for every user. We need to remember the position of existing avatars for others to use. The position of the avatar belongs to each user and this can be done by user variables.

Using user variables in virtual world

User variables are some extra user information in server side. They are designed for developers to temporarily store user-specific data that shares in the same room. For example, storing the user's appearance and position.

Let's continue from our last example. We had a draw function to draw the avatar at random position; now we need another function to draw the avatar in known position.

```
private function drawAvatar(username:String, posX:int,
posY:int):Avatar {
    var avatar:Avatar = new Avatar();
    addChild(avatar);
    avatar.x = posX;
```

```
        avatar.y = posY;

        return avatar;
    }
```

The `onUserVariablesUpdate` event can let us get the newly changed user variables from other users. Therefore we add the listener in the initial function.

```
_sfs.addEventListener(SFSEvent.onUserVariablesUpdate,
                                            onUserVariablesUpdate);
```

We need to save our initial position to user variables after successfully joining the default room. We handle our avatar and other existing avatars separately. We save our avatar position and get other avatar positions. We also set a flag to indicate that this is an initial position update. This flag is useful for other users to know that we are creating a new position or modifying an existing position of the avatar.

```
private function onJoinRoom(e:SFSEvent):void {
    var myAvatar:Avatar = drawAvatarAtRandomPlace(_sfs.myUserName);

    /* save position of myself into user variables */
    var params:Object = new Object();
    params.posX = myAvatar.x;
    params.posY = myAvatar.y;
    params.firstTime = true;
    _sfs.setUserVariables(params);

    /* get current room data */
    var room:Room = e.params.room;

    /* load all users and draw */
    var userList:Array = room.getUserList();
    for each(var user:User in userList){
            /* exclude myself */
            if (user.getName() != _sfs.myUserName){
                    /* get user's position from user variables */
                    var posX:int = user.getVariable('posX');
                    var posY:int = user.getVariable('posY');

                    var avatar:Avatar = drawAvatar(user.
                                        getName(),posX,posY);
```

```
                _avatarList[user.getName()] = avatar;
        }
    }
```

We used to create new avatars for other users in the onUserEnterRoom event handler. However, we need to wait for the new user's updates about their positions before drawing them. We put the avatar drawing responsibility from onUserEnterRoom function to onUserVaraiblesUpdate function and thus the onUserEnterRoom is not needed now.

```
    private function onUserEnterRoom(e:SFSEvent):void {}
```

Any changed variables will fire this event and pass the variables as parameters. There is flag validation to check if the changed variables are a modification or initialization.

```
    private function onUserVariablesUpdate(e:SFSEvent):void {
        /* getting who has updated the variable */
        var user:User = e.params.user;
        var username:String = user.getName();

        /* this is a new user, we create a new avatar movieclip  */
        if (user.getVariable('firstTime') == true){
                var posX:int = user.getVariable('posX');
                var posY:int = user.getVariable('posY');

                var avatar:Avatar = drawAvatar(username,posX,posY);
                _avatarList[username] = avatar;
        }
    }
```

We are getting one step closer now. We have all users' position synchronized in the virtual world but it is not enough. Everyone looks the same in the virtual world and players cannot distinguish themselves from each other. We are going to name every avatar in the next section.

Adding name to the avatar

We logged in to SmartFoxServer using anonymous user name in all previous examples. We are going to ask the user to input the name before logging into the virtual world.

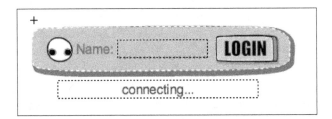

We need to add a text field to the avatar movie clip for the name. We name the text field `nameInput` and place it under the `loginBox` movie clip.

The name input procedure breaks the previous login flow into two parts. We stop and wait for the name input after connecting to server before logging.

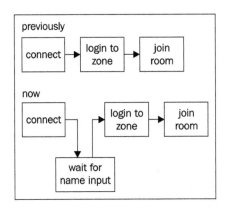

The login box appears at the beginning but we do not want the user to perform the login action before the Flash is successfully connected to the server. The login button is hidden in the initial function.

```
this.loginBox.btnLogin.visible = false;
```

The login button appears and waits for the user action after successfully connecting to the server. We also update the status textfield to display the connected state.

```
private function onConnection(e:SFSEvent):void {
    var ok:Boolean = e.params.success;
    if (ok){
        this.loginBox.statusText.text = "connected to server."
```

```
        this.loginBox.btnLogin.visible = true;
    }
}
```

The user input name is passed to the server instead of anonymous login.

```
private function onLoginButtonClicked(e:MouseEvent):void {
    _sfs.login("simpleChat",this.loginBox.nameInput.text,"");
}
```

After logging into a zone in SmartFoxServer, the server pushes a room list to the Flash client. The Flash client needs the list to join the default room after logging in. When the onRoomListUpdate event is called, we know that we have finished the login procedure, so we can hide the login box.

```
private function onRoomListUpdate(e:SFSEvent):void {
    this.loginBox.visible = false;
    _sfs.autoJoin();
}
```

In the drawAvatarAtRandomPlace and drawAvatar function, we now not only put the avatar movie clip in correct position but also display the username in the nameText textfield.

```
avatar.nameText.text = username;
```

In Adobe Flash CS3, we need to import the flash.text.TextField in the document class when there is text field in timeline to prevent compiler's TextField class not found error. This is fixed after Adobe Flash CS4.

Our virtual world now shows every avatar with the player's name. Players can distinguish each other now but that's not enough. All the avatars have the same outlook and the same color. Let's add some personality to the avatars by customization.

Customizing your avatar

A Flash virtual world is a social community in which players interact with each other and have their own identity. Virtual world usually lets a user decide the avatar's appearance by choosing the combination of different styles and colors.

Customizing different styles

Each part of the avatar will have different styles and shapes to form different combinations of the appearance of the avatar. Thanks to the timeline and movie clip features in Flash, we can put different styles of each part within the movie clip. For example, the following screenshot shows the `head` movie clip with different head styles placed frame by frame and we can use `gotoAndStop` to display the style we want.

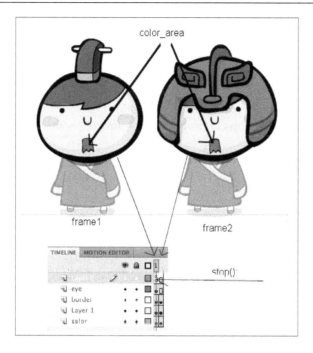

Customizing the color

ActionScript supports changing the color transform for a given movie clip. It supports not only color tint but also applying color filter and detailed RGB transformation. We will use the simple color tint to change the color of the avatar.

As the color transform is applying to the whole movie clip, we cannot simply tint the avatar movie clip because that will make the whole avatar tint to one solid color. In order to tint a partial part of the movie clip, we specifically create a movie clip in each part and name it color_area. We later program the ActionScript to change all movie clip names with color_area to the customized color.

Adding customization to avatar class

We are going to change the style and color by ActionScript in avatar class. We need to import the ColorTransform class in flash.geom package to change the color with ActionScript.

```
import flash.geom.ColorTransform;
```

We need several instance variables to hold the styles and color state.

```
public const totalStyles:Number = 3;
public var currentColor:Number = 0x704F4C;
public var currentStyle:Number = 1;
```

We wrap the whole block of color transform code into one function. The color transform adds RGB color transformation to the target movie clip. We only use `colorTransform` to tint the color here but it also supports percentage transform that adds partial color to the target movie clip. We will apply the color transform to the color area inside the head of the avatar in 4 directions.

```
public function changeColor(newColor:Number = 0x000000):void {
    currentColor = newColor;
    for each(var avatar:MovieClip in _directionArray){
        var avatarColor:ColorTransform = new ColorTransform();
        avatarColor.color = newColor;
        avatar.head.color_area.transform.colorTransform =
                                                avatarColor;
    }
}
```

We modified the color by using color transform and used timeline to style the avatar style. Every frame in the head movie clip represents a style with its color tint area. We display the new style by changing the current frame of the avatar movie clip. It is also necessary to change the color again after switching the style because every style contains its own color area.

```
public function changeStyle(styleNumber:int):void {
    for each(var avatar:MovieClip in _directionArray){
        /* display the giving style in all parts of avatar*/
        avatar.head.gotoAndStop(styleNumber);
        avatar.body.gotoAndStop(styleNumber);
        avatar.lefthand.gotoAndStop(styleNumber);
        avatar.righthand.gotoAndStop(styleNumber);

        /* need to apply the color again after changing the style */
        var avatarColor:ColorTransform = new ColorTransform();
        avatarColor.color = currentColor;
        avatar.head.color_area.transform.colorTransform =
                                                avatarColor;
    }
    currentStyle = styleNumber;
}
```

The purpose of the `avatar` class is to control the appearance of the avatar. We just implemented the direction, color, and style switching methods and it is now ready for customization panel to use.

Designing a customization panel

Avatars in virtual worlds and games often provide players with different kinds of customization. Some games allow users to customize the whole body with lots of options while some games may only provide two to three basic customizations. The layout design of the customization panel is often based on the number of options.

There are two common customization panel layouts in the market. One layout displays arrows for a user to select next and previous styles. The other one displays a thumbnail view of the options within the same category.

The arrows selection layout is suitable for an avatar that contains limited parts for customization. There may be only two to four categories and not many options in each category. Players can easily loop through different style combinations and choose their favorite one using this layout.

The following avatar customization screenshot from the 2D Online RPG called Dragon Fable uses the arrows selection layout:

The thumbnail view layout is suitable for avatars that can be highly customized. There are often many categories to customize and each category provides a lot of options for players to choose. Some virtual worlds even provide micro modification so that players can adjust details on the chosen style such as the distance between the eyes.

Players do not need to iterate the large amount of styles and can quickly choose a style option among them with the thumbnail view.

The following screenshot is an online Mii editor. Mii is the avatar system in the Nintendo Wii console. This is an online clone of the Mii avatar customization. It allows a large amount of avatar customization by the thumbnail view layout with extended features such as scaling and moving the elements.

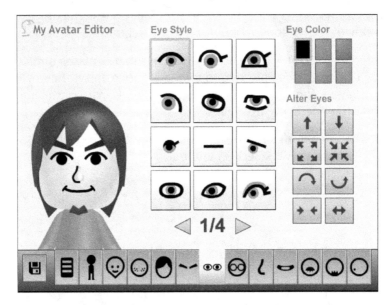

Making our customization panel

In our virtual world, we will use the arrows selection layout for the customization panel because we planned to let players customize the whole avatar style only. There is a color picker with four colors to pick. The color applies to the hair and beard. The following graph is the setup of our customization panel. The avatar movie clip is named `avatar`. The two arrows are named `styleLeft` and `styleRight` accordingly. The four boxes are named from `colorBtn1` to `colorBtn4`. All these elements are placed into a parent movie clip called `customizationPanel`.

Let's start at the initial function of the CustomizationPanel class. What it does is prepare the button events and the color pickers.

```
private function init(e:Event):void {
    /* register the 2 arrows event handler */
    styleLeft.addEventListener(MouseEvent.CLICK,onHeadLeftClicked);
    styleRight.addEventListener(MouseEvent.CLICK,onHeadRightClicked);

    /* prepare the 4 colors for color picker */
    var colors:Array = [0xE1842C, 0xcc66cc, 0xff0000, 0x3399cc];

    /* set the color in the color picker*/
    for(var i:int =1;i<=4;i++){
            var newColor:ColorTransform = new ColorTransform();
            newColor.color = colors[i-1];
            this['colorBtn'+i].color_area.transform.colorTransform =
                                                              newColor;

        /*    register the color picker click event */
    this['colorBtn'+i].addEventListener(MouseEvent.
CLICK,onColorBtnClicked);
    }
}
```

When the left and right arrows are clicked, the avatar will display next styles. Usually the styles will loop back to the first one after reaching the end of the style list.

```
private function onStyleLeftClicked(e:MouseEvent):void {
    if (avatar.currentStyle-1>0){
            avatar.changeStyle(avatar.currentStyle-1);
    }else{
```

```
                    avatar.changeStyle(avatar.totalStyles);
        }
    }
    private function onRightClicked(e:MouseEvent):void {
        if (avatar.currentStyle+1 <= avatar.totalStyles){
            avatar.changeStyle(avatar.currentStyle+1);
        }else{
            avatar.changeStyle(1);
        }
    }
```

Thanks to our easy change color function from the `avatar` class, we only need one line to change the color to the picked color.

```
    private function onColorBtnClicked(e:MouseEvent):void {
        avatar.changeColor(e.currentTarget.color_area.transform.
                        colorTransform.color);
    }
```

The customization panel is ready now. Let's put it to our virtual world to let our players create their own avatars.

Integrating the customization into SmartFoxServer

The customization panel is placed within the login box to let players choose the avatar style when inputting the name.

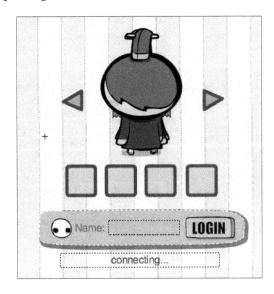

We expand the virtual world document class to support the avatar customization. The styles are stored in the avatar instance inside the customization panel. These styles also need to be saved to the user variables so that all users in the same room can retrieve the styles.

```
private function onJoinRoom(e:SFSEvent):void {
    ...
    /* draw the customization and remember to user variables */

    var myColor:Number = this.loginBox.customizationPanel.avatar.
                                                     currentColor;
    var myStyle:int = this.loginBox.customizationPanel.avatar.
                                                     currentStyle;
    myAvatar.changeColor(myColor);
    myAvatar.changeStyle(myStyle);

    params.avatarColor = myColor;
    params.style = myStyle;

    _sfs.setUserVariables(params);

    var room:Room = e.params.room;
    var userList:Array = room.getUserList();
    for each(var user:User in userList){
            /* exclude myself */
            if (user.getName() != _sfs.myUserName){
                    ...
                    /* draw the style */
                    avatar.changeColor(user.getVariable('avatarColor'));
                    avatar.changeStyle(user.getVariable('style'));
                    ...
            }
    }
}
```

When someone joins the room, we not only need to place the avatar in position but also need to draw the avatar based on that user variable.

```
private function onUserVariablesUpdate(e:SFSEvent):void {
    /* get the avatar of new joined user */
    var user:User = e.params.user;
    ...
    /* draw the style */
```

```
        avatar.changeColor(user.getVariable('avatarColor'));
        avatar.changestyle(user.getVariable('style'));
}
```

Now we added personality to our avatars. We used timeline for the avatar styles, and color array for color customization. It is not difficult to add more new styles from time to time to provide more fun for the avatars. Virtual worlds often release some holiday-specific styles for the avatars. For example, we can release a new head style with a Christmas hat or a collection of Halloween styles. Players may like to hold a virtual party in our virtual world with the new special clothes.

Summary

In this chapter, we have compared several avatar drawing techniques and their usage in Flash. Each of them has its usage and we demonstrated the vector animation methods. It is important to decide which drawing methods to use at the predevelopment stage because that is often difficult to change once the virtual world project is going.

We also discussed on how to work with several user related SmartFoxServer events to manage the user information and graphics when they join or leave the room. We will learn more events in detail because most of the logic is event triggered in a multiplayer virtual world.

We also introduced the usage of user variables, which is a place to store user specific information temporarily. The user variables are useful for sharing some pieces of data between users in the same room.

The avatars now have their own appearance and position. But they cannot move and they are not placed in our isometric map yet. In the next chapter, we will put the avatars on our isometric world and make them walk. We will also discuss the technique of the walking synchronization.

6
Walking Around the World

Walking is an important activity of the virtual world. Most of the time the avatars are walking around to explore the world, to socially interact with people, and to play different types of games inside the world. Moving the avatar in real-time multiplayer network may also have synchronization issues that need to be fixed and for you to be aware of.

In this chapter, we will discuss the synchronization issues of the movement when using either keyboard or mouse input. We will also focus on different path finding approaches and discuss when to use which. We will also discuss some basic movement synchronization techniques.

This is a list of what we are going to learn in this chapter:

- Extend the avatar class to provide walking functions
- Basic movement synchronization over the network
- Basic concept of the path finding technique
- Choosing a right path finding
- Scrolling the world
- Accessing database via server-side extension

Creating the world

To walk around the world, we need the avatar and the isometric map from last two chapters. We are going to integrate them to construct our virtual world.

The movie clip hierarchy of the virtual world now looks like the following graph. The world is responsible to draw the avatars and hold the avatar list. It also creates the isometric world map. The reason of putting the avatars and isometric map into the world movie clip is that we can easily scroll the whole world by only repositioning the world movie clip. All the avatars and the map will scroll together automatically.

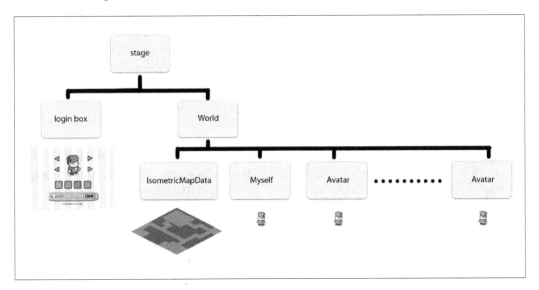

The movie clip architecture

When developing Flash virtual world, it is important to design the movie clip architecture well. A good architecture will glue relative graphic assets together for easy positioning and scaling. It can also make the z-order of the movie clips easier to manage. For example, putting an interface movie clip on top of the world movie clip ensure every UI item is visible without being overlapped by any element in the virtual world. We can also add an empty movie clip on top of everything and put special effects inside it to play some special effect animation.

The `IsometricMapData` class is the collection of the functions we used in *Chapter 4, Creating Map and Ground in Isometric View*. It responds to create the map and ground by loading the map data and providing coordinate conversion functions between the isometric map and screen.

A notable change in `IsometricMapData` class is the local conversion between the screen coordinate and isometric coordinate. We had the conversion between screen coordinate of the stage to the isometric map coordinate. The difference of these two functions is that the local conversion converts the isometric map coordinate into the screen coordinate of the map, instead of the stage. This is useful for positioning the avatars inside the world movie clip.

The implementation difference is that these local conversions will not call the `globalToLocal` and `localToGlobal` function in order to stay on the local coordinate.

```
public function s2iLocal(sx:Number, sy:Number):Point{
    var ix:int = Math.floor((sy*_gridWidth+sx*_gridHeight)/
                            (_gridHeight*_gridWidth));
    var iy:int = Math.floor((sy*_gridWidth-sx*_gridHeight)/
                            (_gridHeight*_gridWidth)) + 1;

    return new Point(ix,iy);
}
public function i2sLocal(ix:int, iy:int):Point{
    var sx:Number = (ix-iy) * _gridWidth / 2 + _gridWidth / 2;
    var sy:Number = (ix+iy) * _gridHeight / 2;
    return new Point(sx,sy);
}
```

 You may notice that we have a lot of coordinate conversion between screen and isometric map. When we are manipulating the data, it usually uses the isometric coordinate. For example, we use isometric when accessing the position of the map data structure. On the other hand, when we are dealing with display, we will use screen coordinate.

The `World` class, on the other hand, integrated the `IsometricMapData` class with the avatar creation functions in *Chapter 5, Creating Avatars*.

The following code snippet is the definition of the `World` class:

```
public class World extends MovieClip{
    // A reference to the isometric map
    public var map:IsometricMapData;
```

```
    /* We have a key-value pair array to store every avatar. Each
avatar represents a logged in player. The key is the username and the
value is the Avatar class  */
    public var avatarList:Array = new Array();


    /* This is the avatar of the player himself. WalkingAvatar is a
subclass of the Avatar class that we are going to implement. */
    public var myAvatar:WalkingAvatar;


    /* This is the function to initialize the isometric map and some
event listeners. */
    private function init(e:Event):void {...}


    /* This function will be called after the map data is loaded into
the IsometricMapData class. It responds to draw the avatars on the
map. */
    public function initWorld(e:Event):void {...}


    /* This is the function to draw the avatar in random place.
Previously we randomly draw the avatars on screen coordinate. Now we
integrated the map and draw them in isometric coordinate in the map. */
    private function drawAvatarAtRandomPlace(username:String):
                                                    WalkingAvatar {...}


    /* Besides drawing the avatar randomly, this function draws the
avatar in specify isometric coordinate. */
    public function drawAvatarInIsometric(username:String,
                            isoX:int, isoY:int):WalkingAvatar {...}


    /* The World class checks every avatars' state to determine what
they should do on every frame. We will control them walking here. */
    private function onAvatarFrame(e:Event):void {...}
}
```

After integrating the isometric map and avatars, the initial process becomes as shown in the following flowchart:

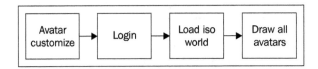

Holding states of the player

Besides the movie clips that are listed in the movie clip hierarchy, there is a class, called `Myself`, to remember all states of the player himself. Every time there will be only one instance of the player so this class is designed to be singleton.

There are several instance variables inside the `Myself` class to remember related states.

The position of the avatar in isometric coordinate:

```
private var _isoPosX:Number;
private var _isoPosY:Number;
```

The customization styles of the avatar:

```
private var _avatarColor:Number;
private var _style:Number;
```

Reference to the current room for easily accessing room-related methods:

```
private var _currentRoom:Room;
```

A reference of the avatar:

```
private var _avatar:MovieClip;
```

Singleton class

It is useful to use singleton pattern when only one instance of the class can exist at a time throughout the whole application life. Normally we initialize new object by calling `new ClassName()`. A singleton class will restrict this normal instantiation way. Instead, we access a singleton class by `Classname.instance` or `Classname.getInstance()`. In this case, there is exactly one instance all the time. `Myself` is a state object for remembering the settings related to the player himself and thus only one instance is needed.

A detailed explanation of ActionScript singleton pattern can be found from gskinner's website:

`http://www.gskinner.com/blog/archives/2006/07/as3_singletons.html`

Moving the avatar

There are two ways to tell the avatar to walk. Either input by pressing the arrows keys or clicking on the destination point by mouse.

Which method is better? We need to consider both the game play and the network synchronization.

The game play of the virtual world is our first consideration. A virtual world with fighting theme requires players to stick on the keyboard to walk and create key combination attack. On the other hand, our virtual world focuses on social interaction so that mouse input will be the main use.

Movement synchronization

When moving the avatars by keyboard, we may keep sending the "move right" command until the right arrow key is released. In this case, the client broadcasts many same messages to synchronize the movement and will slow down the network.

When we are designing the network game, we need to optimize the amount of commands to send over the network. An average TCP connection can have a lag that ranges between 50 ms to 200 ms. The synchronization will fail if we send commands too often.

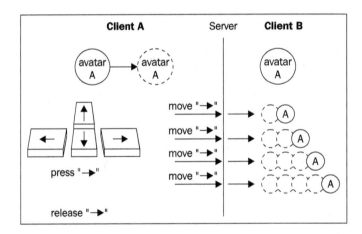

In the second case, we only broadcast the press and release action; the other clients will automatically do the movement until the external release action is received. The final position is not synchronized perfectly because of the network lag of the release message passing. Other clients will receive the release action slightly slower then the original sender.

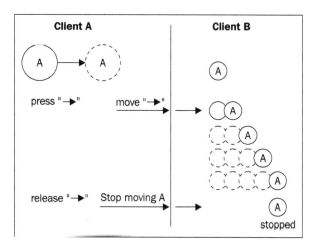

When the avatar movement is by mouse, we can broadcast the destination points and clients will render the movement. As only one message is needed, the movement in other clients lags for only the message passing time and the final position is synchronized.

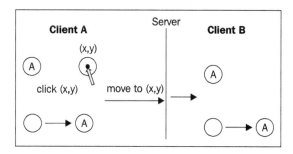

In the virtual world where the avatars are walking around casually, the slightly asynchronous position is acceptable. However, some fixing has to apply in real-time fighting or other games that require precise positioning.

Making avatar able to walk

We need to extend the avatar class to provide walking features. We made another class called `WalkingAvatar` that extends the original `Avatar` class.

```
public class WalkingAvatar extends Avatar{
    ...
}
```

There are some instance variables in the `WalkingAvatar` class.

Every avatar has a **walking speed**. The speed is the pixel displacement every time we draw the walking animation.

```
private var _walkingSpeed:Number = 4;
```

The `isWalking` flag indicates whether the avatar is now walking.

```
private var _isWalking:Boolean = false;
```

A destination point will be set along with the walking command. A loop will keep track if the avatar reaches the destination point.

```
private var _destX:Number;
private var _destY:Number;
```

In isometric coordinate, we may not be able to move the avatar from start point to the destination point in a straight line. We have the limitation of the 4 (or 8) directions movement for which we need to split the path into segments. We need an array to store the segments of the walking path. We will name this array `walkPath`.

```
public var walkPath:Array;
```

The segments are the straight lines of the path. Take the following graph as an example; we need to move three tiles up and two tiles left to the destination. The `walkPath` array will contain the (0,-3) and (-2,0) coordinates.

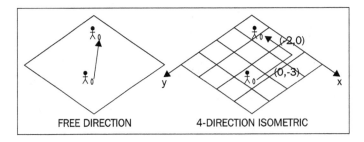

FREE DIRECTION   4-DIRECTION ISOMETRIC

We need to save the current position in the isometric coordinate. It is very useful because we will often calculate isometric coordinate of the avatar, including movement and path finding.

```
public var isoPosition:Point;
```

The avatar class will interact with the world once it can move around. Therefore we have a reference of the world.

```
public var world:World;
```

The walkByPath function will get one segment from the stored path array and call the avatar to walk to the position according to the path segment.

```
public function walkByPath():void {
    if (walkPath != null && walkPath.length>0){
        var nextPathSegment:Object = walkPath.pop();
        var nextDeltaX:int = nextPathSegment.x - isoPosition.x;
        var nextDeltaY:int = nextPathSegment.y - isoPosition.y;
        walkTo(nextDeltaX,nextDeltaY);
    }
}
```

We will also add an entry point to the walkByPath function by creating a startWalkByPath function. This function now only calls the walkByPath function. In later sections, we will add more logic that needs to be executed before starting the walking animation.

```
public function startWalkByPath():void {
        walkByPath();
}
```

This function calculates the destination position to move. The input is the incremental steps from current position. It will then calculate the destination position in isometric coordinate from the input and convert it to screen position inside the world coordinate. This function also faces the avatar to the destination and sets the walking animation.

```
public function walkTo(deltaX:int, deltaY:int):void {
    /* get the destinetion point from the delta*/
    var destIsoX:int = isoPosition.x + deltaX;
    var destIsoY:int = isoPosition.y + deltaY;

    /* calculate the screen point of the destination from isometric */
    var screenPoint:Point = world.map.i2sLocal(destIsoX,destIsoY);
```

```
    var newDirection:String = getDirectionFromDestination(deltaX,
                                                          deltaY);

    _destX = screenPoint.x;
    _destY = screenPoint.y;


    this.showDirection(newDirection);


    /* we only need to set the animation to walk again when not
walking or change direciton */
    if (!_isWalking || _currentDirection != newDirection){

            this.playAnimation('walk');
            _isWalking = true;
            _currentDirection = newDirection;

    }
}
```

The world class checks every avatars' walking state in every frame. When the isWalking flag of the avatar is set to true, the world class will call this walking function to make it walk. This function moves the avatar closer to the destination and stops walking when it reaches there. We play the animation in the walkTo function instead of this function to avoid frequently animation reset and play. The walking animation will be played smoothly without interruption until the avatar stops walking.

```
public function walking():void {
    var remainX:int = _destX - this.x;
    var remainY:int = _destY - this.y;
    var remainLenth:Number = Math.sqrt(remainX*remainX +
                                       remainY*remainY);

    if (remainLenth > _walkingSpeed){
            this.x += remainX/remainLenth * _walkingSpeed;
            this.y += remainY/remainLenth * _walkingSpeed;
    }else{
            this.x = _destX;
            this.y = _destY;

            /* Test if this is the end of the path segment or the end of
the whole path */
            if (walkPath != null && walkPath.length>0){
                    walkByPath();
            }else{
                    stopWalk();
            }
```

```
    }

    /* update the isometric coordinate when walking */
    isoPosition = world.map.s2iLocal(this.x,this.y);
}
```

The `stopWalk` function simply resets the animation to idle and switches off the `isWalking` flag.

```
public function stopWalk():void {
    this.playAnimation("idle");
    _isWalking = false;
}
```

We need to face the direction towards the destination position to make the walking realistic. The directions are based on our isometric coordinate that is used in our virtual world.

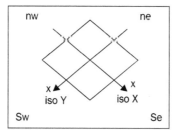

We are using a 4-direction isometric map. We can know which direction the avatar is facing by comparing the next tile's coordinates. If the next tile is in positive x-axis and zero y-axis, the avatar is facing southeast; if the x-axis is negative, it is facing northwest; if the next tile is in positive y-axis and zero x-axis, the avatar is facing southwest; and if the y-axis is negative, it is facing northeast.

```
private function getDirectionFromDestination(deltaX:int,deltaY:int):
                                                    String
{
    if (deltaX > 0 && deltaY == 0){
            return "se";
    }else if (deltaX < 0 && deltaY == 0){
            return "nw";
    }else if (deltaX == 0 && deltaY > 0){
            return "sw";
    }else if (deltaX == 0 && deltaY < 0){
            return "ne";
    }
    return _currentDirection;
}
```

Walking by keyboard

We have made the avatar class able to walk. Let's try to move the avatars by keyboard input and see them walking around.

We set up two event listeners in `World` class. The `onKeyboardDown` and `onKeyboardUp` listeners capture the event when any keyboard key is pressed or released. For each arrow key, we call the `walkTo` methods with one tile movement. For example, when the left arrow key is kept pressed, the avatar will keep moving to the left.

```
private function onKeyboardDown(e:Event):void {
    var c:uint = e.target.lastKey;
    if (c){
        if (c==Keyboard.LEFT){
            _myAvatar.walkTo(-1,0);
        }else if (c==Keyboard.RIGHT){
            _myAvatar.walkTo(1,0);
        }else if (c==Keyboard.UP){
            /* Please note that Y is positive down */
            _myAvatar.walkTo(0,-1);
        }else if (c==Keyboard.DOWN){
            _myAvatar.walkTo(0,1);
        }
    }
}
```

When the key is released, we stop the avatar.

```
private function onKeyboardUp(e:Event):void {
    myAvatar.stopWalk();
}
```

When we test the virtual world, the walking animation is lagged. It is because the walking animation stopped after one walked tile and reset the animation. Then the other one-tile movement started and resulted in non-smooth walking animation. We can improve the animation by moving the avatar two tiles instead of one.

```
...
_myAvatar.walkTo(-2,0);
...
```

The main purpose of this keyboard movement is to test the newly implemented `WalkingAvatar` class. For our virtual world, it is better to use mouse input for the movement which will be discussed later in this chapter.

Introducing path finding

Path finding is the method to find a path between two points in the world. It determines how the avatar moves around the virtual world. There are many different approaches that result differently. Some perform faster while some guarantee a best shortest path. We will discuss how to choose a good path finding method to fit the virtual world design.

Sometimes, finding the direct way from the start point to goal point is possible and trivial. But it can be blocked by non-walkable barrier.

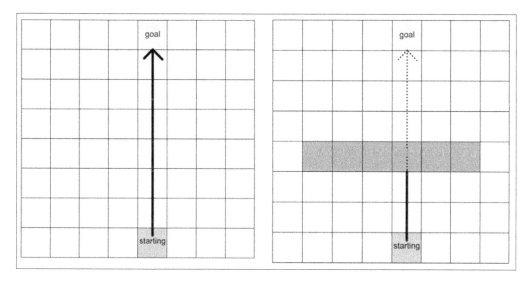

Instead, we may explore all tiles until we find the goal. Then we have shortest path according to the result that was found.

10	-	-	-	10	9	8	9
9	10	-	-	9	8	7	8
8	9	10	9	8	7	6	7
7	8	9	8	7	6	5	6
6	-	-	-	-	-	4	5
5	4	3	2	1	2	3	4
4	3	2	1	0	1	2	3
5	4	3	2	1	2	3	4

10	-	-	-	10	9	8	9
9	10	-	-	9	8	7	8
8	9	10	9	8	7	6	7
7	8	9	8	7	6	5	6
6	-	-	-	-	-	4	5
5	4	3	2	1	2	3	4
4	3	2	1	0	1	2	3
5	4	3	2	1	2	3	4

This method seems to work but it may result in poor performance because it explored almost all tiles on the map to find the result.

Walking is one of the most frequent actions in a virtual world. And it requires path finding for every movement. As in the previous example, path finding is an action that can consume quite a lot of CPU resource if not properly used.

Therefore, choosing the right path finding method is critical and we should use different approaches in different situations when trying to find a path.

How about we modify our previous search to guess the cost from current point to the goal? Suppose we guess the cost from current point to the goal by directly calculating the steps to reach the goal without considering any blocking. The grid value now becomes the steps taken plus the cost we guessed.

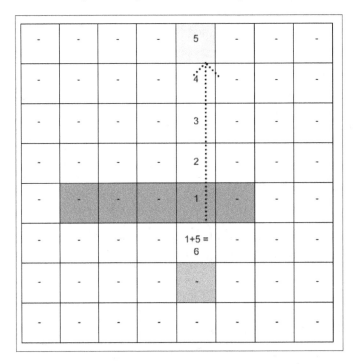

For every step, we will choose the tiles with lowest value to further explore and the result is that we reach the goal in fewer steps.

This is the basic concept of the A* search. Every tile is assigned a score value for determination of the next grid to use. The equation is:

F = G + H

G is the movement cost to move from the start point to the tile. In the example, the cost of each step is one. In some other cases, we may have different terrain on the map with different costs. For example, road costs one, grass costs two, and mountain costs five.

H is the estimated movement cost to move from the tile to the goal and this is often called the **heuristic function**. This is how we guess the cost to reach the goal from the tile. We cannot know the actual cost until we find the final path. There may be a block barrier, grass, or mountain in the way. We used a simple method to count the steps remaining to the goal and ignore all extra costs of those barriers in the example. There are many other ways to guess the cost and this is one main feature of the A* search.

There are two lists during the A* search. One is an open list to remember the tile that is going to explore and the other is a closed list that remembers the grid that is explored. At every step we choose the tile with lowest cost in the open list to explore first. This is the feature of the best-first search algorithm.

Implementing A* search

We used a graphical example and discussed the working principle behind it. We have the pseudo-code of the A* search implementation here to better understand the algorithm.

```
Create an open list with initially contains only the starting point.
Create an empty list for closed tiles.
While we have not reached the goal or the open list is empty {
    Consider the lowest cost grid in the open list. Refer it as
current grid.
    If the current grid is the goal {
        We found the solution and done.
    }
    Else {
        Move the current grid from open list to closed list.
        For each adjacent grid of the current grid {
            If the adjacent grid is not walkable, ignore it.
            Else if the adjacent grid is in either the closed or
open list, and the current F value is lower {
                Update the adjacent grid with new G and F value.
                Update the adjacent grid's parent to current grid.
            }
            Else {
                Add the adjacent grid to the open list and
calculate the G, H and F value.
                Set the adjacent grid's parent to current grid.
            }
        }
    }
}
```

We can avoid re-coding this widely used search algorithm by finding free A* pathfinding ActionScript 3 class on the Internet. In the code example bundle, I used the class from BrainBlitz.com (http://www.brainblitz.org/anthony/as3-a-pathfinding-class). There is another alternative such as the A* pathfinding class from Weekend Code (http://www.weekendcode.com/2009/12/a-pathfinding-in-actionscript-3-0/).

Although the usage of different third-party path finding components may vary, they all have similar input and output. We need to tell the pathfinding class the map information such as width, height, the walkable tiles, starting position, and the destination position. The pathfinding class will output an array containing the path solution.

In the `IsometricMapData` class, we have an instance variable to reference the A* pathfinding class.

```
private var _astarMap.AStarMap;
```

We initialize the pathfinding class with the width and height of the virtual world map.

```
_astarMap = new AStarMap(mapWidth, mapHeight);
```

When loading the map data into IsometricMapData class, we set the tiles in pathfinding class to either walkable (CELL_FREE) or blocked (CELL_FILLED).

```
_astarMap.setCell(i, j, _astarMap.CELL_FREE);
_astarMap.setCell(i, j, _astarMap.CELL_FILLED);
```

After the setup, we can later solve the path solution in this map by giving a starting point and destination point.

We can also check if any tile is walkable by checking if the tile is set to CELL_FREE in the pathfinding class.

```
public function isWalkable(ix:int, iy:int):Boolean {
    return (_astarMap.getCell(ix,iy).cellType == _astarMap.CELL_FREE);
}
```

Understanding the heuristic function

The heuristic function plays an important role in the A* algorithm because different approaches of this function will largely influence the result and performance.

The heuristic function we used is called **Manhattan Distance**, which sums the number of the horizontal and vertical tiles to reach the goal. The Manhattan method considers only the four adjacent and not the diagonal adjacent in an 8-direction map. Using this method in an 8-direction map may slightly overestimate the cost and does not guarantee the shortest path.

Some other heuristic functions like Diagonal distance and Euclidean distance take diagonal adjacent into consideration and get the shortest path result. However, the distance calculations of these methods are often slower. For example, we need the square root for the Euclidean distance, which is CPU resource consuming.

The more accurate the estimation of the heuristic function, the slower A* search to find the result but it guarantees the best shortest path. The less accurate rough estimation will, on the other hand, give the result path faster.

Balancing between accuracy and speed

We know that the behavior of the A* search differs from giving different heuristic function. This is a very useful characteristic for game or virtual world programming. We can easily adjust the heuristic function to shift the balance between the path accuracy and the performance.

For normal walking around the virtual world, we do not need the shortest path between the current position and the destination. Actually, players may not even notice that you are not walking on the shortest path. And most importantly, no one cares about this much because we don't often care whether we are walking the shortest path on the streets. In this situation, it is safe to give up some accuracy to boost the performance.

However, sometimes we always need the shortest and lowest cost path. For example, in a real-time strategy game, we need to ensure every movement of the army is the best shortest path because players take the micro differences of the movement time into the consideration when fighting against enemies.

In some cases, we need to verity accuracy. For instance, the following left image shows many enemies are now chasing the avatar. These enemies will run from a far away position to the adjacent of the avatar and attack. One solution is every enemy calculates their path to the targeted avatar. However, do we need a precise path when the enemy is far away? The answer is no because the avatar may keep moving every second and all enemies need to calculate a new path every second.

 A better approach is to divide the path finding into different states.

In the right image, we can define an area around the avatar. All enemies inside the area will use a better heuristic function to chase the avatar precisely. Enemies outside the area use a faster heuristic function to get a rough path to that area. Sometimes when dealing with a very large number of enemies, we can only direct the enemies to walk towards the avatar and not find any other path until they reach a closer area.

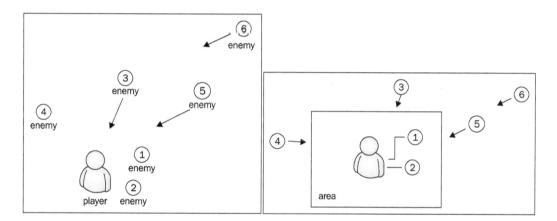

The flexible use of the heuristic function gives the ability to shift between accuracy and speed dynamically, and balancing them in different situations is an important task for the virtual world developers.

The following link contains some examples of heuristic functions and how they can affect the path result: http://theory.stanford.edu/~amitp/GameProgramming/ Heuristics.html.

Walking by mouse click

We modify the World class to listen on mouse click event. When the mouse clicks the world, we get the isometric tile position from the mouse screen coordinate. The map is the reference to the IsometricMapData class which contains the A* pathfinding class. We set up the starting and ending points for the pathfinding class to find a path solution. Then we pass the path to the WalkingAvatar class to follow. At last we need to update the position in the room variables.

```
private function onMapClicked(e:MouseEvent):void {
    var newIsoPosition:Point = map.s2i(stage.mouseX,stage.mouseY);

    if (!map.isWalkable(newIsoPosition.x,newIsoPosition.y)){
        trace("can't walk to there");
        return;
    }

    /* find the path by A* pathfinding class */
    map.astarMap.setEndPoints(myAvatar.isoPosition.x,_myAvatar.
                     isoPosition.y,newIsoPosition.x,newIsoPosition.y);
    var path:Array = map.astarMap.solve();

    myAvatar.walkPath = path;
    myAvatar.startWalkByPath();

    /* update the userVariables*/
    var params:Object = new Object();
    params.isoPosX = newIsoPosition.x;
    params.isoPosY = newIsoPosition.y;
    params.firstTime = false;

    _sfs.setUserVariables(params);
}
```

The updated position in room variables is useful for newly joined players. Existing players in the same room do not need it because they will get the updated position from broadcasted message.

The position set to the final destination in user variables is updated before start to move the avatar. If someone joins the room when you are walking, the new players will see you standing at the destination position instead of walking towards there. It causes a small issue of being asynchronous but it is fine as long as the positioning is not critical.

We can instead do some tricks to make newly joined players see the walking process. We need to put the destination point and the current position on user variables. The user variables need updates every time the walking avatar walks into new position. In this case, the newly joined room players can play the avatar walking by the current position and destination from user variables.

I used the former movement implementation in practical production and it works very well. It is because most of the time we do not need very precise position animation unless the game play requires it.

Broadcasting where you walked

We now can move the avatar locally. The next step is to tell all people in the same room to update your avatar on their screen. A most straightforward way is to tell the others your destination point and then they will calculate the path and move the avatar.

This method may work in development mode because we may have only two to four instances testing the virtual world. Imagine that there are 20 users in the room. Now a user walks a path and broadcasts the destination point. All 20 clients have calculated the path once; that's a total of 20 times. Next we have all 20 people walking at the same time. Twenty destination points are broadcasted and all 20 clients calculated 20 paths. That's a total of 400 times. Assume that the average path finding time take 10 ms. This costs 200 ms on each client and it will absolutely drop the frame rate.

Instead of sending the destination point, we send the path finding result. What we benefit is that the other users do not need to compute the path from the destination point; they get the results already from the broadcasted message and can use them directly. This largely improves the problem. Now when 20 users are walking at the same time, each client only takes 10 ms to calculate their own path and moves the other avatars by the path results.

We will use public message to broadcast the path. Public message is originally designed for chatting but it is useful for sharing temporary information within the same room.

We construct the message in the following format. The | is a delimiter so that we can pack different information into a public message.

```
|path|x1,y1;x2,y2;.....;xn,yn;
```

We broadcast the walking path before starting to walk, so we will put the code inside the `startWalkByPath` function in `WalkingAvatar` class.

```
var message:String = '|path|';
for each (var pathSegment:Object in walkPath){
```

```
        message += pathSegment.x+','+pathSegment.y+';';
    }
    SmartFox.sfs.sendPublicMessage(message);
```

This special format string will be sent out as public message so every one in the room get the latest path to render.

SmartFoxServer provides many ways to communicate and share information with other users. Public message is one of them. We will discuss different information sharing approaches in detail later in *Chapter 9, Communicating with Other Players*.

The following graph shows the result of the code example. When Steve clicks on the map, the `IsometricMapData` class calculates the walking path and the avatar of Steve follows the path. Before the avatar of Steve walks, it broadcasts the path to other players so that they can call the corresponding avatar to walk.

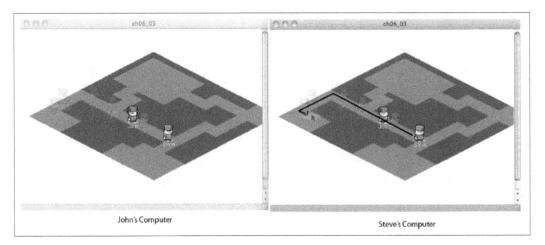

John's Computer   Steve's Computer

Scrolling the world

When the world is becoming bigger, we need to either scroll the world or divide it into smaller parts. We will focus on scrolling the world in this chapter and discuss about dividing the world in next chapter.

We will add a function in `World` class now. The `lookAtAvatar` function offset the world position to have the avatar locate at the center of the screen.

```
    public function lookAtAvatar(avatar:Avatar):void {
        /* the center of the screen */
        var targetScreenPoint:Point = new Point(stage.stageWidth/2,stage.
                                                 stageHeight/2);
```

```
    var localTargetPoint:Point = this.globalToLocal(
                                targetScreenPoint);

    this.x += localTargetPoint.x - avatar.x;
    this.y += localTargetPoint.y - avatar.y;
}
```

In the `walking` function in `WalkingAvatar` class, we can keep putting the controlling avatar in the center of the screen.

```
if (this == world.myAvatar){
    world.lookAtAvatar(this);
}
```

Another common scrolling method is to scroll the world when the avatar is walking into the edge of the screen. We change the preceding code to the following with margin checking when scrolling:

```
var scrollMargin:int = 100;
var globalPosition:Point = this.localToGlobal(new Point());
if ((globalPosition.x > stage.stageWidth-scrollMargin) ||
    (globalPosition.x < scrollMargin) ||
    (globalPosition.y > stage.stageHeight-scrollMargin) ||
    (globalPosition.y < scrollMargin)){
    world.lookAtAvatar(this);
}
```

We can further enhance the world scrolling by adding tweening of the world position when looking at the avatar instead of putting the avatar in the center of the screen directly.

Saving the position for next time

In a virtual world that has a big map, we need to save the current position of the avatar so that we can resume the position next time when we log in again. We can access the database by using server-side extension.

Creating an avatar database table

There are several ways to perform the MySQL tasks. One easy way is to use the PhpMyAdmin, which is a web-based MySQL admin panel provided by the web server bundles.

Windows users can launch the PhpMyAdmin from the taskbar **Wamp2 | phpMyAdmin**.

For Mac OSX:

1. Launch MAMP.
2. Go to `http://localhost/MAMP` in the web browser.
3. Click on the **PhpMyAdmin** link.

Linux users can go to `http://localhost/path_to_phpMyAdmin` in the web browser.

It is optional to create a database before creating our first table. This database will hold all the tables of our virtual world. We create a database name `flash_virtual_world`. In the newly created database, we create a new table named `avatar` with seven fields in `PhpMyAdmin`.

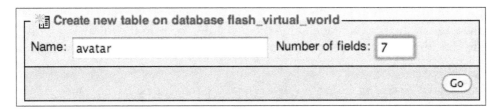

We are going to store following fields into the `avatar` table.

Field name	Type	Description
id	int(11)	A unique ID that is auto incremented.
avatar_name	varchar(50)	A unique name of the avatar.
color	int(11)	The color of the avatar.
head_style	int(11)	The style of the head.
body_style	int(11)	The style of the body.
pos_x	int(11)	The isometric position x of the avatar.
pos_y	int(11)	The isometric position y of the avatar.

We can find more step-by-step tutorials on using `PhpMyAdmin` in following links:

`http://php.about.com/od/learnmysql/ss/create_tables.htm`

`http://php.about.com/lr/phpmyadmin/93864/2/`

Creating a new zone in config.xml

After setting up the database, we need to use extension as a bridge connection between the Flash and the database. In previous chapters, we did not create any dedicated zone for the examples but it is time to create a dedicated zone for the virtual world.

Open the `config.xml` which is located in `Server` folder in the SmartFoxServer installation directory. Right after the `<Zones>`, we create a new zone tag with database configuration.

We also associate the zone extension to `virtualworld.as`, which is placed inside the `sfsExtensions` under `Server` in the SmartFoxServer installation directory.

```
<Zone name="virtualworld" customLogin="false" buddyList="20">
    <Rooms>
          <Room name="Lobby" maxUsers="50" isPrivate="false"
isTemp="false" autoJoin="true" />
    </Rooms>

    <Extensions>
          <extension name="virtualWorld"  className="virtualworld.as"
type="script" />
    </Extensions>

    <DatabaseManager active="true">

          <Driver>org.gjt.mm.mysql.Driver</Driver>
              <ConnectionString>jdbc:mysql://127.0.0.1:3306/flash_
                              virtual_world</ConnectionString>

          <UserName>root</UserName>
          <Password>password of the MySQL user</Password>

          <TestSQL><![CDATA[SELECT NOW()]]></TestSQL>

          <MaxActive>10</MaxActive>
          <MaxIdle>10</MaxIdle>

          <OnExhaustedPool>fail</OnExhaustedPool>
          <BlockTime>5000</BlockTime>
    </DatabaseManager>
</Zone>
```

Programming our first server-side extension

This is our first time for coding the server-side extension. We will walkthrough the steps in detail. The extension acts as a bridge between the Flash client and the database server that handles requests from clients and returns the query results from database.

The syntax of server-side extension is like ActionScript 1.0. It is actually Java on the backend so there are some tricks to keep in mind during the development.

We need the following database manager to hold the reference of the database connection which depends on the database configuration in `config.xml` file:

```
var dbase;
```

The `init` function is called once the extension is loaded successfully. The extension will be loaded on server start up or manually restarted in the server admin tool.

```
function init(){
    dbase = _server.getDatabaseManager();
}
```

The `destroy` function is called when the extension is being destroyed when the server is shutting down or restarting the extension manually. We haven't used it yet but it is useful to save server-side variables to the database before shutting down or restarting the server.

```
function destroy(){}
```

The `sendResponseBack` function wraps the commonly used response codes for reusability purposes. Almost every request from clients will call these three lines to send the result back.

```
function sendResponseBack(obj, user){
    var userList = [];
    userList.push(user);
    _server.sendResponse(obj,-1,null,userList,"json");
}
```

The `handleRequest` function is called when the client send an extension message to the extension. What it is doing here is calling another function according to the command. For example, if the command from the extension message is `getMyLastPosition`, it will then call the `hgetMyLastPosition` function which we defined to get the position from database.

```
function handleRequest(cmd, params, user, fromRoom){
    var str = "h"+cmd;
    var target = eval(str);
```

```
    if (target != undefined) {
        target(cmd, params, user, fromRoom)
    }
}
```

 We seldom define type for the variable in server-side ActionScript file. Even the official examples from SmartFoxServer do not contain type declaration in server-side ActionScript. It may because all the server-side extensions run in Java environment. The ActionScript syntax we code will finally be parsed into Java execution. Therefore, the real type of the objects in the extensions are not ActionScript type. So, we do not declare the type.

For every returning data from database, it is default in Java type instead of ActionScript type. This sounds strange but it is one of the powerful server-side extension features of SmartFoxServer. The server is Java runtime but it supports the extensions that are written in Java, Python, or ActionScript. This greatly helps Flash developers who are not familiar with Java programming and can use ActionScript-like syntax to code the extension into Java runtime. The pay off is that sometimes we need to apply some tricks to make it work perfectly. For instance, we need to convert the Java type to ActionScript object by the following function.

```
function getASObj(row) {
    var map = row.getDataAsMap();
    var mapKeys = map.keySet();
    var mapKeysArray = mapKeys.toArray();
    var asObj = new Object();

    for(var i = 0; i < mapKeysArray.length; i++) {
        var d = map.get(mapKeysArray[i]);

        // force the value to cast into ActionScript string.
        asObj[mapKeysArray[i]] = "" + d;
    }
    return asObj;
}
```

The following function queries the database and prepares the ActionScript results for other functions to use:

```
function getResultArray(sql, list) {
    var queryRes = dbase.executeQuery(sql);
    if (queryRes == null) {
        return 0;
    }

    for(var i=0; i <queryRes.size(); i++) {
```

```
        var tempRow = queryRes.get(i);
        var asObj = getASObj(tempRow);
        list.push(asObj);
    }
    return queryRes.size();
}
```

We will access the position according to the username. That means we can load our last position by using the same username. This is just a simple identification. A more complex login checking process can be further implemented but for now, we will stick to the easier one for the first try on server-side extension.

Next, we create two extension functions to access the position.

The first one is to handle the saved position request. It will search if there exists a record in the database. Then it will either update an existing one or create a new entry with the latest position.

```
function hsavePosition(cmd, params, user, fromRoom){
    var list = [];
    var sql = "SELECT * FROM avatar WHERE avatar_name='"+user.
                                    getName()+"'";
    var count = getResultArray(sql,list);

    if (count>0){
        sql = "UPDATE avatar SET pos_x="+params.posx+",
          pos_y="+params.posy+" WHERE avatar_name='"+user.getName()+"'";
    }else{
        sql = "INSERT INTO avatar(`avatar_name`,`pos_x`,`pos_y`)
VALUES('"+user.getName()+"',"+params.posx+","+params.posy+")";
    }
    var success = dbase.executeCommand(sql);
}
```

The other function is to get last position according to the username from the database. It returns the position to the client.

```
function hgetPosition(cmd, params, user, fromRoom) {
    var res = {};
    res._cmd = cmd;
    var list = [];
    var sql = "SELECT * FROM avatar WHERE avatar_name='"+user.
getName()+"'";

    getResultArray(sql,list);
    if (list[0] != undefined){
```

```
            res.posx = list[0].pos_x;
            res.posy = list[0].pos_y;
    }
    sendResponseBack(res,user);
}
```

There are two functions to query the database within server-side extension. One is `executeCommand` and the other is `executeQuery`.

When fetching the database by using `SELECT` statement, we use `executeQuery`. When accessing the database with commands such as `INSERT` or `UPDATE`, we use `executeCommand` instead.

After modifying the server-side extension, we need to either reload the extension in admin tool or restart the SmartFoxServer. The extension in the admin tool locates in the `Zone Browser | virtualworld | Extension View`. Click on the **RELOAD EXT.** button to reload the extension.

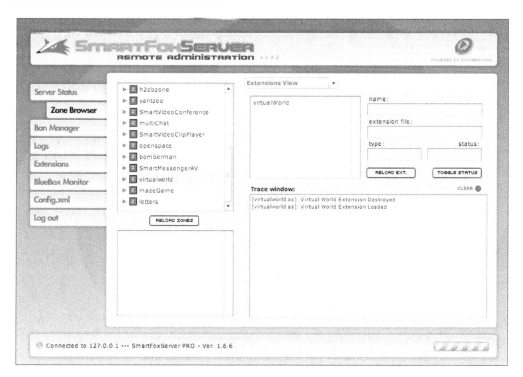

Saving and loading last position

The method to call an extension function in client-side is to send an extension message is this format:

```
_sfs.sendXtMessage(extension_name, command, passing_parameters,
                                              string_format);
```

As configured in the `config.xml`, our `extension_name` is `virtualWorld`; the command will be either `savePosition` or `getPosition`. The `passing_parameters` is an object containing our latest position and we will use JSON as the string format of the message.

We will save the last position after the avatar stops walking.

```
public function stopWalk():void {
    var params:Object = {};
    params.posx = this.isoPosition.x;
    params.posy = this.isoPosition.y;
    SmartFox.sfs.sendXtMessage("virtualWorld", "savePosition", params,
                                                          "json");

    this.playAnimation("idle");
    _isWalking = false;
}
```

And we need to get the updated position in the initial process of the virtual world. Previously, we initialized the World class after joining a room. Now we initialize it after getting the last position from the server response.

```
private function onJoinRoom(e:SFSEvent):void {
    /* handling avatar styling and color */
    ...
    /* get avatar position */
    var params:Object = {};
    SmartFox.sfs.sendXtMessage("virtualWorld", "getPosition", params,
                                                          "json");
}
```

In order to get the response of the extension message, we need to listen to the `onExtensionResponse` event in document class. When the clients receive the extension response, it will check for existence of the latest position and initiate the world and map. This function will also be added to the document class.

```
private function onExtensionResponse(e:SFSEvent):void {
    var data:Object = e.params.dataObj;
    if (data.posx != undefined) {
```

```
        Myself.instance.isoPosX = data.posx;
        Myself.instance.isoPosY = data.posy;
    }

    world = new World();
    addChild(world);
}
```

The virtual world initialization now becomes:

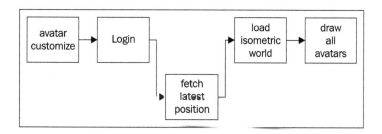

Debugging the code with both Flash client and server-side extension can sometimes be difficult. Here are some tips when facing problems in development:

- Always check the server output log when reloading the extension. If the extension contains syntax errors, it will immediately pop up error message when reloaded.

- We can use trace in server-side extension and the trace message will go to the log in server-side terminal.

- As there are too many places to monitor and compile the code, sometimes it will be confusing. We may forget to reload the extension or look at the wrong place for trace output after coding for hours, and then we think that the bug still exists after modifying the code several times and at last realize that we are debugging in the wrong place.

Summary

In this chapter, we discussed several key techniques to walk around the world. We coded our first server-side extension and created the connectivity between Flash client and the database.

We can walk in our virtual world now, but it seems that we are still missing something. We have basic terrain and avatars. The next step is putting objects in the world. In the next chapter, we are going to discuss the buildings and environments of the virtual world.

7
Creating Buildings and Environments in the Virtual World

In the previous chapter, we learned how to find the shortest path with obstacles in the virtual world. In this chapter, we will discuss the techniques for creating buildings and environments. We will discuss different common problems when putting buildings in the isometric world and the solutions to resolve them. We will also learn how large virtual worlds are divided into small parts and also extend our previous map editor to support buildings.

We will learn the following in this chapter:

- Adding buildings to world
- Sorting the buildings in isometric view
- Techniques of breaking down a large virtual world
- Connecting different parts of the world
- Some tips and tricks when creating the environments
- Implementing a more powerful map editor to design the virtual world

Placing buildings on the map

Similar to drawing the avatars, there are several ways to draw the isometric buildings. We can draw them in any graphical editing tool such as Photoshop or Flash. We can also model them in any 3D software.

When drawing in Flash, we often put some isometric tiles as a guide to keep the correct **orthographic projection**. The size of the building is based on the side length of the tile. A building can occupy a group of contiguous tiles. For example, a tree occupies a 1x1 tile of the map, a fountain occupies 3x3 tiles, and a building may occupy 2x5 tiles. The following graph shows a hand-drawn isometric tree in Flash with a tile as guide:

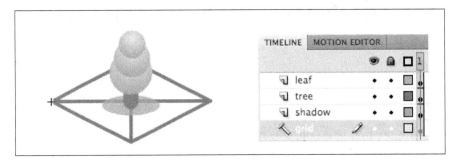

Another common method of drawing buildings is by using 3D modeling tools. Similar to creating the avatar graphics by 3D modeling tools, we can set up an orthographic camera in front of the buildings with the viewing angle matching the Flash virtual world. The advantage of using 3D modeling tools is that we can put texture on the building easily without considering the transformation of the isometric projection.

Outputting building from 3D software

We will show an example on how to output an isometric building in different directions from 3D software. Although every 3D software comes with different interface and commands, the general steps of outputting the building from 3D software to isometric project are almost the same.

1. Modeling the building in 3D software.

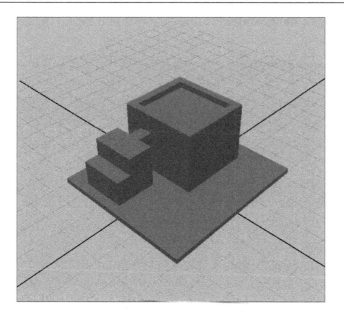

2. Create a camera with Orthographic view.

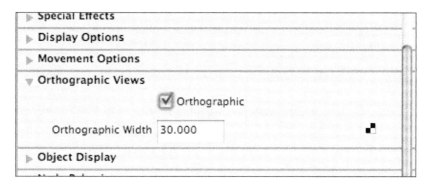

3. Place eight of these cameras with -30 degrees rotation down at every 45 degrees.

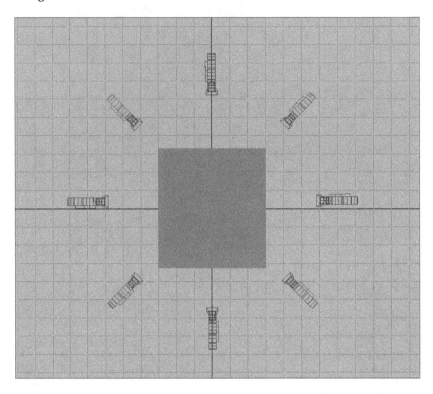

4. For every Orthographic camera, output the images as PNG for Flash.

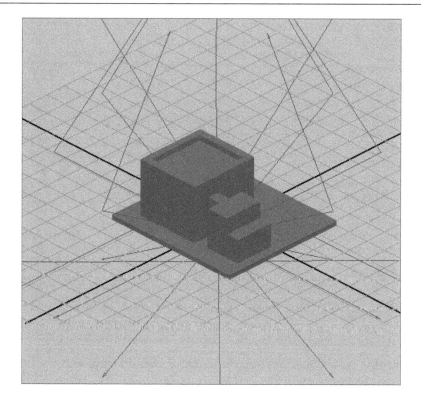

After the eight cameras are set up, we can also write scripts to generate the render of all eight cameras instead of clicking the "render" button eight times per frame. The degree of the downward rotation of the cameras can also be adjusted to fit the isometric view of the map in Flash.

Loading the building map data

We cannot walk on a building in the real world. In virtual world, we need to prevent the avatars from walking on the buildings by using walkable map.

Walkable map is a two-dimensional array with the same size of the terrain map. Each tile of the walkable map declares if avatars can walk on those tiles or not. When we put buildings on the virtual world, we need to mark the tiles that the building has occupied as unwalkable in the walkable map.

The virtual world needs to know all types of buildings in order to draw them and show relative information. The information is basically the ID, name, the length of the side it occupies, and the graphical reference of the class name.

In this example, we will load the data of the buildings externally from an XML file. The `buildingData.xml` is in the following XML structure:

```
<buildingData>
    <building id='1'>
        <size>1</size>
        <name>tree</name>
        <classname>Tree1</classname>
    </building>
    <building id='2'>
        <size>4</size>
        <name>Hotel</name>
        <classname>BuildingHotel</classname>
    </building>
</buildingData>
```

We use `URLLoader` to load this external `buildingData.xml`.

```
_xmlLoader = new URLLoader();
_xmlLoader.addEventListener(Event.COMPLETE, init);
_xmlLoader.load(new URLRequest('data/buildingData.xml'));
```

After the building data is loaded, we put them inside an array with the building ID as key for quick access later.

```
private function init(e:Event):void {
    _xml = new XML(e.target.data);
    for (var i:int = 0; i < _xml.building.length(); i++)     {
        var buildingID:int = _xml.building[i].attribute('id');
        _buildings[buildingID] = new BuildingData();
        _buildings[buildingID].buildingID = buildingID;
        _buildings[buildingID].size = _xml.building[i].size;
        _buildings[buildingID].name = _xml.building[i].name;
        _buildings[buildingID].classname = _xml.building[i].classname;
    }
}
```

 The document and example of using the XML class in ActionScript 3 can be found in the following link: http://www.adobe.com/livedocs/flash/9.0/ActionScriptLangRefV3/XML.html.

We need to be careful of the security problem when putting all building data into an external file. Raw data such as map and buildings should not be accessible directly by users. Players can easily find cheats, tricks, shortcuts, and even hack the virtual world with the access of the raw data. We can deny the public access by putting the XML files outside the web server public folder or adding .htaccess limitation on the file. One advanced way is to load this kind of external raw data via socket connection instead of the traditional URLLoader class. We should also validate each player's movement requests in server-side before putting the virtual world in production.

We need to specify where and which building to show in a map. The following XML shows the building information structure inside the mapdata.xml. There are three fields in every building entry. They are building type and the X/Y in position in map. The building type refers to the ID in our building definition XML file.

```
<map>
    <name>Sample Map</name>
    <width>30</width>
    <height>30</height>
    <terrain><![CDATA[...]]></terrain>
    <buildings>
        <building>
            <type>2</type>
            <x>25</x>
            <y>18</y>
        </building>
        <building>
            <type>1</type>
            <x>16</x>
            <y>17</y>
        </building>
        ...
    </buildings>
</map>
```

In order to display the buildings, we loop through these building nodes when drawing the map. A notable code is the use of getDefinitionByName. This method is used to get the class reference from string of building's name in runtime. Then we can create a movie clip instance of the building from this class reference. Also, we need to set the tiles that are occupied to unwalkable.

```
for(i=0; i<_xml.buildings.building.length(); i++) {
    var buildingXML:XML = _xml.buildings.building[i];
    var ClassReference:Class = getDefinitionByName
    (_buildings[buildingXML.type].classname) as Class;
```

```
var newMC:MovieClip = (new ClassReference as MovieClip);
_mapHolder.addChild(newMC);
newMC.id = Number(buildingXML.type);
var ix:int = int(buildingXML.x);
var iy:int = int(buildingXML.y);
var screenBuildingCoord:Point = i2sLocal(ix,iy);
newMC.x = screenBuildingCoord.x-_gridWidth/2;
newMC.y = screenBuildingCoord.y;

var size:int = _buildings[newMC.id].size;
for(var ii:int = iy-size+1; ii<=iy; ii++){
    for(var jj:int = ix; jj<ix+size; jj++){
        _astarMap.setCell(ii,jj,_astarMap.CELL_FILLED);
        _walkableMap[ii][jj] = 0;
    }
}
}
```

It not only marks the position of the building as unwalkable but also needs to mark those surrounding tiles as unwalkable by the building size.

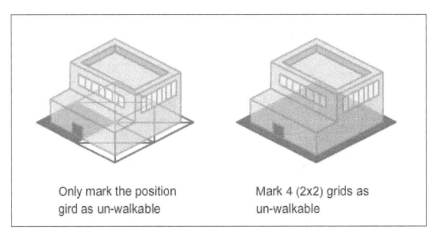

Only mark the position gird as un-walkable

Mark 4 (2x2) grids as un-walkable

Ordering the buildings

Now we are facing a new problem with the buildings. The buildings are not well placed on the map. They overlap with each other in a very strange way. That is because we are now viewing the 3D isometric world in 2D screen with wrong ordering.

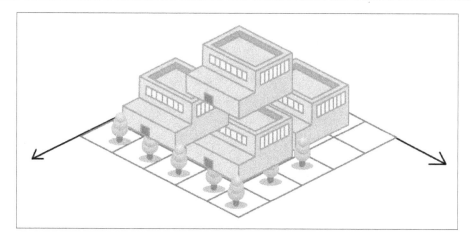

When we view the 3D perspective in the following way, the closer objects should block the view of the objects behind. The buildings in the preceding image do not obey this real-world rule and cause some strange overlapping. We are going to solve this problem in the next section.

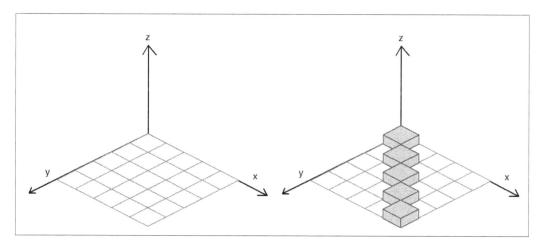

Ordering the movie clips in Flash

In Flash, every movie clip has its own depth. The depth is called **z-order** or the **z-index** of the movie clip. A movie clip with bigger z-order number is higher and covers the others with lower z-order when overlapping. By swapping their z-order, we can rearrange the movie clips on how they overlap and create the correct ordering of isometric buildings.

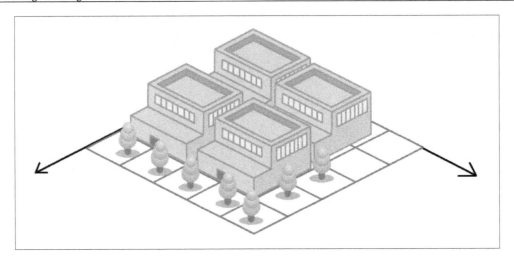

Determining an object's location and view

According to our tile-based isometric map, the object that locates in larger number of the x and y axis is in front of the object that locates in smaller number of the x and y axis. We can thus compare the isometric x and y coordinate to determine which object is in front.

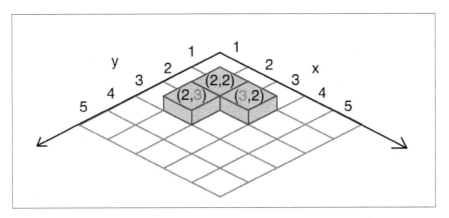

There is a special case when all shapes of the buildings occupy square shapes. In this situation, the order of the movie clip's z order can be easily determined by comparing their y position.

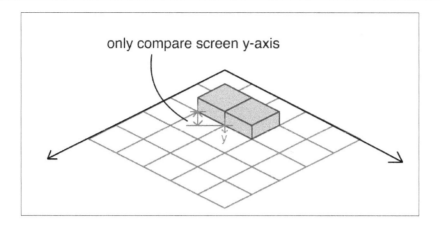

Shaping the buildings

Different buildings occupy different sizes and shapes on the map. We need to be careful of the shapes of the buildings and how it occupies the map. Different sizes and shapes of the buildings result in different ways of sorting the z index of the movie clips to make the three dimensions looks correct.

Rendering z-order for l-shaped buildings

In l-shaped buildings, there is no simple way to render the z-order correctly. No matter how the tree's z-index is, the render result is incorrect. This is because the concave corner of the l-shape makes it difficult to order correctly with other's objects.

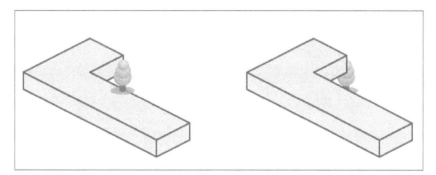

To fix the z-ordering problem of l-shaped buildings, we can either split the l-shaped buildings into several rectangular buildings or mark the whole bound of the building as unwalkable.

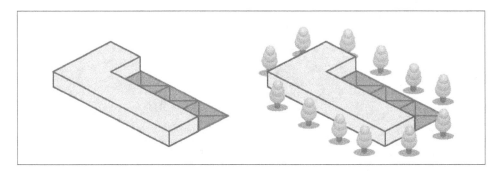

Rendering z-order for rectangle buildings

If the virtual world contains a rectangle shape for building, we have to compare the y-axis and then x-axis of the isometric coordinate to determine the z-order of two buildings or avatars. The buildings or avatars with bigger isometric y and x number are in the front.

Take the following buildings as an example. Building A has bigger y-axis than building B, and building B has bigger y-axis than building C. Therefore, building A is in front of building B which is in front of building C.

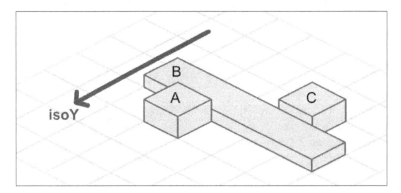

Rendering z-order for square buildings

Square is a special case of a rectangle-shaped building. Because of the special symmetry shape, objects with y position in bigger screen coordinate are always in the front. We can simplify the sorting algorithm by only comparing their y position in screen coordinate to determine the correct z-index if the virtual world contains only square shaped buildings. In our virtual world example, all buildings are in square shape.

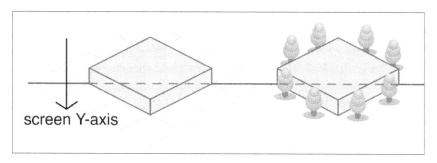

Creating a loop to sort the z-order

We have a loop running every frame for the walking of the avatars. We will insert the sorting z-index code in this loop.

```
for(var i:int =1;i<_sortableContainer.numChildren;i++){
    var mc1:DisplayObject = _sortableContainer.getChildAt(i-1);
    var mc2:DisplayObject = _sortableContainer.getChildAt(i);
    if (mc1.y > mc2.y){
        _sortableContainer.swapChildrenAt(i-1,i);
    }
}
```

Normally, we can use bubble sort for sorting small amount of elements. Bubble sort is easy to implement and it repeatedly compares two adjacent elements and swaps them if the bigger one hasn't come first. The sorting algorithm we used is similar to the bubble sort. However, if you take a closer look at the code, you will find that it is actually a bubble sort without the outer loop. This is a single loop sorting, that only compares and swaps adjacent movie clips' z-index.

There are two reasons that this is not a complete sorting algorithm.

One reason why we omitted the outer loop of the bubble sort is that this function is already executing in every frame. The `enterframe` event acts similar to the outer loop already and the difference is that the `enterframe` event runs 30 times per second according to the frame per second. It will sort all the objects within seconds.

Is this one or two seconds delay of sorting acceptable? Yes, because there is another important reason. When an avatar is walking, it may move from the front of the building to the back and we need to sort them again. In most cases, the avatar only swaps the z-index with its adjacent building each time; this fits our sorting loop because the loop only sorts adjacent objects on each frame.

Moreover, by omitting the outer loop, we can make the sorting much faster which prevents dropping frame rate when there are many buildings and players on the map.

Designing a big virtual world

Normally a virtual world contains several towns and places for players to explore. The following screenshot is from the 51mole, a Flash virtual world for children in China. The whole virtual world contains around 25 places with different themes. Some are inside mountains, some are castle, and some are snowing. Players seldom get bored inside such a large and content-rich virtual world.

Dividing the big world

The virtual world can sometimes be very large. We cannot put the whole world into one SmartFoxServer room when it grows big. Putting a large area into one room means that there are more users inside the room. More users means many more broadcast messages for every player's action and this will cause performance and bandwidth problems.

If all parts of the world belong to the same room, all broadcasted events of the avatar will be accessed by all players. On the other hand, in the partitioned world, the broadcast messages are sent only to those players that are in the same part of the world.

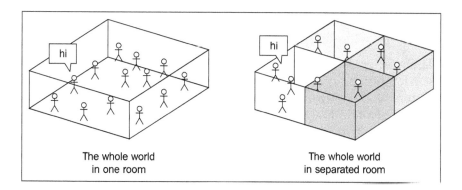

| The whole world in one room | The whole world in separated room |

There is a parameter called `maxUsers` for each room in SmartFoxServer that limits the maximum number of users joining the room. Broadcast messages cost much more bandwidth when there are too many users in the same room. Therefore, we have to break the large world into different rooms, or even different servers to distribute the loading.

When splitting the world, we need to consider the connectivity between different parts of the virtual world. There are two common methods. One is partitioning the rooms as an individual cell. Players cannot see other buildings or players in another cell. The other method is to display the world seamlessly so that the players will not notice the border between different rooms.

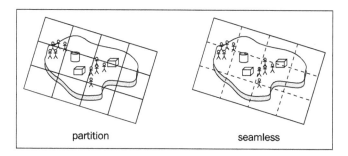

partition   seamless

The pros and cons of the seamless world

In a seamless world, there is no sharp border between different SmartFoxServer rooms of the virtual world. Users can view the other part of the world when they walk near the hidden border of the room. They can cross the border and walk into the other room without notice. They may even be able to see players in other rooms. The seamless world gives the players a larger vision of the virtual world and better interactivity between players.

The seamless world creates a more attractive large world then partitioning the world and thus it is tempting for the virtual world development team to implement the seamless virtual world. However, there are several difficulties in implementing the seamless world. Most difficulties come from the complex exceptions when handling the hidden border of two SmartFoxServer rooms.

- The complexity of a hidden border

  There is a buffer area between two rooms that can share some critical information. For example, a player inside the buffer area has to be viewable from the other room. If there is no buffer area, other players will suddenly appear when crossing the hidden border of the rooms. The buffer area reduces this strange suddenly appearing effect by preloading the avatars that are inside the buffer.

- Complex synchronization between rooms

  However, this buffer area causes another problem. There is one case that player A is in room A outside the buffer area. Player B is in room B inside the buffer area near room A. In this case, player A can see player B but player B cannot see player A. If this virtual world allows a player-versus-player battle, player A can attack player B while player B will not know that player A is there. This causes the imbalance between players.

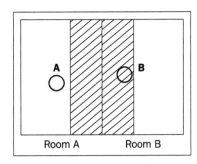

There are often unpredictable synchronization problems between the borders of the rooms. Some players may use these bugs to create an imbalance situation. Some seamless virtual worlds use dynamic border instead of static border to prevent players cheating the border synchronization. Players will not know at any time where the border is and this greatly reduces their chance of cheating the border. However, implementing dynamic border makes the code more complex.

The seamless world give a bigger sight view to players and it is often a bit tempting for a new virtual world designer to try implementing it. However, the decision of using seamless world implementation or not should be considered thoughtfully and made at the very beginning of the virtual world development.

My suggestion is not to use the seamless world because it is not worth putting in so much time implementing it. I will only use the seamless world implementation when the game play requires it as core features and I have a big professional development team.

Partitioning the world into rooms

We will use partition-type virtual world implementation because we should avoid implementing seamless world if it is not necessary. Instead of putting so much manpower on the seamless world, it is worth it to enhance the game player and overall design of the virtual world.

We need to prepare the rooms for the virtual world in the SmartFoxServer configuration. As the rooms for virtual world are something static and will not be destroyed, we can set the rooms in `config.xml` to create the rooms on server start up.

```
<Rooms>
    <Room name="Lobby" maxUsers="50" isPrivate="false" isTemp="false"
autoJoin="true" />
    <Room name="island1" maxUsers="50" isPrivate="false"
                                            isTemp="false" />
    <Room name="island2" maxUsers="50" isPrivate="false"
                                            isTemp="false" />
    <Room name="island3" maxUsers="50" isPrivate="false"
                                            isTemp="false" />
</Rooms>
```

This configuration creates four rooms when the server starts up. More rooms may be needed when the virtual world grows larger.

Connecting rooms with portals

Some special actions or events happen when the player walks near some specific place. This specific place is called **trigger**. One feature of the trigger is to connect two places. It may connect two towns of the virtual world or it may let the players enter some houses. **Portal** is a trigger where avatars teleport to another designed place when stepping on it.

Before implementing the portal functions, we need to modify several codes for preparation.

We used to load the `mapdata.xml` file when initializing the world. As there are different XMLs now to define different maps, we will dynamically load the map data from the room name.

```
loader.load(new URLRequest('data/'+SmartFox.sfs.getActiveRoom().
getName()+'.xml'));
```

The portal XML node is similar to the building XML node; it lists all portals in this room and which room the portal will direct to.

```
<portals>
    <portal id='1'>
        <x>29</x>
        <y>16</y>
        <connectedRoom>island2</connectedRoom>
        <connectedPortal>1</connectedPortal>
    </portal>
    ...
</portals>
```

There are five fields for each portal entry. They are the portal ID, x/y position in map, room name that connected, and the portal ID that connected in that room. We will also define an object called `PortalObject` to store the information of each entry.

The list is loaded after loading the building list in the `onMapDataLoaded` function in `IsometricMapData.as`.

```
for(i=0; i<_xml.portals.portal.length(); i++) {
    var portalXML:XML = _xml.portals.portal[i];
    var portalObj:PortalObject = new PortalObject();
    portalObj.id = int(portalXML.attribute('id'));
    portalObj.x = int(portalXML.x);
    portalObj.y = int(portalXML.y);
    portalObj.connectedRoom = portalXML.connectedRoom;
    portalObj.connectedPortal = portalXML.connectedPortal;
    portalList.push(portalObj);
}
```

We need to check if the avatar stepped on a portal. The checking is executed after the avatar stops walking. The avatar dispatches the `myAvatarStopWalk` custom event to let the `World` class handle.

```
this.addEventListener("myAvatarStopWalk",checkPortal);
```

The `checkPortal` function is located in `World.as`. It loops through the list of portals to see if current stepped tile matches any portals. If they match, it will join the connected room.

```
private function checkPortal(e:Event):void {
    for(var i:int =0;i<_map.portalList.length;i++){
        var portalObj:PortalObject = _map.portalList[i];
        if (portalObj.x == Myself.instance.isoPosX
          && portalObj.y == Myself.instance.isoPosY){
            Myself.instance.nextRoomPortal = int(portalObj.
connectedPortal);
            SmartFox.sfs.joinRoom(portalObj.connectedRoom);
        }
    }
}
```

We also need to teleport the avatars to the connected portal of the new room, so we set the target portal ID before joining the new room and initialize the avatar to the portal position when initializing the new room.

```
public function initWorld(e:Event):void {
    this.x = (stage.stageWidth)/2;
    this.y = (stage.stageHeight-this.height)/2;
    /* if crossing portal */
    if (Myself.instance.nextRoomPortal != -1){
        var portalId:int = Myself.instance.nextRoomPortal;
        var portalObj:PortalObject = _map.portalList[portalId];
        _myAvatar = drawAvatarInIsometric(
                _sfs.myUserName,
                int(portalObj.x),
                int(portalObj.y)
        );
    }else
    ...
}
```

One last thing to do is to clear the old world and map resources before creating the new graphics of the new room.

```
private function onExtensionResponse(e:SFSEvent):void
{
    var data:Object = e.params.dataObj;
    if (data.posx != undefined){
        Myself.instance.isoPosX = data.posx;
        Myself.instance.isoPosY = data.posy;
    }
    if (_world != null){
        removeChild(_world);
        _world = null;
    }
    _world = new World();
    addChild(_world);
}
```

We have created some rooms and connected them. What we have not done is check any failure when joining the new room. Joining room is not always successful. A common error is that the room is full. We can track these errors by handling the onJoinRoomError event.

Besides connecting places, we can also use triggers for some special events. They can discover new items, discover new places, or trigger some mechanism tricks. Adding different types of triggers can enhance the fun of the virtual world—for example, a trigger that switches on or off the streetlight and makes the whole room bright or dark. It provides some fun Easter eggs when the players walk on the street.

Another example from the 51Mole (http://www.51mole.com/), a Flash virtual world that targets Chinese children—when four players sit on the chairs in a room, some fireworks may appear on the screen. These types of triggers are just for fun to enhance the interactivity between players and sometime give them surprises.

Adding sound to the virtual world

Creating realistic sound effects for the environments is important in the virtual world. It can give the players the feeling of immersing inside the world.

The most basic sound handing method is to play all sounds at the same volume. For instance, a bird is singing in the forest and the avatars are walking on the road. In this case, the user should hear at least the music from the bird and the footfalls.

A better way to handle sounds is to consider distance. For example, the following figure depicts the volume of the bird signing in the room:

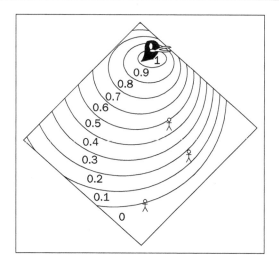

The three avatars in the room should hear different volumes of the music from the bird. The closer the avatar, the louder the music. This enhancement lets the players feel that they are in the realistic world. A classical example of sound control in an environment is Age of Empires. You can feel every single sound from the environment played in a designed volume and balance between left/right channels of stereo.

Let's create a stereo sound example. We create a SoundController class that responds to attach a bird singing sound on every tree. The sound stores the position of the tree for later use to calculate the distance from the tree to the avatar.

```
public function registerSoundSource(sourcePosition:Point) {
    var newSoundSource:Object = {};
    newSoundSource.position = sourcePosition;
    newSoundSource.snd = new Sound(new URLRequest("sounds/bird.mp3"));
    newSoundSource.trans = new SoundTransform(1,0);
    newSoundSource.channel = newSoundSource.snd.
                        play(0,999,newSoundSource.trans);
    _soundSources.push(newSoundSource);
}
```

While the avatar of current user is walking, it keeps the sound controller updated with the latest position of the avatar. When the position changes, the sound controller calculates the distance between the sound source and the avatar. The farther from the tree, the less volume it is. The nearer the avatar to the tree, the louder it plays. It will also determine if the sound source is on the left or right side of the avatar and adjust the pan.

```
public function updateAvatarPosition(position:Point) {
    for each(var soundSource:Object in _soundSources) {
        var newPan:Number = (soundSource.position.x - position.x)/200;
        soundSource.trans.pan = newPan;
        var maxSoundDistance:Number = 500;
        var newVolume:Number = (maxSoundDistance - Math.sqrt(Math.
pow(soundSource.position.x-position.x,2) + Math.pow(soundSource.
position.y-position.y,2)))/maxSoundDistance;
        soundSource.trans.volume = newVolume;

        soundSource.channel.soundTransform = soundSource.trans;
    }
}
```

In the walking function in `WalkingAvatar`, we update the sound controller with the latest avatar's position.

```
_world.soundController.updateAvatarPosition(new Point(this.x,this.y));
```

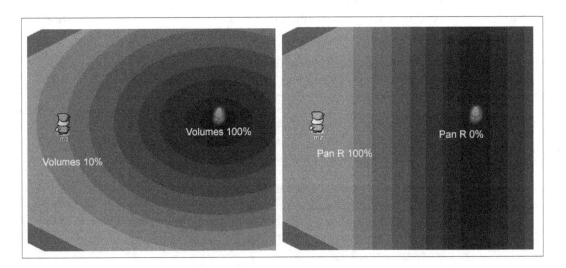

When running this example with headphone, we can notice sound transform differences when the avatar walks to different position on the map.

Mixing art-based background with tile-based map

Our world map now is composited by several pieces of 30x30 tiles. Although it is possible to paint the 30x30 tiles on every map, it is time-consuming and combining the tiles perfectly to build a big terrain texture is difficult.

Another approach is to make a big terrain texture and then set the walkable map manually. We can draw the island in whatever shape we want, then we can use our map editor to mark the walkable grid to prevent the avatar walking into the sea. Please note that the logic is still 50x50 tiles. The only different thing here is that we used one big texture instead of composing the ground with 50x50 tiles.

We will create a movie clip and draw a big texture on it. This movie clip will be exported for ActionScript use with name `BigMap`.

In the `IsometricMapData.as`, we load the `BigMap` movie clip and blend the alpha of the tiles. The reason we keep the 50x50 tiles is that we need them to dispatch the click event in order to walk around.

```
private function onMapDataLoaded(e:Event):void {
    ...
    var bigmap:MovieClip = new BigMap();
    _mapHolder.addChild(bigmap);
    ...
        _map[i][j].alpha = .05;
    ...
}
```

Building map editor for buildings

We have implemented a lot of functions for the buildings and environments of the virtual world. It will now load the terrain map, buildings, and portals to the world. When these basic features are finished, we often begin to input content and shape in the virtual world. We will enhance the map editor for using it to design the whole virtual world. Creating a map editor can highly boost the speed of designing the virtual world because it is—"What you see is what you get"—and prevents inputting boring raw data.

The editor now groups brushes, buildings, and movements into different panels. The following graph shows how we compose the **Building Panel**. The background is static graphic. There is a **ScrollPane** component whose source is pointing to the **Buildings MovieClip**. The **Buildings MovieClip** is controlled by a class which reads the building definition XML file to show the building movie clips.

We will cover key implementations here. The full code of the map editor is in the code example bundle.

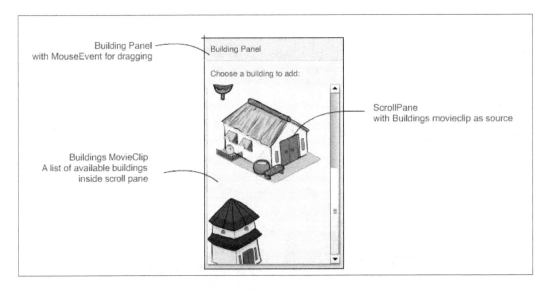

When a map designer selects a building in the **Building Panel**, the new building will follow the mouse. Along the mouse movement, the tiles under the building will highlight in either red or bright colors. Red color means the building cannot be placed there and all bright colors means it can be placed. The following functions show how the highlighted and unhighlighted logic works. We have an `addColor` function to change the color of the building temporarily.

```
private function unhighlightAllTiles():void {
    for(var i:int-0;i<_mapHeight;i++){
        for(var j:int=0;j<_mapWidth;j++){
            addColor(_map[i][j],0,0,0);
        }
    }
}
private function highlightTile(sx:Number,sy:Number,size:int):void {
    unhighlightAllTiles();
    var buildable = false;
    var isoCoord:Point = s2i(sx,sy);
    if (isoCoord.x >=0 && isoCoord.x+size-1 < _mapWidth
     && isoCoord.y-size+1 >=0 && isoCoord.y+size-1 < _mapHeight
    ){
        buildable = true;
        // loop all occupied tile by the building
        for(var i:int = isoCoord.y-size+1;i<=isoCoord.y;i++){
            for(var j:int=isoCoord.x;j<isoCoord.x+size;j++){
                var isoTile:IsoTile = _map[i][j];
                // if any occupied tile is not walkable
                // than it turns red and cannot build.
                if (_walkableMap[i][j] == 1){
                    addColor(isoTile,50,50,50);
                }else{
                    addColor(isoTile,255,20,20);
                    buildable = false;
                }
            }
        }
    }
    _buildable = buildable;
}
```

There are three modes now in the editor; they are move, paint terrain, and add building. These modes are determined by a variable.

```
/* tool type: move, paint, building*/
private var _currentTool:String = 'move';
```

When the mouse is pressed, it will check the mode and perform different actions. It will either start painting the terrain or start dragging the whole map.

```
private function onDown(e:MouseEvent):void {
    if (_currentTool == 'paint'){
        startDraw(e);
    }else if (_currentTool == 'move'){
        _mapHolder.startDrag();
    }
}
```

When the mouse is moving in building mode, the new building follows the mouse and also highlights the tile under the mouse cursor to indicate whether it can be placed.

```
private function onMove(e:MouseEvent):void {
    if ( _currentTool == 'paint'){
        drawing(e);
    }else if (_currentTool == 'building'){
        if (_draggingBuilding != null){
        highlightTile(
            stage.mouseX+_gridWidth/2,
```

```
                stage.mouseY,
                _buildings[_draggingBuilding.id].size);
        }


    }
}
```

When the mouse is released in building mode, it will finalize the building creation and save the data for output later. If the tile under the building is occupied and cannot build anything more, it will delete the newly created building movie clip without saving it.

```
private function onUp(e:MouseEvent):void {
    if (_currentTool == 'paint'){
        stopDraw(e);
    }else if (_currentTool == 'move'){
        _mapHolder.stopDrag();
    }else if (_currentTool == 'building'){
        _draggingBuilding.stopDrag();
        if (_buildable){
            /* map the movie clip to the tile */
            var buildingCoord:Point = s2i(stage.mouseX+_
gridWidth/2,stage.mouseY);
            var alignedBuildingCoord:Point = i2sLocal
                                (buildingCoord.x,buildingCoord.y);
            _draggingBuilding.x = alignedBuildingCoord.x;
            _draggingBuilding.y = alignedBuildingCoord.y;

            /* id 0 is the portal marker */
            if (_draggingBuilding.id == 0){
                var savePortalObj:PortalObject = new PortalObject();
                savePortalObj.id = _draggingBuilding.id;
                savePortalObj.x = buildingCoord.x;
                savePortalObj.y = buildingCoord.y;
                savePortalObj.connectedRoom = "lobby";
                _portalList.push(savePortalObj);
            }else{
                var saveBuildingObj:Object = {};
                saveBuildingObj.type = _draggingBuilding.id;
                saveBuildingObj.x = buildingCoord.x;
                saveBuildingObj.y = buildingCoord.y;

                _buildingList.push(saveBuildingObj);
            }
```

```
                /* mark the place non-walkable after placing the building */
                var size:int = _buildings[_draggingBuilding.id].size;
                for(var i:int = buildingCoord.y-
    size+1;i<=buildingCoord.y;i++){
                    for(var j:int = buildingCoord.x; j<buildingCoord.x+size;
                                                                    j++)
                    {
                        _walkableMap[i][j] = 0;
                    }
                }
            }else{
                _sortableContainer.removeChild(_draggingBuilding);
            }
            unhighlightAllTiles();
            _draggingBuilding = null;

        }
    }
```

The final step is to modify the output code to export the buildings and portals data as well. We just need to trace the building list and portal list variable into our defined XML structure.

Summary

We have discussed building a very basic isometric map, putting avatars on it, and the techniques of creating the buildings and the environment of the virtual world. We ran through some example codes and learned how to build a basic map editor with building supports.

In the next chapter, we will start a new feature of the virtual world. We will discuss the inventory system. We can use the inventory system to collect items and trade them with other users.

8
Creating an Inventory System

In the virtual world, it is common that avatars have their own inventory bag. Users keep and manage their items inside the bag. They collect items for different purposes. They can equip their avatars with items, modify the avatar's appearances with items, they can participate in the virtual world economy through item trading, or they can show off rare items by archiving difficult challenges.

Items and the pricing of the items create an economy system inside the virtual world. We will discuss the influence of the virtual world economy and some methods to prevent the poor impact from imbalance of the economy.

In this chapter, we will learn how to make an item inventory system for an avatar. We will also implement some basic item management with the server-side extensions.

Classifying items in the virtual world

There are several uses of items. Some items are for avatars that change the appearance. Some items equip the avatar to give different special attributes such as weapons or energy healing.

Different themes of the virtual world require different kinds of items. There will not be any sword if the virtual world is focused on farming. And there will be a battery if the virtual world focuses on energy but a battery will not appear in an ancient theme virtual world.

Different types of items

Different types of items define different usages. We will discuss several possible types of items here.

Items for avatar

Some items are only used on the avatar. They include clothes, shoes, and accessories. These items are often used for appearance only and do not have any specified add-on effect.

Weapon

Weapon items add attack and defense attributes to the avatar. It may also be a magic ward to give special attack or healing. Usually weapons have a level system to distinguish powerful and weak weapons.

Tools

Tools items often give the avatar some kind of special feature. For example, an avatar can dig the grass when holding a hoe. And this digging action may increase the probability of finding new items from the ground.

Riding

Riding item is a special item to let the avatar ride on it. Usually it allows a faster movement.

Entertainment

Similar to the items for avatars, entertainment items are often just for some visual display and do not carry any special add-on effect. For example, a firework item will play a firework visually in the sky but it will not affect any game played in the virtual world.

Material item

Some virtual worlds allow users to produce their own items by merging different basic elements. In the following screenshot, players can merge bone, wood, and some mud to create a tool. The tool lets the players remove some obstruction on the road to advance in the virtual world.

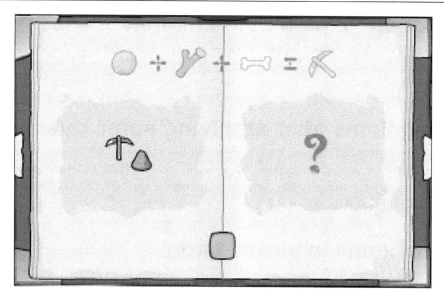

Collecting items

At the initial journey of the virtual world, players only have a few items. They have to collect items during their progress in the virtual world. Some virtual worlds encourage players to collect a whole set of items. For example, a full set of weapons for the whole body includes an axe, body armor, helmet, and shoes. Let's assume there are different axes, armors, helmets, and shoes. When a collection of all four items is mounted on the avatar, the whole performance gains a bonus. Mounting the full set can be a 20 percent bonus over using different parts.

Some other virtual worlds also require collecting a whole set of items to be mixed into one ultimate powerful one. These items are often separated over the whole virtual world. Players have to walkthrough all the places to collect them all.

Players are more likely to stay in the virtual world longer when there is something they have to collect which is still missing. There are several ways in which they can get a new item.

Collecting items that appear in the open

There is a certain probability to drop items on the ground in some events. These items may drop after the player kills a monster, or the items may just drop once in a while and see who is lucky to grab them.

Collecting items that are hidden

Some virtual worlds require players to dig in the ground to find new items. These items are usually some basic elements or cheap healing items. In some rare probability they can discover a relatively expensive item underground.

Getting items after archiving some quests

In order to encourage players to keep playing in the virtual world, there are often many quests for players to challenge. Players will have a chance to get a new item after the challenges. Normally the most difficult challenge will result in more expensive high-level item rewards.

Buying items in virtual shop

Players can buy items in the shops inside the virtual world. They pay virtual money to buy the items.

Trading items with other players

Instead of getting new items, players can exchange or trade items with other players in the virtual world. Exchanging items often happens when two players are collecting a whole set of items and find that the others have the other part of the collection.

Buying from real shop

Some online virtual worlds sell virtual items in real shop. These items are often sold in card form. The card contains the graphic of the item, the name, and most importantly a unique code. The user who buys this card will input this code in the virtual world to obtain the virtual item. When buying the cards, they are often packaged so that the buyer will not know what the actual card is until paying the money and unwrapping the package. Some players will keep paying for a new card package until they get the items they want.

Displaying items in different forms

There are different appearances of items. Players can put items in hands. When they put items in hands, the items can be visually displayed in the hands of the avatars. These require more graphic work. We need to draw several graphics of the avatar mounting the items for each direction. It is four or eight directions for each item; we may have thousands of items and they may even have their own animations.

Therefore, instead of drawing all animation for all items, some low-budget virtual world projects choose to draw only animations of important items. For the other items, they may not even display them on the avatar's graphics.

Some virtual worlds illustrate the items as cards. They add the game play elements of card games into the item's system of the virtual world. The card system can be helpful for players to read different information of the item easily. For example, in the following card inventory panel (http://www.spgame.com/), the cards with gold frame are rare cards that can greatly enhance the power. The sword and shoe cards with the same background color indicate that they are in the same collection.

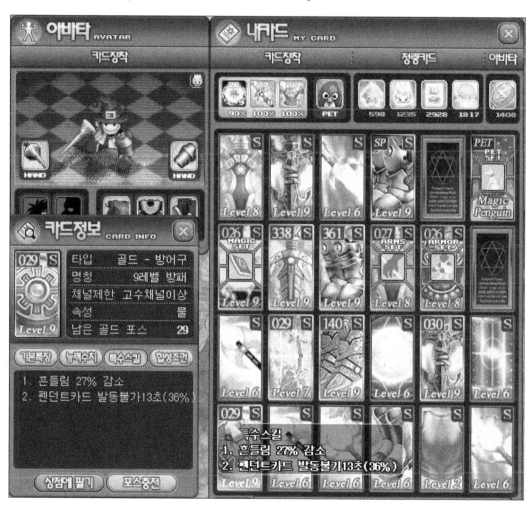

Defining the data structure of inventory items

We will now create a basic data structure of items for our virtual world. Each item has its own type ID, name, description, and corresponding class name in Flash. This item definition is normally stored in the server and the client will get a copy of the latest item definition every time he or she logs in.

```
<itemData>
    <item id='1001'>
        <name>Water Element</name>
        <classname>ItemWater</classname>
        <description>A very basic element of the world.
                                        </description>
    </item>
    <item id='1002'>
        <name>Fire Element</name>
        <classname>ItemFire</classname>
        <description>A very basic element of the world.
                                        </description>
    </item>
    <item id='1003'>
        <name>Land Element</name>
        <classname>ItemLand</classname>
        <description>A very basic element of the world.
                                        </description>
    </item>
    <item id='1004'>
        <name>Rock</name>
        <classname>ItemRock</classname>
        <description>Found everywhere in the world.</description>
    </item>
    ...
</itemData>
```

Setting the item ID

Instead of putting all type IDs in sequence when setting the item type, we can set the IDs with a range of numbers. For example, we can define that all the basic elements start with "10" in four digits and all weapons are "11" followed by other numbers. We will then have the item type list similar to the following table:

Category	Type ID	Item name
Basic elements	1001	Water
	1002	Fire
	1003	Land
	1004	Rock
Weapons	1101	Sword
	1102	Sword Level 2
	1103	Silver Sword
Supports	2001	Health Healing
	2002	Magic Healing
Tools	2101	Hoe
	2102	Hammer
	2103	Key

The benefit of distributing the type ID into a wide range is that it easily allows the addition or removal of new items types in the same group. Virtual worlds often release new items and the distribution provides rooms for new items to be grouped together within same category. For example, next new Sword can be 1104 instead of 2104.

Implementing inventory in the SmartFoxServer

We need to create a table in our virtual world database to store the items. Similar to creating a table player's position in *Chapter 6, Walking Around the World*, we use PhpMyAdmin to create the items table with the following schema. The id is an auto incremental primary key.

Field	Type	Description
id	int	Auto incremental ID for reference to a unique item entry.
type	int	The type ID of the item, specifying which item it is.
owner	varchar(50)	The owner avatar name of the item.
bag_id	int	The bag that this item is in.
position	int	The position of the item inside the bag.
create_time	datetime	The creation time of this item.
extra_info	varchar(255)	Some string extra information.

As items can be in the avatar's bag or placed somewhere else, the bag ID is used to indicate if the item is carried with the avatars.

The creation time of the item is useful to calculate the fatigue of the item. The longer it is created, the lesser performance it provides.

The extra information stores some item-specific information in string serialization format. How this field is used depends on the design of the virtual world. For instance, it may indicate how many monsters were killed with the sword. The more the kill count of the weapon, the more powerful it is.

Coding the server-side extension

We need to store the items permanently instead of storing for only a short period. We need a database to store how users own their items. We use server-side extension to connect to the database and retrieve items when the users log in to the virtual world. We also need to modify the records when the items are being used or sold.

The first reason why we need server-side extension is we cannot access the database directly from Flash. Server-side extension acts as a middle bridge between the Flash clients and the database.

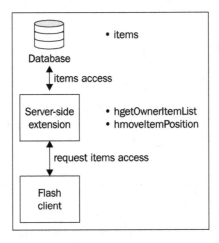

The second reason why we usually put items modification logic in server-side is to protect the items and prevent cheating from client-side, instead of handling the items flow in client-side. Server-side provides further validation and protection when modifying the items' information or ownership.

We will now locate our virtual world extension file in server-side to add the item-related functions. The file is in SmartFoxServer's installation directory | `Server` | `sfsExtensions` | `virtualworld.as`. The following extension function queries the owner's item from database and returns it to the virtual world:

```
function hgetOwnerItemList(cmd, param, user, fromRoom) {
    var res = new Object();
    res.cmd = cmd;

    res.list = [];
    var sql = "select * from items where owner='" + user.getName() +
                                        "' and bag_id is null";

    getResultArray(sql, res.list);
    sendResponseBack(res, user);
}
```

We will update the position in database when the item is moved to its new position.

```
function hmoveItemPosition(cmd, param, user, fromRoom){
    var res = new Object();
    res.cmd = cmd;

    var sql = sql = "update items set position=" + param.position +
                                    " where id=" + param.id;
    var success = dbase.executeCommand(sql);

    if(!success){
            res.err = "Error updating item position";
    }
    sendResponseBack(res, user);
}
```

We need to modify the code of handling response from server a little bit. The code is located in the document class on the client-side. In the previous examples, we only had position update response from server. Now we are handling several different command responses and need to distinguish them.

```
private function onExtensionResponse(e:SFSEvent):void {
    var cmd:String = e.params.dataObj.cmd;
    var data:Object = e.params.dataObj;

    if (cmd=='getPosition')     {
            if (data.posx != undefined){
                    Myself.instance.isoPosX = data.posx;
                    Myself.instance.isoPosY = data.posy;
```

```
            }

            if (_world != null){
                    removeChild(_world);
                    _world = null;
            }

            _world = new World();
            addChild(_world);
            if (_panels == null) {
                    _panels = new Panels();
                    addChild(_panels);
                    _panels.controller = this;
            }

            this.setChildIndex(_panels,this.numChildren-1);
    }
    else if (cmd == 'getOwnerItemList') {
            _panels.currentDisplayingPanel.dataArrived(data.list);
    }
}
```

Let's get a closer look at the function.

The server-side extensions always return the command itself so that we can distinguish which command is the response message for on client-side.

```
var cmd:String = e.params.dataObj.cmd;
```

The return data includes different useful information and it depends on the extension command. For example, we have the updated avatar position in the getPosition command and a list of items for getOwnerItemList.

```
var data:Object = e.params.dataObj;
```

The server response comes with a list of items that the player owns. We call the current displaying item panel to display them.

```
else if (cmd == 'getOwnerItemList'){
    _panels.currentDisplayingPanel.dataArrived(data.list);
}
```

Implementing the item panel

Item panel is a place where players organize their items. The following graph shows how we composite the item panel in Flash. The panel consists of a close button and 19 item slots. The `itemSlot0` and `itemSlot1` represent both hands, and `itemSlot2` represent the riding. Players can arrange items within slots. They can put riding item in the riding slot. **Riding item** is a special item that players can ride on for faster movement. We are going to query items from server-side and display them in this panel according to the position.

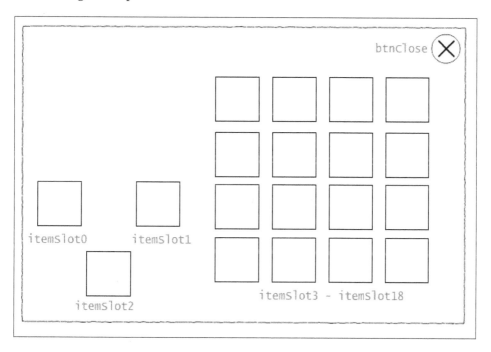

Loading the item definition

Similar to the buildings in the previous chapter, we have a definition for all items. We reference items by using their ID and the definition lets us get all the information of the item from the item ID. In this example, we put the item definition in an XML file. In production virtual world, we should keep the definition in the server to prevent users from modifying it in client-side.

```
public function ItemDefinition():void {
    _xmlLoader:URLLoader = new URLLoader();
    _xmlLoader.addEventListener(Event.COMPLETE, onItemDataLoaded);
    _xmlLoader.load(new URLRequest('data/itemData.xml'));
}
```

This function creates the item definitions according to the data structure we defined for the items.

```
private function onItemDataLoaded(e:Event):void {
    _xml = new XML(e.target.data);
    for (var i:int = 0; i < _xml.item.length(); i++) {
        var itemID:int = _xml.item[i].attribute('id');
        _items[itemID] = new ItemData();
        _items[itemID].itemID = itemID;
        _items[itemID].name = _xml.item[i].name;
        _items[itemID].classname = _xml.item[i].classname;
        _items[itemID].description = _xml.item[i].description;
    }
}
```

Loading the items list from the server

We have the items information and the extension ready. Now we can call the extension in the `ItemPanel` class and display the items according to the item definition. As long as the `ItemPanel` initializes, we ask the server to get the list of items that belongs to this avatar.

```
private function init(e:Event):void {
    _itemDefinition = new ItemDefinition();
    this.btnClose.addEventListener(MouseEvent.CLICK,closeItemPanel);

    /* get the item list from server */
    var params:Object = {};
    SmartFox.sfs.sendXtMessage("virtualWorld", "getOwnerItemList",
                            params, "json");
}
```

When the server response data arrives with the list, we construct the item panel.

```
public function dataArrived(data:Array):void {
    for each(var anItem:Object in data){
        var itemDef:ItemData = _itemDefinition.
                                getDefinitionFromID(anItem.type);
        if (itemDef == null){
            throw new Error("Error accessing an undefined data:
                            "+anItem.type);
            return;
        }

        var itemClassname:String = itemDef.classname;
```

```
    /* Create the Item from classname */
    var ClassReference:Class = getDefinitionByName(itemClassname)
                                                        as Class;
    var newItem:MovieClip = (new ClassReference as MovieClip);

    addChild(newItem);
    newItem.x = this['itemSlot'+anItem.position].x;
    newItem.y = this['itemSlot'+anItem.position].y;
    newItem.itemID = anItem.id;
    newItem.position = anItem.position;
    newItem.panel = this;
    Myself.instance.itemList[anItem.position] = newItem;
    }
}
```

Let's discuss this function in detail part by part.

The returning item list has the same field of the database schema. We know which item it is by finding the definition by the item type.

```
for each(var anItem:Object in data){
    var itemDef:itemData = _itemDefinition.getDefinitionFromID
                                                    (anItem.type);
```

We need to ensure that we have a matching item type here. Otherwise there is something wrong in the development.

```
if (itemDef == null){
    throw new Error("Error accessing an undefined data: "+anItem.type);
    return;
}
```

Every item has its own class. We create the movie clip according to the item's class name, so we can show the specific item in the item panel.

```
var itemClassname:String = itemDef.classname;

/* Create the Item from classname */
var ClassReference:Class = getDefinitionByName(itemClassname) as Class;
var newItem:MovieClip = (new ClassReference as MovieClip);
```

We set up the newly created item movie clip and then put it in the right position.

```
addChild(newItem);
newItem.x = this['itemSlot'+anItem.position].x;
```

```
newItem.y = this['itemSlot'+anItem.position].y;
newItem.itemID = anItem.id;
newItem.position = anItem.position;
newItem.panel = this;
```

At last, we put the item on the client-side item list and the item panel is ready.

```
Myself.instance.itemList[anItem.position] = newItem;
```

Displaying items in the item panel is just the first step. The next step is to let the user organize the items. Players can organize their items by dragging items inside the item panel. They can even put items in other bags or exchange items with others.

Moving items

Now we will implement the feature of moving items around the item panel. There are a total of 19 slots right now. They are the left-hand, right-hand, riding slots, and 16 normal slots.

When the mouse is down, we glue the item on the mouse pointer and bring it to the front of the display list.

```
private function mouseDown(e:MouseEvent):void {
    this.startDrag();

    /* put the dragging item on the top of the display list*/
    parent.setChildIndex(this,parent.numChildren-1);
}
```

When the mouse is up, the item is probably dragged to a new position. We should check if there is any empty slot nearby and snap the dragging item to the empty slot. Otherwise, the dragging operation is not valid and the item returns to its original position.

```
private function mouseUp(e:MouseEvent):void {
    this.stopDrag();

    /* snap to a nearby grid */
    var isPutInNewGrid:Boolean = false;
    for (var i:int =0;i<19;i++){
            if (this.hitTestObject(_panel['itemSlot'+i])){
                    /* check occupied or not*/
                    if (Myself.instance.itemList[i] == undefined){
                            /* clear reference of the old position*/
                            Myself.instance.itemList[_position] =
                                                          undefined;
```

```
                        /* create new reference on new position*/
                        this.x = _panel['itemSlot'+i].x;
                        this.y = _panel['itemSlot'+i].y;
                        _position = i;
                        isPutInNewGrid = true;
                        Myself.instance.itemList[i] = this;
                        break;
                    }
                }
            }
        /* If there is no room nearby to place the item, return the item
    to original grid */
        if (!isPutInNewGrid){
                this.x = _panel['itemSlot'+_position].x;
                this.y = _panel['itemSlot'+_position].y;
        }else{
                /* And we need to save the new position in server too */
                var params:Object = {};
                params.position = _position;
                params.id = _itemID,
        SmartFox.sfs.sendXtMessage("virtualWorld", "moveItemPosition",
                                    params, "json");
        }
    }
}
```

The following screenshot is the result of our example. We can open up the item panel and move the items around. The server will update the position in the database so next time we log in, they are in the right order.

Now each position update operation requires a database access. There is one performance issue here. What if users in our virtual world keep moving items? The database access is a file-based operation that costs time. In order to use the benefit of socket server, we should implement a RAM-based operation rather then a file-based operation when possible.

Instead of updating the database immediately, we can cache the server item list in RAM for a moment and access the database in a batch operation once a while.

Implementing the item operation in RAM

We discussed that the database is required for the inventory system. However, we may not need to access the database every time we have item transaction. If the virtual world features frequent items trading or exchange, we need to take some further steps instead of accessing the database often. We can store the items' ownership changes in the server's RAM instead of temporarily in the database. After a period of time or after the user log is out, we can save the modification to the database permanently.

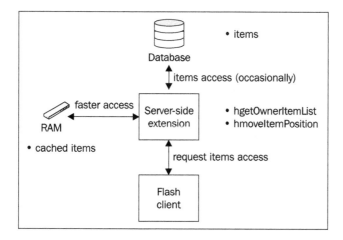

In order to store a clone of the item list in RAM, we have to get all the field names of the item table in server-side extension. The field name is stored as an instance variable within the server-side extension. We can get the field names by calling the describe SQL command.

```
var itemFields;

function initItemFieldNameArray(){
    itemFields = [];
    var sql = "describe items";
    var queryRes = dbase.executeQuery(sql, _server.QUERY_INT_KEYS);
    for(var i=0; i <queryRes.size(); i++){
        var tempRow = queryRes.get(i);
        var tmpFieldName = tempRow.getItem(1);
        itemFields[i] = tmpFieldName;

        /* confirm that we get the field name */
        trace(i+":"+itemFields[i]+" : "+tmpFieldName);
    }
}
```

We will call this initItemFieldNameArray method when the server-side extension initializes.

```
function init(){
    dbase = _server.getDatabaseManager();

    /* get the fields of items from database once after server
initialization*/
    initItemFieldNameArray();
}
```

Then we will store the item list in the server too. We can attach user-related variables in server by accessing the user properties.

According to the document from SmartFoxServer:

> *It is also possible to "attach" your own custom properties to the* User() *object by using the public "properties" object. The object works like an associative array.*

The following table shows a list of methods available:

Method name	Description
put(key, value)	Put a new value/object.
get(key)	Retrieve the value/object for the passed key. If the object doesn't exist it returns null.
remove(key)	Remove the value/object.
size()	Return the size of the properties array.

Maybe you will ask, "What is the difference between properties and user variables?" The difference is that a user variable is populated to all clients and clients can modify it anytime. Properties are different. Server properties only persists in server-side and will not be sent to the client. They persist in the server-side's RAM and can only be modified by extensions. They will also only be passed to client through custom extensions.

There are two benefits for saving the item list as properties instead of user variables. First, properties will never populate to all clients and it saves the bandwidth because not every one needs this piece of information. Second and importantly, using properties in the server can prevent client-side invalid modification of the item list.

Before we modify the code from database operation to RAM-based operation, we need to get the items from the database to the server-side properties.

```
function getItemFromDatabase(user){
    var arr = [];
    var sql = "select * from items where owner='" +
                                    user.getName() + "'";

    var queryRes = dbase.executeQuery(sql, _server.QUERY_INT_KEYS);
    for(var i=0; i <queryRes.size(); i++){
            var tempRow = queryRes.get(i);
            var itemRow = new Object();
            for(var j=0; j<itemFields.length; j++){
                    itemRow[itemFields[j]+""] = ""+ tempRow.getItem(j+1);
```

```
        }
        /* mark how this item status will be when operating database
later */
        itemRow["modified"] = 0;
        itemRow["new"]     = 0;
        itemRow["removed"] = 0;

        arr.push(itemRow);
    }

    /* remember the item list in user variables*/
    user.properties.remove("item");
    user.properties.put("item", arr);

    /* we do not need to return anything because client can access the
user variable */
}
```

Besides the original fields, we added three special fields to the item list. They are modified, new, and removed.

The modified is false by default. It indicates if this item is modified after it is queried from database. If it is modified, we need to save it back to database before the user logs out.

The new and removed indicate if this item is newly created or deleted without database access yet. We need these flags because we have to create or delete the entry in database during the database operation.

Next we modify the two extensions we had from database access to RAM-based access.

Compare to the old moveItemPosition extension; we do not need any SQL or database query anymore. All we need is to access the properties and return it back. All operations are from RAM only. We just need to mark the item as modified and it will get saved into the database later.

```
function hmoveItemPosition(cmd, param, user, fromRoom){
    var res = new Object();
    res.cmd = cmd;

    var items = user.properties.get("item");

    for(var i = 0; i < items.length; i++){
        if (items[i]["id"] == param.id){
            items[i]["position"] = param.position;
```

```
                      items[i]["modified"] = 1;


            }
        }
        user.properties.put("item", items);

        sendResponseBack(res, user);
    }
```

The same applies to the `getOwnerItemList`. It returns the item list from RAM directly.

```
function hgetOwnerItemList(cmd, param, user, fromRoom) {
    var res = new Object();
    res.cmd = cmd;
    res.list = [];

    var items = user.properties.get("item");

    for(var i = 0; i < items.length; i++){
            if (items[i]["bag_id"] == 'null'){
                    res.list.push(items[i]);


            }
        }
        sendResponseBack(res, user);
    }
```

RAM is a temporary storage of the items. We need to save the data back to the database when the user logs out.

Here we have two similar functions, one is designed to be called by the client and the other is to be called within the extension scope. They are executed by the same code and just different in the calling parameters.

```
function hsaveItemToDatabase(cmd, param, user, fromRoom){
    saveItemToDatabase(user);
}
```

This saving function contains three main blocks. They are the `update`, `create`, and `delete` blocks.

```
function saveItemToDatabase(user){
    var arr = [];
    var sql = "";
```

```
var items = user.properties.get ("item");

for(var i=0;i< items.length;i++){
        if (items[i]["modified"] == 1){
                /* Update items block */
                ...
        }
        if (items[i]["new"] == 1){
                /* Create items block */
                ...
        }
        if (items[i]["removed"] == 1){
                /* Delete items block */
                ...
        }
    }
}
```

In the Update items block, it saves all fields back to the database for a modified item entry.

```
if (items[i]["modified"] == 1){
    // start from 2, ignore 0 which is 'id', and 1 which is 'type'
    var str = itemFields[2] + "='" + items[i][itemFields[2]]+"'"
    for(var j=3;j<itemFields.length;j++){
            if (items[i][itemFields[j]] == 'null'){
                    str += ", "+itemFields[j] + "="
                                            + items[i][itemFields[j]]+""
            }else{
                    str += ", "+itemFields[j] + "='"
                                            + items[i][itemFields[j]]+"'"
            }
    }
    var sql = "UPDATE items SET " + str+ " WHERE id="+items[i]["id"];
    var success = dbase.executeCommand(sql);
    if (success){
            items[i]["modified"] = 0;
    }
}
```

In the Create item block, it will execute the INSERT command instead of the UPDATE.

```
if (items[i]["new"] == 1){
    var str1 = itemFields[1];
    var str2 = "'"+items[i][itemFields[1]]+"'";
    for(var j=2;j<itemFields.length;j++){
```

```
        if (items[i][itemFields[j]] == 'null'){
              str2 += ", "+itemFields[j] + "="
                                  + items[i][itemFields[j]]+""
        }else{
              str2 += ", "+itemFields[j] + "='"
                                  + items[i][itemFields[j]]+"'"
        }
    }
    var sql = "INSERT INTO items ("+str1 +") VALUES ("+str2+")";
    var success = dbase.executeCommand(sql);
    if (success){
          items[i]["new"] = 0;
          items[i]["modified"] = 0;
    }
}
```

For the `Delete` block, it is relatively short because it does not need to handle any fields. It just deletes the entry in both the database and the server properties.

```
if (items[i]["removed"] == 1){
    var sql = "DELETE FROM items WHERE id="+items[i]["id"];
    var success = dbase.executeCommand(sql);
    if (success){
          delete items[i];
    }
}
```

That is the extension to save back the data from RAM to the database. And our next question is when to save it.

The server "properties" persist during the user's session. That means this exists after the user successfully logs on the server and is destroyed when the user exits or loses connection. Therefore, the simplest way is to save the data back to database during the `userExit` or `userLost` internal event. In server-side extension, we can handle the internal events as follows:

```
function handleInternalEvent(e){
    if (e.name == "userExit" || e.name == "userLost")     {
          var user = e.user;
          saveItemToDatabase(user);
    }
}
```

The server-side extension modification is completed. We now move back to the client-side. We have to get the data from database to server properties before accessing the items. We need to call the getItemFromDatabase extension method sometime after the user logged in and before accessing the items. Therefore we put it in the room list updated function. Another suitable time to call the getItemFromDatabase extension method is when the server handles the userJoin internal event .

```
private function onRoomListUpdate(e:SFSEvent):void {
    /* hide the login box after login */
    this.loginBox.visible = false;

    /* Join the room 1 after receiving the room list */
    _sfs.joinRoom("island1");

    /* get the item list from database to RAM in server */
    var params = {};
    SmartFox.sfs.sendXtMessage("virtualWorld", "getItemFromDatabase",
                               params, "json");
}
```

Creating items

We have implemented several features for users to manage their items. But we haven't created the items yet. Here we have the server-side extension to create an item in the database.

The function will first search for an empty item slot to place the new item. The item creation will fail if there is no empty slot.

```
function hcreateItem(cmd, param, user, fromRoom){
    // get a free position
    var items = user.properties.get("item");
    var position = -1;
    var occupied = false;
    do{
        position++;
        occupied = false;
        for(var i = 0; i < items.length; i++){
            if (items[i]["position"] == position){
                occupied = true;
            }
        }
        if (position > 18){
```

```
                break;
        }
    }while(occupied);
    if (occupied){
            trace("Error creating items. The bag is full.");
            return;
    }
    ...
```

The item creation can either be a database operation or RAM-based operation. If it is RAM-based, we can create a new item entry of the user item list and mark the new flag as true. Here we will instead use the database operation to demonstrate how to mix these two operation methods.

We are executing a database operation in extension with the latest item data in RAM instead of the database. We need to save the data from RAM to the database for data synchronization. After creating the new item in the database, we need to query the data from the database back to the RAM.

```
    ...
    saveItemToDatabase(user);

    var res = new Object();
    res.cmd = cmd;
    res.list = [];
    res.position = param.position;

    var sql = "insert into items (type, owner, avatar_id, bag_id,
     position, create_time, extra_info) values
     ("; sql = sql + param.type + ", '" + user.getName() +
     "', 1 , null, "+ position+ ", NOW(), ''"; sql = sql + ")";
    trace(sql);
    var success = dbase.executeCommand(sql);
    if(!success){
            res.err = "Error creating new item.";
    }

    /* since create item is an database operation, we need to update
the item list */
    getItemFromDatabase(user);
    sendResponseBack(res, user);
}
```

We have created the server-side extension methods and now need some client code to test them. Let's call the create item extension method somewhere in the client to create some items for testing. We are going to create items after successful temporary login to get some items. We will discuss about buying items in *Chapter 10, Interacting with NPC*.

We need to pass the item type as parameters to tell the server which item we are requesting to create.

```
params = {};
params.type = 1002;
SmartFox.sfs.sendXtMessage("virtualWorld", "createItem", params,
                           "json");
```

Right now in our item panel, all items occupy one item slot no matter what size they are. In some virtual worlds, the item size is involved in the calculation and thus players need to organize their inventory to put all useful items inside the bag. This is one of the designs to let players choose between more useful but bigger items or less powerful but smaller items. The following screenshots taken from MMOG and Diable show how you can either keep the item size uniform or different as per your choice:

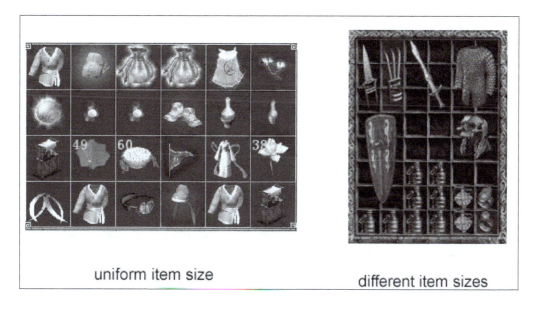

uniform item size   different item sizes

Some virtual worlds even count the weight of the items. When the weight of all carried items is over some preset limit, the avatars move more slowly. We have a property called `walkingSpeed` in the `WalkingAvatar` class. We can change it in different situations. This can be some design to balance the benefit of carrying more items or the benefit of moving faster.

Exchanging items with other players

Allowing trading and exchanging items with other players provides a lot of possibilities for game play in the virtual world. For example, players can work as a group to collect different items for the same collection. Or they can focus on finding specific elements and collect them to mix some high-level items. However, allowing trading between players may also cause some problems. It is difficult to totally prevent players from paying real money for virtual items. If the design of the virtual world does not allow trading with real money, the virtual world designers have to think carefully on the trading mechanism to prevent it.

Trading items with other players requires a complex data flow between two clients. We will further discuss the implementation methods in the next chapter, which will focus on the communication between players.

Introducing the economy in virtual world

We discussed how to exchange or trade items with other players. The flow of the items in virtual world forms an economy system. It can be a simple economy system or a complex one depending on the virtual world design.

For example, a virtual world may let players farm together. The players plant the seeds items and harvest the product item, and sell it to the system. This virtual world does not allow any item exchange between players. The money they earn from the farming product can be spent on buying new clothes, new cars, or new houses. Those cars or houses are designed for the system to reclaim the money from the users. This is a simple economy system and the world focuses on giving the users fun in farming.

Take a look at a complex economy system. A virtual world may allow players to equip their avatars with weapons and armor. They can collect woods and rocks to create weapons themselves. They can exchange or trade items with other players. The virtual world may even allow the players to trade the virtual items with real money. As there are many ways of gaining items and using them in this virtual world design, the economy system is complex and any little part of the system failure will cause an unbalancing problem.

We will discuss the balancing of the items and the influences of the economy system on the virtual world.

Balancing the items virtual economy

Balancing the virtual economy inside the virtual world is not easy. It is especially true for a massive multiplayer virtual world.

We have discussed that players have many methods to gain items. These items are created from nothing but just a SQL command. After running the virtual world for a while, players may have already created tons of items inside the world. The excess of items may cause inflation in the virtual world. The virtual world economy applies the same demand and supply rule from the real world. We will see how to balance the virtual world from the pricing of the item.

Setting the price of the items

A careless pricing method will cause a lot of problems. The first problem is letting the players own a lot of money.

Players collect items when playing in a virtual world. These items are worth a certain amount of money. Normally it costs more when the items are rare and it is cheaper when they are easy to obtain. The cost of the item depends on how much time the players need to devote before getting it. Rare items may require players to archive a difficult challenge which need weeks to practice.

However, cheap items sometimes are not cheap enough. Although it is cheap in the developer's mind, the time that players need to devote is very short. Short enough for players to keep collecting these kinds of cheap items and sell the huge amount of it to trade back a lot of virtual money.

Some virtual worlds adopt a flexible pricing system, so that when the same kind of item is traded in a large amount, the single price will drop. In another words, the more a kind of item sells, the cheaper it is. This allows the market to adjust the price itself. But it may cause another balancing problem on how flexible it is.

Preventing the inflation

The second problem is the inflation. In a virtual world, players need different levels of items in different stages. At the beginning, players can only afford low-level items. After the avatar grows up to a higher level with more difficult challenges, they need higher-level items. The problem is when the average-level of all avatars rises, lower-level items will drop value. Most players need high-level items and no one want those cheap and low-level items anymore. If players do not have interest in lower-level items, they start to stock up a lot of money. High-level items are usually rare and players with a lot of money are willing to pay more to own those rare items.

This situation then becomes a loop. More players own the rare items and use them in higher-level challenges. That means the rare items become common and more rare items appear and are waiting for players to grab them. The money that required to obtain common items becomes higher and higher and causes inflation.

Hosting special event

A good virtual world design will always give players just enough money at different stages. One way to prevent the inflation is to control the total amount of the money inside the virtual world. The virtual world can periodically host some special event and encourage players to join. In these special events, players are asked to buy special items such as clothes and special decoration items. The purpose of the event is to reclaim the virtual money from the players. On the other hand, these events can also gain attraction and have a positive marketing purpose too.

For example, in 51 Mole virtual world, they host a special Chinese New Year event with New Year decorations on buildings. Players can buy special clothes or even special building decorations to decorate their home. These items are sometimes expensive and only high-level players can afford them. As these special items are individual to the game play of the virtual world, they can effectively reclaim money from players.

Some virtual worlds also allows players to buy fireworks and play the fireworks inside the virtual world. When they are fired, every player can watch and enjoy the fireworks. High-level players are willing to buy these kinds of expensive entertainment items to show off themselves or gain a higher popularity.

Adding fatigue to items

Sometimes players can easily collect money by using some kind of items. For example, using weapons to kill monsters and collecting the dropping items. In this situation, we can add fatigue as one of the properties of the item. Every item has its own usage time and after using it for a specific time, it will stop working. Players need to pay to repair an item or replace it with a new one.

Limiting the total amount of high-level items

Another method to prevent the inflation and excess of money is to limit the total number of the high-level items. When an item reaches the upper limit of existing in the virtual world, the system will not create anymore of this kind of item. This virtual item is locked for creation until some of them are ironed out from fatigue.

Preventing the virtual economy from affecting the real world

The items and pricing in virtual not only affect the game balancing of the virtual world but also influences the real world. It will cause some real world social problems if the virtual economy system is not handled carefully.

Trading with real money

Collecting high-level items often means players need to put a huge amount of time into the virtual world. Some players want to enjoy the virtual world without putting much effort into collecting items. They will often acquire virtual items or virtual money with real money. This extends the virtual world economy to the real world.

Trading virtual money with real money cause a lot of social problems. Some teenagers may use all their pocket money on buying some digital virtual items. Some may even attempt suicide just because a rare virtual item has been stolen by others.

Some virtual worlds prohibit users from trading the virtual items with real money. World of Warcraft is one of those. The virtual economy inflation in other existing virtual world games also affects real money. Players in Mu Online, a Korean virtual world, bought a set of high-level items with around USD $150. After six months, those items became common and were not worth $150 anymore.

Government policy on virtual items

Some countries have a tax policy for their earnings on the virtual items. China and South Korea are some of them. In China, when users earn money by selling the virtual items at higher price, this earning is counted as personal earning and needs to be included in the tax calculation. In the latest regulation issued from China (`http://english.gov.cn/2010-06/23/content_1634750.htm`):

> *"Minors will also be prohibited from buying or selling items with virtual currencies, which the regulations say must be exclusively used to purchase the products or services of online games."*

The responsibility to maintain a good economy system

Whether or not to allow trading between players depends on the design of the virtual world and target users. If the virtual world mainly focuses on children or teenagers, the virtual world should avoid real money trading. Even trading virtually between players should be disabled or handled very carefully. Unlike adults or teenagers, kids do not have enough knowledge to trade with other players and may cause a lot of problems.

Therefore, most clean virtual worlds for children do not allow exchanging items between players. Instead, the virtual world should focus on other aspects to give the players fun.

Summary

We have discussed the implementation of a basic inventory system in SmartFoxServer. We also took a look at how the items and pricing affects the whole virtual world. Balancing the virtual economy system is challenging and different virtual world designs requires different approaches. Virtual world economy is a relatively new area and not every country has mature law to protect it. It is the developer's and company's responsibility to protect the virtual world from negative economic impact.

9
Communicating with Other Players

A major difference between an online virtual world and a traditional single-play game is the communication between players. Players connect to the socket server and share real-time information. Successful virtual worlds encourage users to interact and exchange useful information and resources. They allow players to divide their works inside the virtual world and group into different parties to explore different parts of the virtual world.

In this chapter, we will discuss several implementations of the communication methods with the help of SmartFoxServer. We will create a basic chat system and buddy list. We will also use some new server API to implement the item trading feature that was discussed in the last chapter.

We will use quite a lot of server build-in APIs in this chapter. It is because the server acts as an important role during the communication between players.

Communicating using several methods

There are different methods to communicate between players.

We can send public messages, team messages, private messages, or voice chat. They can also be either in public or private. We need different types of approaches during different scenes. Let's discuss when to use which approach.

Sending public messages

Normal public messages are the basic method. This allows people in the same room to see all the messages. It is useful when the players are casually chatting in a room of the virtual world. Or it is useful for group chat if the room only contains some specific users. Some virtual worlds may also provide a feature for users to create a temporary empty room for a group of people chatting and exchanging items inside.

Sending private messages

Private messages can be used to chat between two specific avatars. This is like an instant message or private e-mail inside the virtual world. Private messages do not have the limitation that both players have to be in the same room. This is convenient for players to find their friends.

Sending group messages

Teams often need some kind of group messages besides public messages to all people within the room or a private message to one user. These group messages are a chat channel that all team members within a team can read and post messages to. These messages may be cross-roomed and may limit to the same room. This team private chat channel is useful when the virtual world requires a team to discuss a strategy to finish some tasks.

Communicating in real-time voice

Sometimes virtual worlds may contain a real-time cooperation challenge for a group of players. We may consider providing a voice chat to these players. Instead of typing messages when playing a real-time action game, they can communicate with their voice and free the hands for the challenge.

SmartFoxServer provides a solution to the voice chatting by using the build-in media server, RedBox. RedBox is a modification of an existing open source Flash media server called Red5 (http://code.google.com/p/red5/). The SmartFoxServer document provides some guidance on using the RedBox add-on (http://smartfoxserver.com/docs/).

Potential problems of using voice communication

Consumes a lot of server bandwidth

Allowing voice chat in virtual world means we require a faster network with more bandwidth. In a server, bandwidth costs money and we have to consider if it is worth paying for extra bandwidth on this feature.

Message filtering problem

We can easily filter text messages in our virtual world. The filtering is just some kind of text word and pattern search. However, it is difficult to filter the content from a voice.

Number of users limitation

Audio chatting experience is good when there are few users participating in the chat. The experience will become worse when there are more and more users joining the same voice chat because more people means there are more chances that voices are overlapped. For text messages, we can have logs to trace the whole conversation. For voice, the overlapped voice means that the chat content is not fully delivered to the players. This problem makes it unusable for a chat group with many users.

Logging and revisit problem

We can have log in text messages so users can revisit the history to find some important information, for example, keywords of time and place. This is not easy to implement for the voice conversation. Players cannot search for specific keywords among the voices. If the virtual world logs all the voice conversation, they can only revisit them by listening and seeking the whole conversation. It is as if we are seeking a position with a large MP3 file. It is time-consuming and not efficient.

Chatting with public messages

The most basic communication method in a virtual world is public chat channel. A public message is populated to all players within the same room. The public message mechanism is like people talking loudly in a room. All people can listen and join the conversation. However, when they leave the room, they cannot listen to the conversation anymore. This is exactly how public message behaves in a virtual world.

We are going to make a chat dialog for public chat. The chat is composited by two parties—the sender and the receiver. The sender is a client which speaks the message out loud. The receivers are the clients which are in the same room and listening to the public chat message event. The chat dialog acts as both; the conversation log in the upper half acts as receiver and displays the messages. The lower half allows users to send out messages. This chat dialog is exported as ChatBox ActionScript class and we will implement the behavior with the following code snippets.

In the constructor, we have event listeners for clicking the **Send** button and receiving public messages.

```
public function ChatBox() {
    _sfs.addEventListener(SFSEvent.onPublicMessage,onPublicMessage);
    this.btnSend.addEventListener(MouseEvent.CLICK,clickBtnSend);
}
```

When the player clicks the **Send** button, we construct the message and send it out via sendPublicMessage call. Actually, we have used this public message in the previous example. We sent out the walking path in the virtual world via public message in *Chapter 6, Walking Around the World*. We constructed the public message in the following format:

```
|Action|Parameters
```

Here we follow the message format to construct our chat message. The format is:

```
|chat|The content of chat message
```

```
    private function clickBtnSend(e:MouseEvent):void {
        if (txtMessage.text.length > 0) {
            _sfs.sendPublicMessage("|chat|"+txtMessage.text);
            txtMessage.text = '';
        }
    }
```

When a new public message arrives, this event listener function will handle it. Not every public message is the chat message. It can be either the chat or a walking path. We deserialize the message into two segments—the action and the parameters. If the action shows that it is a chat message, we will print the message in the conversation log area.

```
    private function onPublicMessage(e:SFSEvent):void {
        var username = e.params.sender.getName();
        var msg = e.params.message;
        var splitArray = msg.split('|');
        var starting = splitArray[1];

        /* This is a chat message */
        if (starting == 'chat') {
            var message:String = splitArray[2];

            txtChatLog.appendText("\n"+username+" said: "+message);

            // scroll the textfield to show the latest messages
            txtChatLog.scrollV = txtChatLog.maxScrollV;
        }
    }
```

Showing chat bubble

Showing chat messages inside the chat panel is good. However, it is more common to have a chat bubble appear above the avatar.

In the `World.as`, we add a function to attach the chat bubble inside the avatar's movie clip. The function references the avatar movie clip by looking up the username.

```
public function showChatBubble(username:String,message:String):void {
    var chatBubble:ChatBubble = new ChatBubble(message);

    /* if it is my avatar */
    if (username == _sfs.myUserName) {
            _myAvatar.addChild(chatBubble);
    } else {
            _avatarList[username].addChild(chatBubble);
    }
}
```

Take a look at our `ChatBubble.as`. The chat bubble normally lasts for only a certain period. Therefore we will have a timer to track the showing time.

```
private var _timer:Timer = new Timer(3000);
```

We display the message in the text field inside the bubble and start counting the timer in the initialize function.

```
private function init(e:Event):void {
    this.txtChat.text = _message;

    _timer.addEventListener(TimerEvent.TIMER,tick);
    _timer.start();
}
```

The bubble has been showing up for three seconds when the timer event fires for the first time. We will now remove the timer event listener and remove the bubble itself. Please note that we have to remove the timer event listener manually. Otherwise the timer will still exist inspite of the movie clip being removed, and keeps firing and accessing non-existing references.

```
private function tick(e:TimerEvent):void {
    _timer.removeEventListener(TimerEvent.TIMER,tick);
    parent.removeChild(this);
}
```

When do we pop up the chat bubble? It is a good idea to put it inside the public message event handler. Besides appending the chat message into the conversation log, we show the chat bubble too.

```
private function onPublicMessage(e:SFSEvent):void {
    var username:String = e.params.sender.getName();
    var msg:String = e.params.message;

    var splitArray:Array = msg.split('<,>');
    var starting:String = splitArray[1];

    /* This is a chat message */
    if (starting == 'chat'){
        var message:String = splitArray[2];

        txtChatLog.appendText("\n"+username+" said: "+message);
        txtChatLog.scrollV = txtChatLog.maxScrollV;

        /* tell the world to show the chat bubble */
        _worldRef.showChatBubble(username,message);
    }
}
```

Scaling the chat bubble

We may have different lengths of chat messages. When the message varies in different lengths, we will try to scale the bubble to fit the message. The bubble contains four round corners for which we need to apply the **9-slice scaling**. The text field is made scalable by setting the autoSize property to TextFieldAutoSize.LEFT.

The chat bubble movie clip is exported as `ChatBubble` class with the following structure. The `bubble` movie clip turns on the 9-slice scaling. This chat bubble will be added to the stage once the public chat message arrives.

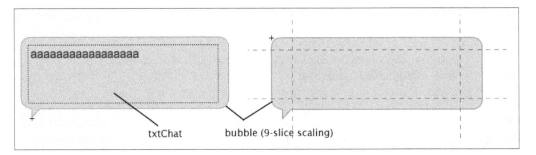

txtChat   bubble (9-slice scaling)

When the chat bubble is displayed on screen, we set up the text field with the chat message content and scale the bubble to fit the message. We also position the chat bubble above the avatar by moving it up.

```
private function init(e:Event):void {
    this.txtChat.autoSize = TextFieldAutoSize.LEFT;
    this.txtChat.text = _message;
    this.bubble.height = this.txtChat.height+40;
    this.y = -this.bubble.height+30;

    ...
}
```

Implementing the buddy list

Besides public chatting, players often want to communicate with their own friends. The friend list in virtual world is called **buddy list**.

Buddy list is like the friend list in an instant messenger application. Players can add other players as friends into their buddy list. The design of buddy list is to help them communicate easily. They can know which friends are online. They can know the latest status of their friends. They may know where their friends are now and they can send private messages to them easily.

There are two modes of buddy list provided by SmartFoxServer — the basic version and an advanced version. This setting can be set in the `config.xml` in server.

By default, the old depreciated buddy list setting is located as an attribute in the `Zone` tag.

```
<Zone name="virtualWorld" customLogin="false" buddyList="20">
```

The new method is to delete the `buddyList` attribute and use the `BuddyList` tag as the following:

```
<BuddyList active="true">
    <mode>basic</mode>
</BuddyList>
```

Creating buddy list panel

SmartFoxServer provides us the API to access the buddy list features and data but not the user interface. We will create our buddy list panel to display the buddy list.

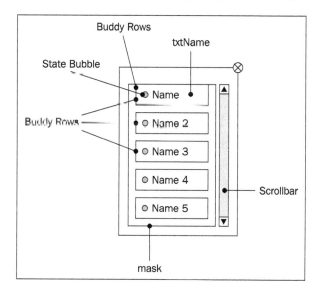

The buddy list uses a scrollbar to control the rows under the mask area. We list the rows of buddies and show the status accordingly to the buddy list data from the server. In the basic version, we will only display the buddy name and the online status.

We export the buddy list movie clip as `BuddyPanel.as`. There are two new server events in the constructor of the `BuddyPanel` class. They are the `onBuddyList` and `onBuddyListUpdate`. The `onBuddyList` event is dispatched when the list is first loaded from server or when there is a buddy entry modification on the list. On the other hand, `onBuddyListUpdate` is dispatched when there are status or variable changes from a buddy in the buddy list. For example, we get this even when one of our buddies is going offline.

```
public function BuddyPanel() {
    _sfs.addEventListener(SFSEvent.onBuddyList,loadedBuddyList);
```

```
    _sfs.addEventListener(SFSEvent.onBuddyListUpdate,
onBuddyListUpdateHandler);
    _sfs.loadBuddyList();
    addEventListener(Event.ADDED_TO_STAGE,init);
}
```

We often need to check if a user is in our buddy list. The buddy list is loaded into the client SmartFoxServer so we can check if the user exists in that array.

```
public function isBuddy(username:String):Boolean {
    for each(var buddy:Object in _sfs.buddyList) {
        if (buddy.name == username) {
            return true;
        }
    }
    return false;
}
```

This function constructs the buddy rows as our design. It will put every buddy data into one row and list them one by one vertically.

```
private function displayBuddyRows():void {
    /* remove all existing elements in the buddy list area */
    while(_buddyRows.numChildren>0) {
        _buddyRows.removeChildAt(0);
    }

    /* scrollbar steps according to the count of the buddy list */
    this.scrollbar.maxScrollPosition = _sfs.buddyList.length-6;
    for(var i:int = 0;i<_sfs.buddyList.length;i++) {
        var row:BuddyRow = new BuddyRow();
        _buddyRows.addChild(row);
        row.txtName.text = _sfs.buddyList[i].name;
        row.y = i*row.height;
            _buddyRowHeight = row.height;

        if (_sfs.buddyList[i].isOnline) {
            row.stateBubble.gotoAndStop(2);
        }
    }
}
```

Once the buddy list is loaded from server, we draw the buddy list on the panel.

```
private function loadedBuddyList(e:SFSEvent):void {
    _buddyLoaded = true;
    displayBuddyRows();
}
```

When there is any update of the buddy list, we redraw the buddy list to update the latest buddy information.

```
private function onBuddyListUpdateHandler(e:SFSEvent):void {
    displayBuddyRows();
}
```

Knowing others with profile panel

While communicating with other people, we often want to know their basic information. In the real world, we have name card exchange. In a virtual world, we can get others' profiles with profile panel.

Buddy list panel is just a list to display an existing buddy list. We need a panel that is related to the player for the buddy add/remove operations. We will create an info panel to display information related to that player and also some operation buttons such as **ADD FRIEND**.

The info panel appears whenever the avatar in the world or the buddy row in the buddy list is clicked.

We will create two custom events to dispatch the click event that needs to display the info panel.

In `Avatar.as`, we convert the click event to an event called `avatar_clicked`.

```
dispatchEvent(new Event('avatar_clicked',true));
```

Similarly, we dispatch the click event when a buddy row is clicked in the buddy panel.

```
dispatchEvent(new Event("display_info_panel",true));
```

Dispatching custom event in ActionScript 3

We dispatch custom events to trigger and display the profile info panel. The `Panels` class uses `stage.addEventListener` to catch our custom event from the avatars.

```
stage.addEventListener("avatar_clicked",onAvatarClicked);
stage.addEventListener("display_info_panel",onDisplayInfoPanel);
```

In the `avatar_clicked` event handler from an avatar, we need to loop through the avatar list to get the username of the avatar and then display it in the info panel.

```
private function onAvatarClicked(e:MouseEvent):void {
    var username:String;

    /* clicking myself */
    if (e.target == Myself.instance.avatar) {
        username = SmartFox.sfs.myUserName;
    } else {
        for(var u:String in _controller.world.avatarList) {
            if (_controller.world.avatarList[u] == e.target) {
                username = u;
                break;
            }
        }
    }

    var infoPanel:InfoPanel = new InfoPanel(username);
    addChild(infoPanel);
    infoPanel.x = (stage.stageWidth-infoPanel.width)/2;
    infoPanel.y = (stage.stageHeight-infoPanel.height)/2;

}
```

We also support showing the info panel from clicking the buddy list. The buddy row dispatches the `display_info_panel` event to tell the `Panels` class displaying it.

```
private function onDisplayInfoPanel(e:Event):void {
    var username:String = e.target.txtName.text;

    var infoPanel:InfoPanel = new InfoPanel(username);
    addChild(infoPanel);
    infoPanel.x = (stage.stageWidth-infoPanel.width)/2;
    infoPanel.y = (stage.stageHeight-infoPanel.height)/2;}
```

We have just created the basic buddy list system and we need to test the code:

1. Create several browser instances and browse to the virtual world HTML file.

2. Log in to the virtual world by using 'player1', 'player2', 'player3', ... 'player 5' as username.

3. We toggle to display the buddy list in all virtual world instances so that we can know what is happening when adding friends.

4. In the control of player 1, we add player 2 as friend. We see player 2's name appear on the buddy list of player 1. This is because the server dispatches the `onBuddyListUpdate` event to the buddy list panel.

5. Player 1 adds player 2 as friend but we notice that player 1 is not a friend with player 2. It is because in the basic version of the buddy list, the friend-adding feature is not mutual. We will cover this later in the advanced version.

6. Now we add friends randomly among those players.

7. Then, we can test if user login and logout will update the buddy list by closing the browser instance and logging again.

8. The buddy list should update when someone logs out or logs in. It is because the server dispatches the `onBuddyListUpdate` event even when the buddy state changed.

Creating an advanced buddy list

The latest SmartFoxServer comes with a bundle of advanced features for the buddy list. It enhances the buddy list system to allow permission control, offline buddy variables, and custom server-side code to store the buddy list information.

Adding buddy mutually

In order to use the advanced features, we need to first ensure that the depreciated old buddy list setting is deleted in the `config.xml` from the server.

Change from:

```
<Zone name="virtualworld" customLogin="false" buddyList="20">
```

to:

```
<Zone name="virtualworld" customLogin="false">
```

The buddy list tag setting will not be active if the depreciated buddy list attribute exists. Then we can change the buddy list to advanced mode. In order to add the buddy mutually, we need to enable the permission setting. When both `addBuddyPermission` and `mutualAddBuddy` setting is true, the add buddy process works like this:

1. When player A adds player B as friend, an event dispatches to player B.
2. Player B can choose to accept or refuse the add buddy request.
3. If player B refuses it, both players are not in each other's buddy list.

4. If player B accepts the request, both players are in each other's buddy list.

```
<BuddyList active="true">
    <mode>advanced</mode>
    <addBuddyPermission>true</addBuddyPermission>
    <permissionTimeOut>120</permissionTimeOut>
    <mutualAddBuddy>true</mutualAddBuddy>
</BuddyList>
```

The SmartFoxServer dispatches the `onBuddyPermissionRequest` event to the user that someone has requested to add him as a buddy. We listen to this event in `BuddyPanel` class and prompt a permission panel when someone wants to add the user as a buddy. The user can then choose to respond the server with accept or refuse action.

```
private function onBuddyPermissionRequest(e:SFSEvent):void {
    var permissionPanel:PermissionPanel = new PermissionPanel
                                        (e.params.sender);
    addChild(permissionPanel);
    permissionPanel.x = -250;
}
```

After the permission panel prompts, we can respond the add buddy requests by sending the buddy permission response to the server with a Boolean to indicate whether to accept or refuse the request. The following code sends permission response to the server in `PermissionPanel` class:

```
private function clickAddFriend(e:MouseEvent):void {
    SmartFox.sfs.sendBuddyPermissionResponse(true,_targetBuddyName);
            parent.removeChild(this);
}
private function clickRefuse(e:MouseEvent):void {
    SmartFox.sfs.sendBuddyPermissionResponse(false,_targetBuddyName);
            parent.removeChild(this);
}
```

We will use two browser instances to test the code and it should work by following these steps:

1. Create two virtual world browser instances.
2. Log in as "player A" and "player B", and open the buddy list.
3. In player A's browser, click player B and add him as friend.
4. A permission window appears on player B's browser.
5. When player B clicks **ADD FRIEND**, both players appear on the buddy list.

Introducing the buddy variables

One of the benefits of socket server is real-time information sharing among users. We discussed chat messages, room variables, user variables, and server-side user properties that are all real-time information sharing. We are going to learn another variable type, buddy variables.

Buddy variables are a set of properties related to the current user that are only visible to the friends. Other users who have the current user in the buddy list will receive these variables and the modification notice.

These variables are useful for sharing user's information with all other friends. For example, this information can be playing audio track, online status, or some emotion messages.

We will make a feature to let players input their emotion messages. Emotion messages are something similar to current status or current emotion. Players can use this field to share their current feeling and help messages. For example, a player may say, "I'm bored and finding friends to play together" or "Help me to get the golden apple item". These messages will be displayed on their friends' buddy list and friends will know each other's current feeling on the virtual world.

In the `InfoPanel` class, we provide a text field for the current user to set the emotion message and view other's emotion message. We check if the info panel is showing the current user or other users, and display the input text field or dynamic text field. The buddy variables of the current user can be accessed via the `myBuddyVars` in the SmartFoxClient API. The variables from other buddies can be accessed via the `buddy.variables` property. The buddy variable is an array with both key and value as string.

```
private function init(e:Event):void {
...
    if (_username == SmartFox.sfs.myUserName) {
            this.txtEmotionMessage.visible = false;
            /* Resume the emotion message */
            if (SmartFox.sfs.myBuddyVars['emotionMessage'] != null) {
                    this.txtInputEmotionMessage.text = SmartFox.sfs.
                                myBuddyVars['emotionMessage'];
            }
    } else {
            var buddy:Object = SmartFox.sfs.getBuddyByName(_username);
            if (buddy != null && buddy.variables['emotionMessage'] !=
                                                null)
            {
                    this.txtEmotionMessage.text = buddy.
                                variables['emotionMessage'];
            }
            this.txtInputEmotionMessage.visible = false;
    }
}
```

We save the emotion message when we close the info panel. We can call `setBuddyVaraibles` to sync the updated buddy variables to the server. The server will immediately populate the update to other buddies.

```
private function clickCloseBtn(e:MouseEvent):void {
    if (_username == SmartFox.sfs.myUserName) {
            /* set the emotion message to buddy varible */
            var vars:Array = [];
            vars['emotionMessage'] = this.txtInputEmotionMessage.text;
            SmartFox.sfs.setBuddyVariables(vars);
    }
    parent.removeChild(this);
}
```

We extend the row of buddies to display emotion message.

```
private function displayBuddyRows():void {
    ...
    if (_sfs.buddyList[i].variables['emotionMessage'] != undefined) {
        row.txtEmotionMessage.text = _sfs.buddyList[i].
                                     variables['emotionMessage'];
    }
    ...
}
```

Offline buddy variables

There is one option to access some buddy variables even when buddy is not online. This is called offline buddy variables. A virtual world can have millions of registered users and thousands of active users every minute. By default all buddy variables are populated only when the buddy is online. With the `offLineBuddyVariables` setting turned on in server's `config.xml`, we can set offline buddy variables by starting the variable key with "$". SmartFoxServer grabs all offline buddy variables that start with "$" when loading a buddy list.

Because there can be very large amount of registered users, all offline buddy variables should be considered carefully to reduce the loading time cost.

With our previous example, we can easily modify all variable keys from `emotionMessage` to `$emotionMessage`.

```
var vars = [];
vars['$emotionMessage'] = this.txtInputEmotionMessage.text;

SmartFox.sfs.setBuddyVariables(vars);
```

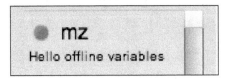

When we test the example now, we can see that the emotion message still exists even when the buddy is offline.

Creating custom buddy list persistence class

The advanced buddy list uses the build-in H2 database engine to store the data. SmartFoxServer provides us the flexibility to implement our own buddy list storing. We can program a Java class in server-side and set the persistence class path in server configuration XML file.

```
<persisterClass>classpath.to.SFSCustomBuddyPersiter</persisterClass>
```

With our custom buddy list persistence class, we can store the data in the MySQL database that we have been using in the examples.

We are not going into detailed Java implementation of the class here. SmartFoxServer documents the usage and example of Java custom buddy list persistence class in the following URL:

```
http://smartfoxserver.com/docs/docPages/sfsPro/buddyList2.htm
```

Summarizing buddy list configuration setting

We have discussed several buddy list configurations and their unique features. Let's have a summary of all the buddy list configuration settings, including those that we have not used in the examples.

We can enable or disable the buddy list feature by using the `BuddyList` tag.

```
<BuddyList active="true/false">
</BuddyList>
```

The buddy list features are divided into either **basic** or **advanced** mode.

```
<mode>basic/advanced</mode>
```

A `size` tag can set the maximum size of the buddy list. When a player tries to add a buddy and exceeds the maximum size, an error message will dispatch to the user. The default size is `50`.

```
<size>50</size>
```

This sets the maximum number of variables that a buddy is allowed to set. The default value is `10`.

```
<maxBuddyVars>10</maxBuddyVars>
```

When this setting is true, the addBuddy request will wait until the buddy accepts or refuses the permission request.

```
<addBuddyPermission>true/false</addBuddyPermission>
```

Timeout can be set to a permission request. It is in seconds unit and a expired permission request becomes void.

```
<permissionTimeOut>60</permissionTimeOut>
```

We can turn this on to enable the mutually-added buddy features. The addBuddyPermission setting has to be true for this setting to work.

```
<mutualAddBuddy>true/false</mutualAddBuddy>
```

Similar to the mutualAddBuddy setting, with this setting on, both players will be removed from their buddy list when either one deletes the other.

```
<mutualRemoveBuddy>true/false</mutualRemoveBuddy>
```

This setting enables the offline buddy variable features to access some buddy variables even when the buddy is not online.

```
<offLineBuddyVariables>true/false</offLineBuddyVariables>
```

This is the path to the custom persister class. The class path follows the naming convention from Java. For example, if the class is in package a | b | c, the class has to be under this directory structure: class path/a/b/c/CustomPersisterClass.

```
<persisterClass>class.path.to.CustomPersisterClass</persisterClass>
```

The server will send this message to the users when they try to add buddy in a full buddy list.

```
<ownerListFullErrorMsg>message</ownerListFullErrorMsg>
```

When a user tries to add a buddy mutually and the target user's buddy list is full, we get the target-list-full error. This tag defines the message that the server sends to the user when this error occurs.

```
<targetListFullErrorMsg>message</targetListFullErrorMsg>
```

Sending private messages

A common use of buddy list is sending private messages to buddies. In some cases, we may be playing a game in virtual world and want to ask whether my friend wants to join it. We can open up the buddy list within the game and send a private message out. We are going to implement it by using the built-in private message feature.

We added a private message button in the info panel. A private message panel prompts out when we click on the button. After the player inputs some text and clicks on **send**, we construct the private message in a format to include the recipient's name. We need the recipient's name to display in the chat dialog panel. The chat message is composed in following format:

```
Sender|recipient|private message
```

The following code in `PrivateMessagePanel.as` sends out the private message. We need to check if the recipient is from current room or buddy list in order to get the recipient's user ID.

```
private function clickSendBtn(e:MouseEvent):void {
    var targetBuddyId:int;
    var targetBuddy:User = SmartFox.sfs.getActiveRoom().getUser
                                             (_targetBuddy);
    if (targetBuddy != null) {
        targetBuddyId = targetBuddy.getId();
    } else {
        targetBuddyId = SmartFox.sfs.getBuddyByName(_targetBuddy).id;
    }

    /* prepare the chat message */
    var message:String = SmartFox.sfs.myUserName+"|"+_
                    targetBuddy+"|"+txtInputContent.text;

    SmartFox.sfs.sendPrivateMessage(message,targetBuddyId);
    parent.removeChild(this);
}
```

We will display the private message in chat box. The private message handler deserializes the message and gets the sender name, recipient name, and the content of message.

The reason we put the sender and recipient into the message is that the default private message will store the sender as null if the sender is not from current room of the user. We need to know who sends the message to us, so that we can include the sender's and recipient's name inside the message.

We listen to the `onPrivateMessage` event in `ChatBox` class and decode the private message to display it in the chat log.

```
private function onPrivateMessage(e:SFSEvent):void {
    var msg:String = e.params.message;

    var splitArray:Array = msg.split('|');
    var sender:String = splitArray[0];
    var recipient:String = splitArray[1];
    var message:String = splitArray[2];

    if (sender == _sfs.myUserName){
        txtChatLog.appendText("\nYou said to "+ recipient+": " +
                                message);
    } else {
        txtChatLog.appendText("\n"+sender+" said to you: " +
                                message);
    }
    txtChatLog.scrollV = txtChatLog.maxScrollV;

}
```

Capturing private message in server-side with internal event

There are several internal events available in server-side extension. These internal events are useful for us to extend several internal behaviors such as sending public and private messages. Whenever the internal event dispatches, the extension can handle it via the `handleInternalEvent` function. We are going to save the messages on server-side when buddies are chatting with private messages.

By default, the internal event of the private messages is not created. In order to handle this internal event, we have to configure the server by using the `setPrivMsgInternalEvent` to turn on this event.

We can enable the private message internal event on server-side to extend the default private message feature. We will extend the private messages to log them in the database. Players can access all their private message logs so it will look like an e-mail system between players.

We create a table called `chatlog` in database with following schema:

Field name	Type
sender	varchar(50)
recipient	varchar(50)
message	text
logtime	datetime

In the server-side `virtualworld.as` extension, we need to enable the internal private message event in the `init` function.

```
_server.getCurrentZone().setPrivMsgInternalEvent(true);
```

We can then handle the private message via the `handleInternalEvent` function. After we save the message into database or do anything we want, we need to dispatch the private message manually. The SmartFoxServer will not send the private message to the recipient automatically once handled in extension.

```
function handleInternalEvent(e){
    if (e.name == "userExit" || e.name == "userLost")     {
            var user = e.user;
            saveItemToDatabase(user);
    } else if (e.name == "privMsg") {
            var sender = e.sender.getName();
            var recipient = e.recipient.getName();
            var msg = e.msg.split("&lt;,&gt;");
            var message = msg[3];


            var sql = "INSERT INTO chatlog(`sender`,`recipient`,`message
`,`logtime`) VALUES
                ('"+sender+"','"+recipient+"','"+message+"',NOW())";
            var success = dbase.executeCommand(sql);


            _server.dispatchPrivateMessage(e.msg, e.room, e.sender,
                                        e.recipient);
    }
}
```

The following graph shows the differences of handling the private messages on the server. When the private message internal event is turned off, the message is sent to the recipient directly through the server. With the private message internal event turned on, it is the extension's responsibility to dispatch the private message.

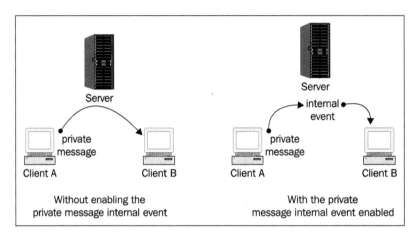

With the internal event and the saved private messages, it is not far off to implement the offline message feature. We can load the saved message from the database when the player logs in and design a panel such as message inbox to show the unread messages. Playing with messages in a virtual world can be far more creative than this. We may also create a common chat room within friends. They will be able to comment on chat messages or status. This becomes a basic form of social networking. We are not going to implement these features here but thinking about a creative way to let players communicate with friends is good for selling the virtual world.

Sharing object data between players

We have discussed how to communicate with text messages. In many cases, we need to share some pieces of information with other players. For example, we want to update others with our location. In previous chapters, we used serialization and deserialization methods to put information inside the private and public messages in some special format. This is a useful method where we can only send out and receive text messages.

Recently the SmartFoxServer introduced the `sendObject` and `sendObjectToGroup` functions to broadcast data object to all players or specific players. The data communication flow of the two methods is basically the same. The difference is public message serializes all data into strings and `sendObject` does not. We do not need to deserialize the strings back to complex objects and arrays when receiving it.

Making the trading items system

With the `sendObjectToGroup` function, we can share data between specific players. It is useful to implement the **trading items** feature. In the trading items system, both players select one or two items that they want to exchange. The items information is sent to each other. If they both agree to the item exchange, they click a **CONFIRM** button to tell the server to exchange those items.

Let's take a step-by-step look to see how `sendObjectToGroup` works. The full code example is available in the code example bundle.

At first, we design an exchange item panel. The exchange item panel contains two parts—the owner's inventory list and the exchange area. Players drag files from their inventory to the exchange area. The exchange area contains four slots—two slots for the owner to drag in items and two slots to preview what the other player wants to give the owner.

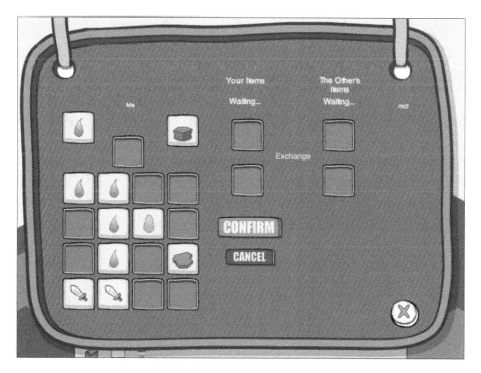

We will focus on the exchange area now. When player A requests to trade items with player B, both player's virtual world prompts the exchange item panel.

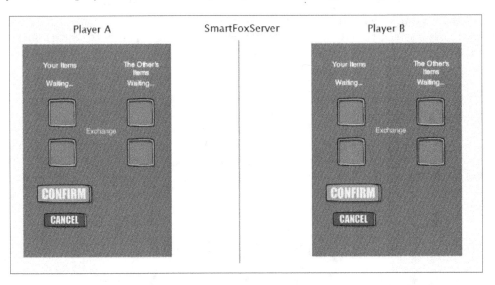

When either of the players drag items to the exchange area, the virtual world client packs the exchange item's type and item ID into an object and sends it to the other by calling `sendObjectToGroup` with player B's player ID as target recipient.

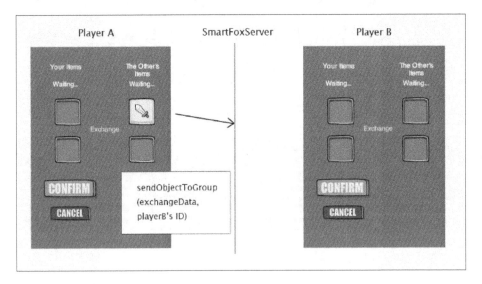

SmartFoxServer handles the `sendObjectToGroup` command and dispatches an event to player B. Player B handles the `onObjectReceived` event to receive and display the item data that player A wanted to exchange.

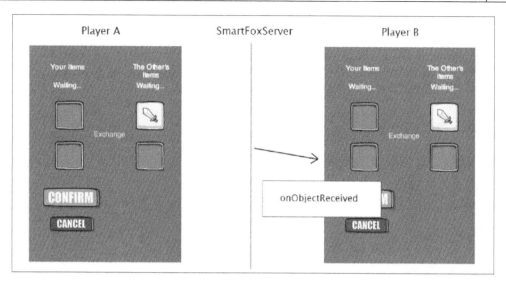

The process from player B to player A is similar. Player B drags items to the exchange area and sends this information to player A to display them.

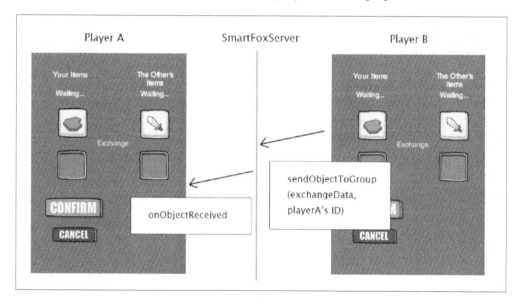

The players will press the **CONFIRM** button if they agree with this trading or the **CANCEL** button if they do not agree. When either player confirms the trading, we send an extension call to server-side extension. The extension call contains the player's information and the exchange items' information. We create an array `waitingExchange` on server-side to store this information.

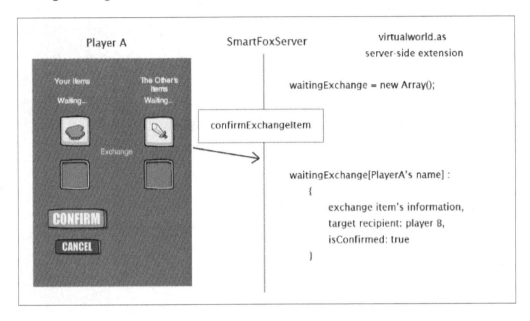

When another player confirms the trading, another confirmation message is sent to the server-side extension. The following extension function receives both confirmations and performs the item exchange process in the database.

```
function hconfirmExchangeItem(cmd, param, user, fromRoom) {
    var res = new Object();
    res.cmd = cmd;

    /* store the exchange item confirmation into the waiting exchange
list. */
    waitingExchange[user.getName()] = {};
    waitingExchange[user.getName()].userReference = user;
    waitingExchange[user.getName()].user2Id = param.user2Id;
    waitingExchange[user.getName()].myNewItem1 = param.myNewItem1;
    waitingExchange[user.getName()].myNewItem2 = param.myNewItem2;
    waitingExchange[user.getName()].othersNewItem1 =
                                        param.othersNewItem1;
    waitingExchange[user.getName()].othersNewItem2 =
                                        param.othersNewItem2;
    waitingExchange[user.getName()].isConfirmed = true;
```

```
    /* check if the target exchange user also confirmed this exchange
by checking the waiting exchange list with user2's name as key. */
    if (waitingExchange[param.user2] != undefined &&
waitingExchange[param.user2].isConfirmed)    {
        /* MySQL query to exchange the items when both sides are
confirmed. */
    }

}
```

SmartFoxServer provides us the sendObject, sendObjectToGroup, sendPublicMessage, and sendPrivateMessage. By using these four functions, we can communicate with other players in different forms and create different applications.

Summary

Communication is important in an online virtual world because it provides methods for players to exchange information. And this is one of the advantages of an online virtual world when compared to a single play game.

We discussed several methods of communicating with others and tried to implement some of them. We showcased how and when to use public message, private message, and object sharing among players. We also discussed the usage of buddy list provided by SmartFoxServer.

We can further enhance the communication by integrating existing social network technology or creating a social community inside the virtual world. We will discuss the social network integration in *Chapter 12, Integrating Social Community.*

10
Interacting with NPC

In a virtual world, there are some characters that are not controlled by the users. These characters are called **Non-Player Characters**, or **NPC** in short. Traditionally, NPCs are controlled by the game master in role-playing board games. In virtual a world, the NPCs are controlled by the server or the computers that serve some distinguished purposes. They can range from a house guard to the king in the castle.

In this chapter, we will discuss the purpose of having non-player characters in the virtual world. We will control the NPC to move around the world. We will also let players interact with the NPC by chatting or trading items.

We will also cover an advanced server-side extension technique to use Java extension instead of ActionScript extension to gain performance.

Running virtual world smoothly with NPCs

The main purpose of the non-player character is to help the virtual world run smoothly. The NPCs are like the characters in a novel. The purpose of each character is different and depends on the type of the novel. But the final purpose of the characters are to shape the novel in a smooth way.

The purpose of each NPC in a virtual world is different. A newbie guide will provide basic information to the new players and guide them through some newbie practices. For instance, a guard in front of the castle will stop the players from entering without meeting some requirements; a shopkeeper will provide some trading services to players; some other NPCs may be talkative and provide different background information of the virtual world. Every NPC has its own purpose and their final purpose is to make the players play in the virtual world smoothly.

In some online virtual world, NPC will act as player replacement. Sometimes players want to play in the virtual world without interacting with other players. Let's assume there is a real-time action game that requires four players to start the game. A player can add NPCs as opponents to join the game. An NPC will have its own AI script to run the game.

Classifying different roles of NPC

There are two types of NPC, one is essential to the virtual world and the other is non-essential.

Those essential NPCs are important to the virtual world and carry specific purposes. For instance, the shopkeeper that sells items, the guides that help players, or the enemies that interact with players.

Besides those essential NPCs, there are often other NPCs in the virtual world. The virtual world can run smoothly without these non-essential NPCs. The role of these NPCs is to enhance the game experience or to provide some sidetrack background information.

For example, when the player walks into a restaurant, the main NPC is the cashier to whom the player needs to place the order. This NPC is important because players need the food to recharge their energy or finish quests. Besides the cashier, there may also be waiters and other clients. The waiters may say welcome to the player and different clients may share their thoughts on the food. Some may say that the food is delicious while some may be drunk and may be saying something funny. These NPCs give players a feeling as if they have actually walked into a real restaurant. Without these waiters and clients, the player can still buy foods and refill his energy. But the existence of these non-essential NPCs enhance the player's experience.

Assume there is a virtual world where players need to rescue the princess. Players need to chat with those major NPCs to get hints on where the princess is locked. Besides this major story of the virtual world, there are some sidetrack challenges that the players can complete as a bonus. Those non-essential NPCs can reveal the information or hints about these non-critical challenges.

Placing NPC in virtual world

The placement of the NPC will affect where players gather, especially for those essential NPCs. Players often need to interact with NPCs for certain actions such as selling items. Players will most likely gather around these NPCs.

If we want to separate the high-level players and low-level players into different places, we can distribute the NPCs that serve different levels of players in different places. Similarly, if the virtual world encourages the interaction between different levels of players, we can design a place with an NPC that serves a large range of players. For example, there may be two NPCs that sell different levels of items with expensive prices in the virtual world. We can add an NPC seller that sells all levels of items with a cheaper price in the place we designed to gather the players.

Putting our first NPC in the virtual world

SmartFoxServer provides build-in NPC features. The mechanism behind the NPC features from SmartFoxServer is to connect a new player to the server internally. In other words, SmartFoxServer creates a new socket connect for the NPC. The server treats the NPC as a normal user that connects from localhost.

We can enable the NPC feature in the `config.xml` configuration file.

```
<EnableNPC>true</EnableNPC>
```

The NPCs will be controlled in the server-side extension. We have created a server-side extension to handle the players' request. Now we will create an extension dedicated to control the NPC logic.

```
<Extensions>
    <extension name="virtualWorld"  className="virtualworld.as"
type="script" />
    <extension name="VirtualWorld"  className="VirtualWorld"
type="java" />
    <extension name="npc" className="virtualworld_npc.as"
type="script" />
</Extensions>
```

The `createNPC` server-side API call will let us create the NPC and "connect" it to the server. It needs four parameters to create the NPC.

Parameters	Description
username	The username of the NPC
ipAddress	The IP address of the server that NPC connects
port	The port number of the server that NPC connects
zoneName	The zone that NPC will log in to

As the NPC creation is a real socket connection to the server, it is just like connecting a player to the server that requires both server IP address and port number. The NPC connection will receive server messages and events the same as players. In order to get the best performance, most of the time we should connect the NPC with the IP address set to 127.0.0.1.

```
_server.createNPC("NPC name", "127.0.0.1", 9339, _server.
                        getCurrentZone().getName());
```

 Please note that we should not call the NPC creation function in the init function of the extension. We create the NPCs after the serverReady event.

It is because the server is not ready yet when the init function is executed. We have to wait till the whole server initializes to create our NPC. The server will dispatch a serverReady internal event after the initialization. We will create our NPC at that time and join the room island1.

```
function handleInternalEvent(e){
    if (e.name == "serverReady") {
        theNpcUser = _server.createNPC("TestNPC", "127.0.0.1", 9339,
                            _server.getCurrentZone().getName());
        var ok = _server.joinRoom(theNpcUser, -1, true, _server.
            getCurrentZone().getRoomByName('island1').getId());
    }
}
```

After players connect to the server, they have to choose our style before logging in to the server, and so does the NPC. In our virtual world, the NPCs need to set their appearances in user variables so that other players can draw them. We will assign the styles and position user variables to the NPC.

```
function handleInternalEvent(e){
    if (e.name == "serverReady") {
        theNpcUser = _server.createNPC("TestNPC", "127.0.0.1", 9339,
                            _server.getCurrentZone().getName());
        var ok = _server.joinRoom(theNpcUser, -1, true, _server.
            getCurrentZone().getRoomByName('island1').getId());
```

```
var uVars = {}
uVars.avatarColor = 0xccffcc;
uVars.isoPosX = 8;
uVars.isoPosY = 16;
uVars.fistTime = 1;
uVars.style = 1;

// Set the variables for this client
_server.setUserVariables(theNpcUser, uVars)
        }
    }
```

Preventing the NPC from disconnecting

After restarting the server and logging in to the virtual world, we will see our NPC. However, if we wait for approximate five minutes in the virtual world, we will find that the NPC is disconnected by the server because of the excess of the maximum user idle time. It is because that NPC connection is same as the player's in the view of the server.

The disconnect message will be shown in the server prompt.

[INFO] > Disconneting idle user: TestNPC

In order to keep the NPC alive in the virtual world, we can schedule a loop for the NPC to update the server. We create an interval to execute the loop in a certain period. The time of the period can be of any value as long as it is shorter than the MaxUserIdleTime in the configuration file.

```
function init(){
    myInterval = setInterval("npcLoop", 8000)
}
```

Inside the loop, we will call the updateMessageTime server-side API. This function will refresh the timestamp of the last message of the user to current time. That is to let the server know that the user is still alive in the world and not idling.

```
theNpcUser.updateMessageTime()
```

Besides updating the message time, we will also dispatch a public message by the NPC. It is useful for us to test the code and check if the loop is executing correctly.

```
function npcLoop() {
    if (theNpcUser != null) {
        theNpcUser.updateMessageTime()
        var rooms = theNpcUser.getRoomsConnected();
        _server.dispatchPublicMessage("|chat|Hello Virtual World",
            _server.getCurrentZone().getRoom(rooms[0]), theNpcUser)


    }
}
```

Resolving a potential problem of using provided NPC feature

In SmartFoxServer 1.6.5, there is a known issue with the NPC feature. According to the documentation from SmartFoxServer, all NPC connections will not be closed completely after the NPC disconnects. The connections remain in a CLOSE_WAIT state in TCP layer.

This problem will not affect the NPCs that are created once and last for the whole server life cycle. That is because the shut down process can remove all NPC connections.

However, if the NPCs are being created or destroyed repeatedly, the remaining incomplete and closed connections will eventually exhaust the number of sockets available in the operating system.

We can avoid this problem by writing an external application to connect to the server and act as the NPC.

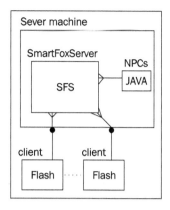

We will create a basic NPC by using the Java API. It creates the NPC instance and holds the process until the terminate command. Create a new file anywhere on the server-side and name it NPC.java. We will implement a basic NPC within this file.

```java
public class NPC implements ISFSEventListener{
    public static void main (String[] args) {
        NPC npc = new NPC();

        try{
            System.in.read(); // Wait until ctrl-C
        }
        catch(Exception e){}
    }
    ...
}
```

The NPC client reads a configuration XML with the server IP, port, and the zone to connect.

```java
private SmartFoxClient sfs;

public NPC() {
    sfs = new SmartFoxClient(true);
    sfs.addEventListener(SFSEvent.onConfigLoadSuccess, this);
    sfs.addEventListener(SFSEvent.onConfigLoadFailure, this);
    sfs.addEventListener(SFSEvent.onConnection, this);
    sfs.addEventListener(SFSEvent.onLogin, this);
    sfs.addEventListener(SFSEvent.onRoomListUpdate, this);
    sfs.addEventListener(SFSEvent.onJoinRoom, this);

    // Load the config file
    sfs.loadConfig("config.xml", false);
}
```

Similar to the ActionScript SmartFoxClient, there are different events to indicate the state changes of the application. We will log in the NPC to the server step-by-step and finally set the user variables.

```
public void handleEvent(final SFSEvent event){
    if(event.getName().equals(SFSEvent.onConfigLoadSuccess))      {
            sfs.connect(sfs.ipAddress, sfs.port);
    }
    else if(event.getName().equals(SFSEvent.onConfigLoadFailure)) {
            System.out.println("ERROR: Connect Failed.");
    }
    else if(event.getName().equals(SFSEvent.onConnection)) {
            sfs.login(sfs.defaultZone, "JavaNPC", "");
    }
    else if(event.getName().equals(SFSEvent.onLogin)) {
    }
    else if(event.getName().equals(SFSEvent.onRoomListUpdate)) {
            System.out.println("Login Successful");
            // join the island1 room
            sfs.joinRoom("island1","",false);
    }
    else if(event.getName().equals(SFSEvent.onJoinRoom)) {
            Map<String, SFSVariable> uVars = new HashMap<String,
                                         SFSVariable>();
            uVars.put("isoPosX", new SFSVariable("4", SFSVariable.TYPE_
                                         NUMBER));
            uVars.put("isoPosY", new SFSVariable("4", SFSVariable.TYPE_
                                         NUMBER));
            uVars.put("firstTime", new SFSVariable("true", SFSVariable.
                                         TYPE_BOOLEAN));
            uVars.put("avatarColor", new SFSVariable("0xff0000",
                                         SFSVariable.TYPE_NUMBER));
            uVars.put("style", new SFSVariable("2", SFSVariable.TYPE_
                                         NUMBER));
            sfs.setUserVariables(uVars);
    }
}
```

To compile and run the code, we need the SmartFoxClient Java API library and some related utilities. These libraries are packed in the download file of the API.

1. Create a new folder called lib in the same directory of NPC.java.

2. Go to http://smartfoxserver.com/labs/API/ and download the Java API.

3. Uncompress the ZIP file and go into the `bin` directory.

4. Copy all `.jar` files into the `lib` directory.

After installing the required libraries, we can type the following command in the terminal to compile the Java NPC code.

```
javac -cp "lib/*" NPC.java
```

After successful compilation, we can run the NPC Java client within the same machine of SmartFoxServer.

```
java -cp "lib/*:./" NPC
```

The NPC will appear in the virtual world after running the NPC Java client.

Advanced SmartFoxServer extension technique

Within the server-side extension environment, it is not limited to using the provided ActionScript API. We can use Java class to extend the extension.

One benefit of mixing Java class into our ActionScript extension is that we can gain extra performance with the precompiled native code. It is especially useful for complex codes such as path finding or XML parsing.

The other benefit is that we can archive a lot more possibility in extension with the Java programming.

We can use native Java class directly in the following way:

```
var javaList = new java.util.LinkedList();
var message = new java.lang.String("This is a JAVA string");
```

We can also access the SmartFoxServer Java API in ActionScript extension. For example, we can access the zone.

```
var javaExt = Packages.it.gotoandplay.smartfoxserver.extensions.
ExtensionHelper;
var helper = javaExt.instance();
var zone = helper.getZone("virtualWorld");
```

Or we can access any custom class by using the Packages class. To use our custom class, we need to put the Java class in the classpath of the server. We can put them in the sfsExtensions directory or Server directory. Then we can access our class through Packages class.

```
var customClass = Packages.path.to.our.customClass;
trace(customClass.hello());
```

Controlling NPC movement

NPCs can walk around the virtual world as the players. The movement is controlled in server-side extension.

Controlling NPC to walk in predefined path

Some NPCs' movement is fixed to a predefined path. For these NPCs, we can dispatch the path directly without path finding algorithm. In the following example, we will repeatedly control the NPC to walk between two points.

As we treat the NPC as a normal player in the logic, we will use the same walking mechanism from the player. The NPC will dispatch a public message with specific walking path to other players in the same room. Every client will then move the NPC according to the path. We have an npcLoop function in server-side extension. We will put the NPC movement logic there.

```
function npcLoop(){
    if (theNpcUser != null)      {
        theNpcUser.updateMessageTime();
        var rooms = theNpcUser.getRoomsConnected();
        if (theNpcUser.getVariable("isoPosX").getValue() == 8){
            _server.dispatchPublicMessage("|path|4,16;", _server.
                getCurrentZone().getRoom(rooms[0]), theNpcUser)
            var uVars = {}
            uVars.isoPosX = 4;
            _server.setUserVariables(theNpcUser, uVars);
        }else{
```

```
_server.dispatchPublicMessage("|path|8,16;", _server.
    getCurrentZone().getRoom(rooms[0]), theNpcUser)
var uVars = {}
uVars.isoPosX = 8;
_server.setUserVariables(theNpcUser, uVars);
            }
        }
    }
```

Directing NPC to walk using path finding algorithm

Controlling the NPC to walk in predefined path sometimes looks too mechanical. We may want some NPC to walk randomly within the world, or even follow the players. We used A-star search algorithm in *Chapter 6, Walking Around The World*, for the movement of the player in client-side. We need the same algorithm in server-side now.

Path finding algorithm is relatively resource consuming. In order to gain performance on calculating the path, we will use Java implementation instead of the ActionScript. As the SmartFoxServer is running on Java environment, we can benefit from the performance of running native Java. We will apply the advanced extension techniques we just discussed to use the Java path finding class inside the ActionScript extension.

We can use an existing A-star Java class from Internet and integrate it with our map. We created a class called AStarSolution to load the map data on server-side and provide a getPath method to solve the path finding with a downloaded A-star class. The full code is in code example bundle and we will take a look at the getPath method.

The getPath method calls the A-star algorithm to calculate the path by providing the starting point and ending point. Later we put the path into the format that we used to send out the walking message.

```
public String getPath(int originX, int originY, int destX, int destY)
{
    NodoAstar nodeInit = mapData[originY][originX];
    NodoAstar nodeFinal = mapData[destY][destX];

    Astar pathfinder = new Astar(mapData, nodeInit, nodeFinal, false);
    ArrayList result = pathfinder.calcularCamino();
    String path = "|path|";
    if (result != null) {
```

```
                for (int i = result.size()-1; i >= 0; i--)       {
                        NodoAstar node = (NodoAstar) result.get(i);
                        path += node.getX()+","+node.getY()+";";
                }
        } else {
                System.out.println("path not found");
        }
        return path;
}
```

We will control an enemy NPC to follow the first player in the virtual world to demonstrate the server-side path finding. We will use the current NPC position and the player's position to ask the Java A-star class to generate the path. Then we will dispatch the path to all players in the room.

```
function npcLoop() {
    if (enemy != null) {
            enemy.updateMessageTime();
            // follow the 1st player.
            var rooms = enemy.getRoomsConnected();
            var currentRoom = _server.getCurrentZone().
getRoom(rooms[0]);
            var allUsers = currentRoom.getAllUsers();
            if (allUsers[1] != undefined){
            // get the position of the NPC and the 1st player.
                    var selfIsoX = Number(enemy.getVariable("isoPosX").
                                            getValue());
                    var selfIsoY = Number(enemy.getVariable("isoPosY").
                                            getValue());
                    var destX    = Number(allUsers[1].
                                getVariable("isoPosX").getValue());
                    var destY    = Number(allUsers[1].
                                getVariable("isoPosY").getValue());
                    // calculate the path to walk towards the 1st player
                    if (selfIsoX != destX || selfIsoY != destY)      {
                        var uVars = {}
                        uVars.isoPosX = Number(destX);
                        uVars.isoPosY = Number(destY);
                        _server.setUserVariables(enemy, uVars);
                        var enemy_astar = new Packages.
                                        AStarSolution('island1');
                        var path = enemy_astar
                                .getPath(selfIsoX,selfIsoY,destX,destY);
                        _server.dispatchPublicMessage(path, _server.
                            getCurrentZone().getRoom(rooms[0]), enemy)
                    }
```

```
                        }
                    }
                }
```

Talking with NPC

The players need to interact with the NPCs. Most often players need to ask the NPCs something or chat with them to share information. There are several types of conversation system. Each one comes with its pros and cons.

 It is important to choose a right conversation system for the virtual world.

Communicating with NPC using text parsing

Text parsing conversation is a prompt box with a text input box for a player to input the sentence they want to say. After which, the NPC will parse the sentence and respond to the player with related information. It is similar to talking with a chat bot.

Text parsing interaction existed for a long time as old text game without graphic user interface. At that time, the computer was not fast enough so that the system would only parse certain patterns of sentence and certain keywords. It is called **Ask/Tell conversation**.

Ask/Tell conversation means the player will either ask the NPC something or tell the NPC something. As each NPC has its own knowledge base, the player has to try asking or telling the NPC different keywords to get a response. If the NPC knows that keyword, it will respond with some useful information to the player. Otherwise, it may simply respond not understood or some unrelated thing.

For instance, we can ask an NPC about the keyword "king" by input:

Where is King?

The NPC will parse the word king and respond something like the following:

The king is hunting in the forest.

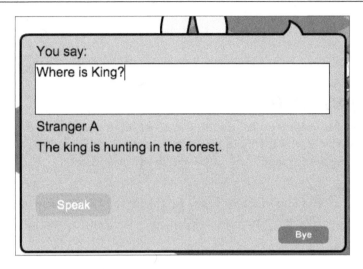

By asking the NPC several keywords, the players can collect more information to progress in the virtual world.

Nowadays the parsing system is more powerful then just parsing a word. We can improve it by parsing the words What, Where, How, and so on.

For instance, let's assume that we meet a farmer NPC in the virtual world.

We ask: "Where is town A?"

The farmer NPC will parse the words Where and town A, and may respond with:

Town A is in the west.

The advantages of text parsing conversation

Flexible conversation content:

Text parsing conversation is an open conversation. Players can type in whatever they want without limitation. The NPC will answer the one it knows.

It is flexible and the players need to think of the right question to ask. The player needs to consider the current problem and raise a possible solution. For example, they need to ask the shopkeeper to sell items or give the medicine item to the doctor NPC. In contrast, there will be no effect if the players ask the doctor to sell them items.

The disadvantages of text parsing conversation

- **Fragmentation conversation**

  One disadvantage of this conversation system is that the conversation will become segments of asking and responding. The player asks a keyword and the NPC responds something. There are no links between each conversation. It may let players feel strange and not natural.

- **Guess in blink**

  Another disadvantage is that the player needs to guess what to say. Sometimes it is difficult to determine the right keyword to ask the NPC. Players may feel frustrated after several failed tries on the NPC. The frustration will finally lead to the loss of players.

In order to not let the players get confused in front of the conversation input box, we should give hints to the player. That is suggesting to the players some topics that they should talk about next.

The text parsing conversation is not common in virtual world design and we are not going to get into detailed implementation here. A basic code example of the text parsing conversation is available in the code bundle.

Menu-driven conversation

Another conversation approach is to provide a list of options for player to choose. The player selects one of the sentences to speak to the NPC and the NPC responds according to the selection. Then the player is provided a new list of options. This iteration repeats until the player ends the conversation or runs through the whole conversation. Each NPC has its own conversation branches according to its knowledge.

The advantages of the menu-driven conversation

There are several advantages of using the menu-driven conversation:

- **The conversation can be well selected and fine-tuned**

  One advantage of this conversation system is it strictly limits the input from players to several specify options. As we only need to handle several options at each time, we can set how NPC response to the options. With the limited and predefined sentences, we can fine-tune every sentence in the conversation to be full of emotion.

- **Easy for thread conversation**

  We can also make the conversation in thread. One player's response leads to the NPC's response and leads to a more specific topic. The whole conversation will look like a tree graph with branches of different topics. It is more natural compared to the segments from the text parsing conversation.

- **Avoid the keyword guessing:** Another benefit of using menu-driven conversation than the text parsing is this that the system avoids the guessing problem. The options are listed in front of the players and they do not need to guess and try different keywords to test the NPC.

The disadvantages of the menu-driven conversation system

This system also comes with a disadvantage:

Restrict Options:

One disadvantage of the menu-driven conversation is that it is too restrictive. Players can only choose from the provided options. They can travel the whole conversation branches by selecting all the options and know everything from the NPC and never come back again to this NPC.

An improvement to this disadvantage is to add some selective branches. Some options may only appear when matched with some criteria. For example, a soldier will tell the players how they can get in the castle only when the country is not at war. Otherwise, the solder will respond to the players that he cannot tell. The players will then know that there is still something this NPC knows and will visit this NPC later.

Let's get into detail of how we implement the menu-driven conversation system.

Every node in the conversation contains the response message, the options for player, and the next node after the choice. The following table shows the properties of a conversation node:

Property name	Type	Description
messages	String	The chat message that NPC says.
choices	Array of integer	Each choice refers to the next conversation node index to be used.
choiceMessages	Array of string	Each choice message is for the player to choose in order to respond to the NPC.

Many conversation nodes composite a conversation in the NPC's class. The whole conversation branch is a tree graph in data structure.

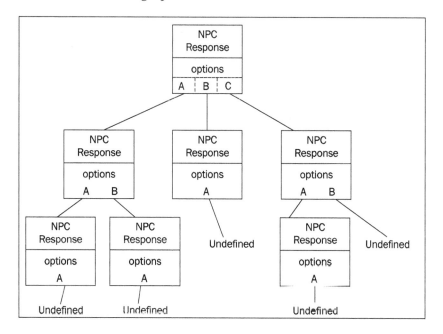

For example, we design a conversation tree for a stranger NPC. We will use the zero nodes to indicate the end of the conversation.

```
public function StrangerA() {
    var playersName:String = SmartFox.sfs.myUserName;
    _conversation[1] = new ConversationNode();
    _conversation[1].message = "Hello, Nice to meet you.";
    _conversation[1].choices = [2,0];
    _conversation[1].choiceMessages[0] = "Nice to meet you too, I am "
                                        + playersName;
    _conversation[1].choiceMessages[1] = "Sorry, Bye.";

    _conversation[2] = new ConversationNode();
    _conversation[2].message = "Hi " + playersName + ". Can I help
                                                    you?";
    _conversation[2].choices = [4,0];
    _conversation[2].choiceMessages[0] = "I want to know where I am.";
    _conversation[2].choiceMessages[1] = "No. Bye.";
    ...
    _conversation[0] = new ConversationNode();
    _conversation[0].message = "Good bye. Chat later.";

}
```

The following graph shows the outlook and parts of the menu-driven conversation dialog:

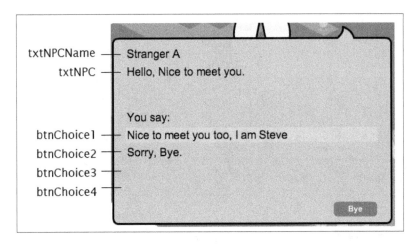

After the player chooses an option, we display the content in the next conversation node according to the option. If there is no further conversation for the current node, we will end the conversation.

```
private function displayConversation(i:int):void {
    _currentNodeIndex = i;
    txtNPCName.text = _npc.name;
    txtNPC.text = _npc.conversation[i].message;

    for(var j=0;j<4;j++) {
            if (_npc.conversation[i].choices[j] != undefined) {
                    this["btnChoice"+j].txtChoice.text = _npc.
                                        conversation[i].choiceMessages[j];
                    this["btnChoice"+j].visible = true;
                    this["btnChoice"+j].addEventListener(MouseEvent.
                                        CLICK,clickChoice);
            }else{
                    this["btnChoice"+j].visible = false;
            }
    }
    /* when the index is 0, it means it is the ending node*/
    if (i==0)
    {
            txtYouSay.visible = false;
            _timer.addEventListener(TimerEvent.TIMER,tick);
            _timer.start();
    }
}
```

Keyword-based conversation

A variation of the menu-driven conversation is keyword-based conversation. The keywords are often some names of places, items, or NPCs that the players need to know. During the chat with the NPC, players will learn some new keywords. They can then click on one of the keywords to progress the conversation. Keyword-based conversation is sometimes mixed with the menu-driven conversation as one of the options.

Keywords are often marked in highlighted color for easy recognition. We can specify which branch the keyword will link to by using the following format:

```
<a href="event:conversation_node_ID">keyword</a>
```

In this example, we will highlight a word and make it a link. The link will lead to another conversation branch related to the word.

```
_conversation[4] = new ConversationNode();
_conversation[4].message = "You are in <a href='event:5'>Flash Virtual
World</a> now.";
_conversation[4].choices = [0];
_conversation[4].choiceMessages[0] = "Ok, Bye";

_conversation[5] = new ConversationNode();
_conversation[5].message = "Flash Virtual World is an example world
to demonostrate how to make a multiplayer online virtual world with
ActionScript.";
_conversation[5].choices = [0];
_conversation[5].choiceMessages[0] = "Thanks a lot. Bye.";
```

We also need to highlight the keywords for players to recognize. An underline style is applied to a keyword.

```
var style:StyleSheet = new StyleSheet();
style.setStyle("a:link", {textDecoration:"underline"});
txtNPC.styleSheet = style;
```

The link is linked to event so we can catch it by listening to the TextEvent.LINK.

```
addEventListener(TextEvent.LINK, clickTextLink);
```

We have embedded the conversation node ID inside the link in the following format. We can show the next conversation content based on the node ID.

```
<a href='event:ID_of_conversation_node'>Keyword</a>
```

One feature of the keyword-based conversation is the learning of keywords. During the play in the virtual world, players may gradually meet new items and learn new keywords. NPC can be designed to hide some information until the players know a specific keyword. For instance, an NPC will not talk about his wife until the player meets her somewhere in the virtual world.

We modify the Myself class to add the mechanism of adding and checking known keywords. We add an array variable knownKeywords to store all known keywords. Then the following two functions add new keywords to the array and check if a keyword is already in the known keyword list:

```
public function addKnownKeyword(newKeyword):void {
    _knownKeywords.push(newKeyword);
    /* code to tell sever-side extension to save the new keyword */

}
public function checkKnownKeyword(keyword):Boolean {
    for each(knownKeyword in _knownKeywords) {
            if (knownKeyword == keyword) {
                    return true;
            }
    }
    return false;
}
```

In order to create the conditional branching, we add a property to the conversation node called `preRequest` which is in `Function` type to the conversation node.

```
public var preRequest:Function = undefined;
```

Take the keyword "Flash virtual world" as an example; we add an option that the player can ask about the virtual world. But this option will only appear after the player knows the keyword "Flash virtual world".

```
_conversation[3] = new ConversationNode();
_conversation[3].message = "Yes, you're right.";
_conversation[3].choices = [0];
_conversation[3].choiceMessages[0] = "Thanks, bye";
_conversation[3].preRequest = function(){
    if (Myself.instance.checkKnownKeyword('Flash Virtual World')) {
        return true;
    }
    return false;
}
```

When displaying the options in the chat dialog, we will check the preRequest function to determine whether they are displayed or not.

```
private function displayConversation(i):void  {
    ...
    if (_npc.conversation[i].choices[j] != undefined)
        ((_npc.conversation[nextChoice].preRequest == undefined) ||
         (_npc.conversation[nextChoice].preRequest())))) {
    ...
}
```

After the player clicks on a keyword, we will mark this keyword as known.

```
Myself.instance.addKnownKeyword(keyword);
```

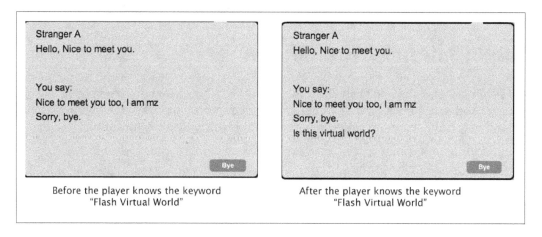

| Before the player knows the keyword "Flash Virtual World" | After the player knows the keyword "Flash Virtual World" |

Choosing the right conversation system

Different conversation systems are suitable for different types of virtual worlds. Menu-driven conversation may not be suitable for a virtual world that requires players to reveal the mysteries. It is because players can travel all the possibilities by choosing every choice in the conversation branches tree to get the answer. Instead, the openness text parsing conversation system fit the investigating type because players need to use the hints provided by the NPC to reveal the mysteries behind.

Designing the characteristic of the NPC

Designing NPCs is somewhat like writing a novel. We have to define their role and background information. They will have their own personality and thus result in different conversation tones and styles.

The chatting style should also fit the role of the NPC. For example, if the NPC is a strong soldier, his tone should be certain and solid. On the other hand, if the NPC is a little girl, her tone should be slow and shy.

Trading with NPC

We discussed item trading between players in the last chapter. We are going to discuss trading items with NPC now. The difference in trading between NPC and trading between users is that the former creates a new item and sells it to the player and the latter just passes an item from one player to another. The item creation process means the total amount of the items inside the virtual world increases, and it may lead to a virtual economy problem such as inflation. Therefore, some virtual worlds will set a limit to some rare items that even the NPC will not always sell. Instead, they will mark it as no stock until the amount of the items is below the upper limit.

Buying items from NPC

Not every NPC sells the same items. Some NPCs may sell weapons and some may sell healing tools. It is one of the task for players to find out where the specific NPC appears and sells items. And also it is a challenge to find an NPC who sell rare items but appears only at certain times in a place that is difficult to be found.

We will design a trading panel for the player to buy items from NPC. Players chat with the shopkeeper to ask him to pop up the trading panel. Then they buy items by dragging them from the shell to their own item inventory.

We modify the conversation node to add an action variable. This action variable defines an extra action when the player chooses this chat option.

```
public function ShopKeeper() {
    ...
    _conversation[2] = new ConversationNode();
    _conversation[2].message = "Sure.";
    _conversation[2].choices = [0];
    _conversation[2].choiceMessages[0] = "Thank you, Good bye.";
    _conversation[2].action = "npc_sell_item_panel";
    ...
}
```

When the player chooses the conversation option with action defined, the action will be dispatched as an event. We can then catch the action somewhere to perform specific actions according to the options.

```
if (_npc.conversation[i].action != '') {
    dispatchEvent(new Event(_npc.conversation[i].action, true));
}
```

In Panels.as, we will catch the event to display the trading panel.

```
stage.addEventListener("npc_sell_item_panel",onDisplayNPCSellPanel);
private function onDisplayNPCSellPanel(e):void {
    if (_currentDisplayingPanel != null){
        closeItemPanel();
    }
    _currentDisplayingPanel = new BuyItemPanel();
    _currentDisplayingPanel.controller = this;
    addChild(_currentDisplayingPanel);
}
```

Each NPC seller has its own list of items for selling. We display the item on the shopping shell according to this list.

```
private function setupNPCItems():void {
    var npc:* = Panels(parent).targetNPC;
    var i:int = 1;
    for each (var itemType:int in npc.itemList){
        var itemDef:ItemData = _itemDefinition.
getDefinitionFromID(itemType);
        if (itemDef == null){
            throw now Error("Error accessing an undefined data");
            return;
        }
        var itemClassname:String = itemDef.classname;
        /* Create the Item from classname */
```

```
var ClassReference:Class = getDefinitionByName
                                (itemClassname) as Class;
var newItem:MovieClip = (new ClassReference as MovieClip);
addChild(newItem);
newItem.x = this['npcSlot'+i].x;
newItem.y = this['npcSlot'+i].y;
newItem.panel = this;
newItem.type = itemType;
/* this item data is in system, not belongs to any players*/
newItem.belongsToSystem = true;
i++
            }
        }
```

The items from the NPC are marked as belongsToSystem. When the item is dragged to the player's item inventory, this flag will be checked to determine that this is a buying action instead of a normal positioning action.

```
if (_belongsToSystem){
    params:Object = {};
    params.type = _type;
    params.position = _position;
    SmartFox.sfs.sendXtMessage("virtualWorld", "createItem", params,
                            "json");
}
```

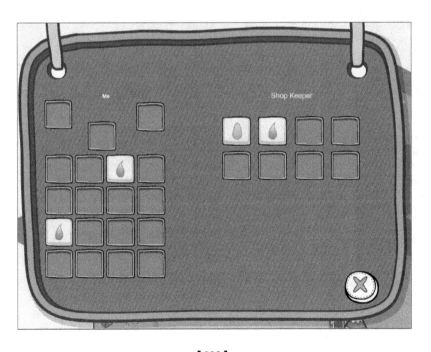

Selling items to NPC

Similar to the buying items example, a trading panel for selling items to NPC will pop up when the player chooses the conversation marked with action for selling items.

```
_conversation[2].action = "player_sell_item_panel";
```

In contrast to the item creation when buying items from NPC, we need to delete the item after selling it. We do not have any item deletion function yet so we need one on server-side extension.

```
function hdeleteItem(cmd, param, user, fromRoom){
    var res = new Object();
    res.cmd = cmd;

    var items = user.properties.get("item");
    for(var i = 0; i < items.length; i++){
            if (items[i]["id"] == param.id){
                    items[i]["removed"] = 1;
            }
    }
    user.properties.put("item", items);
    sendResponseBack(res, user);
}
```

When the player clicks the **Sell** button, we will tell the server to sell this item. Now it means telling the server to delete it.

```
private function sellItem(e:Event):void {
    var itemList:Array = Myself.instance.itemList;
    // get the item to sell
    var targetItem:Item = itemList[19];
    if (targetItem != null)    {
            var params:Object = {};
            params.id = targetItem.itemID;
            SmartFox.sfs.sendXtMessage("virtualWorld", "deleteItem",
                                      params, "json");
            removeChild(targetItem);
            itemList[19] = undefined;
    }
}
```

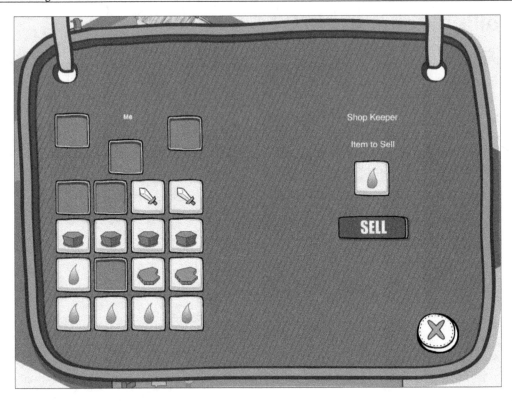

Summary

We have discussed how NPC is added to a virtual world. The NPCs appear in the virtual world with different purposes. Some of them tell stories or information whereas some of them serve players such as item trading.

We discussed how players interact with the NPCs. They can chat or trade with them. We compared several methods to chat with the NPCs. Every conversation system has its advantages and disadvantages, and we need to choose a right one for our virtual world. We can even mix their mechanisms together to supplement the system.

Also, we learned an advanced technique of mixing Java classes into the ActionScript server-side extension. This technique improves the performance in critical parts of the code and provide more possibilities to the extensions.

In the next chapter, we will discuss how to challenge our players by design quests in the virtual world.

11
Designing Quests

Players will make a lot of actions in the virtual world. They will walk around the world, talk with NPC, kill monsters, and interact with other players, or play some mini games. Quests are some tasks that require players to do these actions within a meaningful story. Instead of killing monsters for fun, players will be told to kill monsters to save the village. Instead of walking around the world without any purpose, players complete achievements while logging in the world. These pieces of purpose and reasons compose the main storyline of the virtual world.

We are going to discuss the flow from accepting a quest to completing it. We will also discuss different ways of presenting quests.

We will discuss the following topics in this chapter:

- The database and server set up for quests
- Listing available quests in the quests panel
- Methods of getting new quests
- Logic structure to maintain the in-progress quests
- Some tricks to make quests interesting

Introducing quests

Quests are some tasks that players can accept and complete in the virtual world. The content of the tasks is often related to the places or people nearby. For instance, a farming quest will most likely appear from a farmer in countryside.

Most probably there is a theme for every virtual world. The world can be set in modern age, middle age, or ancient. The theme can be around pirate, elf, or villages. The tasks and quests will be based on the theme of the virtual world. Players may need to kill sea monsters in a pirate theme virtual world. They may need to make friends to earn points in a social-based virtual world. In our theme, the players may need to contribute to build the town and quest around the town.

One feature of the quest is to tell stories. There is a reason for every quest that makes it meaningful. Pieces of the story will focus one at a time when players are working on the quests. Completing the quests is like putting missing puzzles at the correct place. As the player plays longer in the world, these pieces will gradually shape the storyline of the virtual world.

Triggering quests

When players reach some specific quest event trigger points, available quests will be listed for the player to choose to accept them. The straightforward way to trigger the quest is through the conversation with NPCs. While chatting with NPCs, they may require the players to archive some tasks. For example, a farmer may ask players to buy some seeds in the other town; a solider may ask players to kill a monster in order to get into the castle.

Besides triggering quests from NPCs, quests can also be triggered from reading documents, collecting items, or completing a quest. We will discuss them one by one.

Getting quests from NPC

In the last chapter, we created the NPC conversation system which is able to dispatch specific event when the player reaches that conversation node. We will make use of this feature to dispatch the quest triggering event.

When we design the conversation, a `quest_list_panel` event will be dispatched somewhere.

```
_conversation[5].action = "quest_list_panel";
```

The `Panels` class will then catch the event and display the quest-listing panel. We are going to create this quest-listing panel in the next section.

```
stage.addEventListener("quest_list_panel",onDisplayQuestListPanel);
```

Getting quests from reading documents

In the environment, there may be some poster stuck on the wall or some paper documents put up on the desk. Players may be able to read the content inside those documents when they walk near by and click on them. This can be done by checking the player's position and dispatching an event to trigger the document reading. The content of these documents may be just telling some facts or they can be a starting point of the quest. For example, if players read the wanted poster on wall, a people hunting mini game may be launched.

Getting quests from collecting items

Players may be able to collect items on the ground. Some of these items may contain special quests. A player may pick up a mystery key that triggers the quest of finding the treasure or a rubbish paper that contains a secret of a mad scientist.

Getting quests from the last quest

Sometimes, quests can be chained together to composite a large mission. A new quest appears when a player finishes a quest in the chain. The new quest is usually a continuation of the last quest for the player to explore the next part of the story. This is also called **Quest Chain**.

The following graphs shows how a quest is disabled until the pre-requirement is fulfilled:

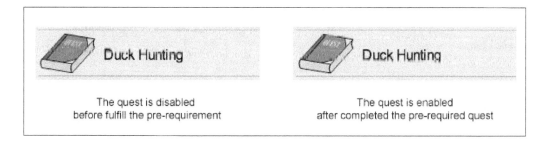

We have discussed some basic quests concepts and we will move on to setting up quests in our virtual world.

Setting up server environment for quests

Before we start coding, we need to store a list of quests information and also the progress of each quest for each player. We are going to create two tables in the MySQL database. The virtual world client-side will retrieve this information through server-side extensions.

Setting up database

We need to create two tables in PhpMyAdmin, one for storing the quests data and the other for storing the relationship between each avatar and each quest.

Let's take a look at the table structure of `quests`:

Column	Type	Description
id	int	The unique ID to reference a quest.
title	varchar(50)	The title of the quest.
description	text	Some background information and requirements to let players know about.
holder	varchar(50)	This states which NPC holds the quest.
pre_ requirement	int	When a prerequired quest ID is set to the quest, players need to complete the prerequired quest in order to accept this quest.
is_achievement	int(1)	Achievement quests will be automatically added to the player.
daemon	varchar(50)	The name of the class that is in charge of the quest.

The `avatar_quests` table stores the status and progress for each player on each quest:

Column	Type	Description
quest_id	int	The ID of the quest.
avatar_name	varchar(50)	The name of the player who took this quest.
status	int	The status of the quest. We will use 1 for quest in progress and 2 for completed quest.
progress	int	Every quest has a different number of steps to complete. This field stores the progress of the quest.

Designing the quest panels

Quest panels are used to display a list of quests to players and perform several quest-related actions such as accepting a quest. There are two quest panels in our virtual world. One is the panel that lists the available quests from an NPC. The other panel lists the player accepted quest log with completed and in-progress quests.

Displaying available quests

When a player triggers the quests event, we will pop up a panel to list the available quests from the NPC. Some quests are disabled because the player has not fulfilled the requirement of the quest. We will focus on listing the quests here and discuss the quest pre-requirement later.

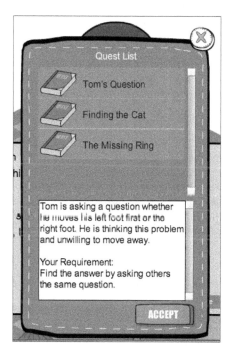

Getting available quests in server-side extension

We retrieve the list of quests for a given NPC. Every quest entry in the database contains a `holder` field which is the NPC's name that own that quest. We need a server-side extension to query the database and pass the quest list to the quest panel, which is on client-side. We will expand our `virtualworld.as` extension with the following functions:

```
function hgetQuestListFromHolder(cmd, param, user, fromRoom) {
    var res = new Object();
    res.cmd = cmd;
    res.list = [];
    var holder = param.holder;
    var sql = "SELECT * FROM quests WHERE holder='" + holder + "'";
    var resultCount = getResultArray(sql, res.list);
    sendResponseBack(res, user);
}
```

When we accept a quest, we insert the relationship of the avatar and the quest as a new entry. We also mark the status to be 1 which means it is in progress.

```
function hacceptQuest(cmd, param, user, fromRoom) {
    var res = new Object();
    res.cmd = cmd;
    var sql = "INSERT INTO avatar_quests (quest_id,
avatar_name,status,progress) VALUES
                    ('"+param.questId+"','"+user.getName()+"','1','0')";
    var success = dbase.executeCommand(sql);
    sendResponseBack(res, user);
}
```

With an in-progress quest, a player can choose to abandon it. We simply delete the entry from database so the quest look as if the player never accepted it.

```
function habandonQuest(cmd, param, user, fromRoom) {
    var res = new Object();
    res.cmd = cmd;
    var sql = "DELETE FROM avatar_quests WHERE
      quest_id="+param.questId+" AND avatar_name='"+user.getName()+"'";
    var success = dbase.executeCommand(sql);
    sendResponseBack(res, user);
}
```

Displaying the quests in different statuses

There are four statuses of a quest. We will display the statuses in the quest panel.

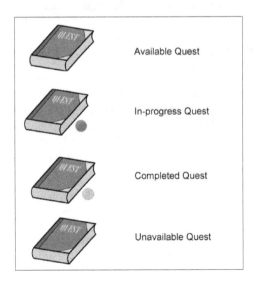

While we are displaying the quest's information in the `QuestListPanel` class, we will check which status of the quest it is and display the corresponding status icon. We use the technique that is similar to the avatar styles to display different quest status icons. The four status icons are put into four frames inside a movie clip called `questStat` and we can display different quest status by using `gotoAndStop`.

```
for each (var inProgressId:int in inProgressList){
    if (row.questId == inProgressId){
        row.questState.gotoAndStop(2);
        break;
    }
}
```

Displaying quests for the avatar

Similar to the listing of available quests, we need a panel to display the quests that are completed or are in-progress from an avatar. Players are able to open this quest panel from the bottom bar. As these quests are from avatars, the status of the quest must be either completed or in-progress.

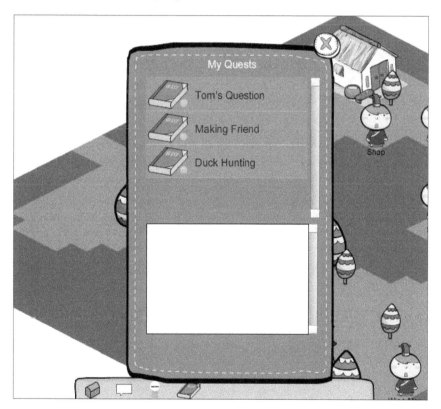

We need another server-side extension to the query the quests of the avatar from the database. We join the `quests` table and `avatar_quests` table to get all information of the quest that is related to the given avatar.

```
function hgetAllQuestsFromAvatar(cmd, param, user, fromRoom) {
    var res = new Object();
    res.cmd = cmd;
    res.quests = [];
    var sql = "SELECT quests.daemon daemon, quests.id id, quests.
title title, quests.description description, avatar_quests.status
status, avatar_quests.progress progress FROM avatar_quests, quests
WHERE quests.id = avatar_quests.quest_id AND avatar_name =  '"+user.
getName()+"'";
    var resultCount = getResultArray(sql, res.quests);
    sendResponseBack(res, user);
}
```

We have prepared the panels for listing the quests. Next, we need some classes to help us manage our quests status and progress.

Running daemons for quests

For some quests, we may want to apply some special effects on the players before they finish the quest. We may want to restrict them from going somewhere, adding special visual effects to their screens, or may be disable some attributes of the avatars.

Take the Fantastic Age virtual world as an example. There is a quest that is telling the story about the mad scientist's invention of a machine that makes the whole virtual world cloudy and stormy. A cloudy visual effect is then added to the players who are working on this quest until they finish it by destroying the machine.

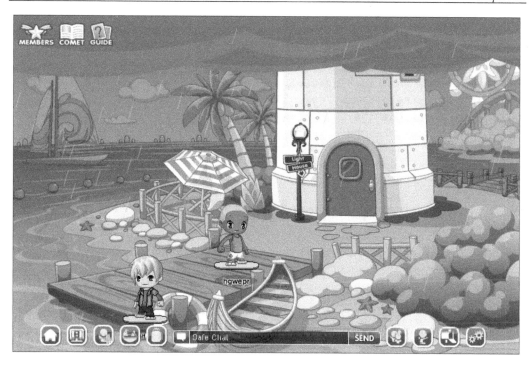

Moreover, each daemon class is also in charge of keeping track of the progress of the quest. Quest progress is advanced when the player plays in the game. The daemon's role is to track the progress and determine when to show something and when to hide it to make the quest run smoothly. Also it will determine if the quest is completed.

Before coding our daemons, we need some server-side extensions to help us access the database. The commands we need are getAllInProgressQuests, loadCompletedQuestList, getQuestStatus, updateQuestProgress, and completeQuest. We will go through them one by one now.

We will need to get all in-progress quests from database so that we can restore the quests every time that the players log in.

```
function hgetAllInProgressQuests(cmd, param, user, fromRoom) {
    var res = new Object();
    res.cmd = cmd;
    res.daemons = [];
    res.inProgressList = [];
    var quests = [];
    var sql = "SELECT quest_id FROM avatar_quests WHERE
            avatar_name='"+user.getName()+"' AND status=1";
    var resultCount = getResultArray(sql, quests);
```

```
    for(var i=0;i<quests.length;i++){
        var quest = [];
        var sql = "SELECT daemon,id FROM quests WHERE
                id="+quests[i].quest_id;
        getResultArray(sql,quest);
        res.daemons.push(quest[0].daemon);
        res.inProgressList.push(quest[0].id);
    }
    sendResponseBack(res, user);
}
```

We will load the completed quest from server. The status is marked as 2 for completed quest.

```
function hloadCompletedQuestList(cmd, param, user, fromRoom) {
    var res = new Object();
    res.cmd = cmd;
    res.completedList = [];
    var sql = "SELECT quest_id FROM avatar_quests WHERE status=2 AND
            avatar_name='"+user.getName()+"'";
    var resultCount = getResultArray(sql, res.completedList);
    sendResponseBack(res, user);
}
```

For a quest daemon, it will need to load the status and progress of a specific quest. The daemon needs the status to check if the working quest has fulfilled the completed criteria.

```
function hgetQuestStatus(cmd, param, user, fromRoom) {
    var res = new Object();
    res.cmd = cmd;
    res.status = -1;
    var quest = [];
    var sql = "SELECT * FROM avatar_quests WHERE
      quest_id="+param.questId+" AND avatar_name='"+user.getName()+"'";
    var resultCount = getResultArray(sql, quest);
    if (resultCount > 0){
        res.status = quest[0].status;
        res.progress = quest[0].progress;
    }
    sendResponseBack(res, user);
}
```

While players are playing in the virtual world, the daemon will track the changes of the quests and update the progress in the server. The updated progress will be saved in the database so that the user can restore the progress at next login.

```
function hupdateQuestProgress(cmd,param,user,fromRoom) {
    var res = new Object();
    res.cmd = cmd;
    var sql = "UPDATE avatar_quests SET progress="+param.progress+"
    WHERE quest_id="+param.questId+" AND avatar_name='"+user.
    getName()+"'";
    var success = dbase.executeCommand(sql);
    sendResponseBack(res, user);
}
```

We will mark the quest as complete in database after the user fulfills the completion criteria. There are several ways to complete a quest and we will discuss that later.

```
function hcompleteQuest(cmd,param,user,fromRoom) {
    var res = new Object();
    res.cmd = cmd;

    var sql = "UPDATE avatar_quests SET status=2 WHERE quest_
    id="+param.questId+" AND avatar_name='"+user.getName()+"'";
    var success = dbase.executeCommand(sql);
    sendResponseBack(res, user);
}
```

Let's move to the client-side. We create a daemon base class for all daemons to extend it. The Daemon class contains the following properties and functions:

Properties or function name	Type	Description
progress	Number	Stores the progress of the quest.
status	Number	States whether the quest is in-progress or completed.
name	String	The quest name.
run	Function	Periodic running logic that is related to the quest.
onAccept	Function	Called once when the player accepts the quest.
onRemove	Function	Called once when the player abandons the quest.

Managing quest daemons

Daemon manager is a class to manage all quest daemons at one central place. It is also responsible to keep a list of completed quests and in-progress quests. There is a timer in the Daemon Manager that runs every second. This timer will call every monitoring daemon to run a periodic logic which is useful for some quests that require some periodic checking.

Property name	Type	Description
daemons	Array	A list of active quest daemon references.
timer	Timer	A timer to execute the periodic logic of active daemons.
inProgressList	Array	A list of quest IDs for the quest that is in-progress.
completedList	Array	A list of quest IDs for the quest that is completed.

The daemon manager will load the completed and in-progress quests from server when the user logs in to the virtual world.

```
public function restoreRunningDaemon():void {
    _daemons = new Array();

    var params:Object = {};
    SmartFox.sfs.sendXtMessage("virtualWorld",
                        "getAllInProgressQuests", params, "json");

    params = {};
    SmartFox.sfs.sendXtMessage("virtualWorld",
                        "loadCompletedQuestList", params, "json");
}
```

The daemon manager provides a function for other classes to register a daemon into the monitoring list and a function to remove it from the active quest list.

```
public function registerDaemon(d:String):Daemon {
    // dynamically initialize the daemons class from string
    // the daemon classes are placed inside npcs | daemons classpath.
    var classReference:Class = getDefinitionByName("npcs.daemons."+d)
                        as Class;
    var daemon = new classReference(_stage);
    _daemons.push(daemon);

    // start the timer when there is any active quest.
    if (_daemons.length == 1){
        _timer.start();
```

```
        }
        return daemon;
    }
    public function unregisterDaemon(daemonName:String):void{
        for(var i:int=0;i<_daemons.length;i++){
            var d:Daemon = _daemons[i];
            if (d.name == daemonName){
                d.onRemove();
                _daemons.splice(i,1);
                d = null;
            }
        }

        // no daemon in the list now, stop the timer.
        if (_daemons.length <= 0){
            _timer.stop();
        }
    }
```

When other classes need to reference the daemon instance, they can access it by providing the daemon name in string. We need to get the instance from string instead of directly referencing the instance because sometimes this daemon name is stored in string format in the database.

```
    public function getDaemonByName(daemonName:String):Daemon {
        for each(var d:Daemon in _daemons){
            if (d.name == daemonName){
                return d;
            }
        }
        return null;
    }
```

During the initialization process, the daemon manger will load all in-progress quests and register the daemons to restore the working quests' status.

```
    private function onExtensionResponse(e:SFSEvent):void {
        var cmd:String = e.params.dataObj.cmd;
        var data:Object = e.params.dataObj;

        if (cmd=='getAllInProgressQuests') {
            for each(var daemon:Daemon in data.daemons){

                registerDaemon(daemon);
            }
```

```
        for each(var quested:Number in data.inProgressList) {
            _inProgressList.push(questId);
        }
    } else if (cmd=='loadCompletedQuestList')        {
        for each(var quest:Object in data.completedList) {
            _completedList.push(quest.quest_id);
        }
    }
}
```

Creating our first quest—Tom's Question

We are now going to create an example to demonstrate what we just implemented. The quest is called **Tom's Question**. There is an NPC called Tom who blocked the player's road. When the player asked Tom to walk away, Tom said he didn't know which foot to move first. If the player chooses to help Tom find the answer, a quest panel will prompt to let the player accept the quest.

The player then needs to ask a wise man, another NPC, the same question and seek the answer from him. When player gets the answer and gets back to Tom, an option appears in the conversation to let the player answer Tom's question.

Finally, Tom gets the solution and the quest daemon will track the completion and update the status in the database.

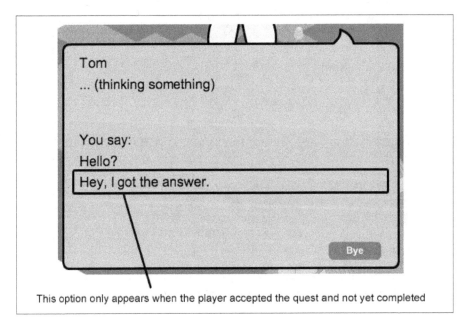

This option only appears when the player accepted the quest and not yet completed

The quest daemon that is in charge of the Tom's Question quest will keep the latest progress and status of the quest. The conversation menu can use this information to check if some options in the conversation tree are displayed or not.

```
_conversation[6].preRequest = function(){
    // check if the quest "Tom's Question" is completed
    // if the quest is complete, we hide this option
    var completedList:Array = DaemonManager.instance.completedList;
    for each(var questId:Number in completedList){
            if (questId == _questId){
                    return false;
            }
    }

    // get the daemon of the quest "Tom's Question"
    var daemon:Daemon = DaemonManager.instance.getDaemonByName
                                    (_daemonName);
    if (daemon == null) return false;

    /* get the progress of the Tom's Question quest, if the game is in
progress,
    display this conversation, otherwise, hide it. */
    var progress:Number = DaemonManager.instance.getDaemonByName
                                        (_daemonName).progress;
    var status:Number = DaemonManager.instance.getDaemonByName
                                        (_daemonName).status;
    if (status < 2 && progress > 0){
            return true;
    }
    return false;
}
```

When players reach the conversation node where the wise man gave the answer, an event is dispatched to inform the daemon to update the progress.

```
_conversation[5] = new ConversationNode();
_conversation[5].message = "Ahha, what a good question. Why not take a
wheelchair? Then you don't need to move either one.";
_conversation[5].choices = [0];
_conversation[5].choiceMessages[0] = "Thank you!";
_conversation[5].action = 'found_answer_of_tom_question';
```

Here is the flow of the whole quest.

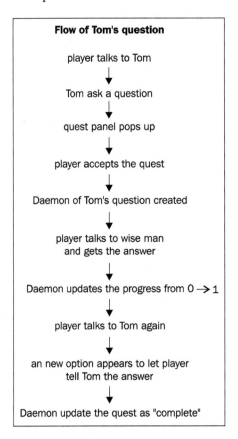

The `TomQuestionD.as` quest daemon listens to the found_answer_of_tom_question and complete_tom_question event to update the progress. The found_answer_of_tom_question event will be dispatched when the player talks to the wise man NPC and gets the answer. The complete_tom_question is dispatched when the player talks to Tom again and tells him the correct answer.

```
public function TomQuestionD(stageRef) {
    // execute the superclass's constructor code.
    super(stageRef);

    _name = "TomQuestionD";
    _stage.addEventListener(
                    'found_answer_of_tom_question',onFoundAnswer);
    _stage.addEventListener('complete_tom_question',onComplete);
```

```
SmartFox.sfs.addEventListener(SFSEvent.onExtensionResponse,
                         onExtensionResponse);
var params:Object = {};
params.questId = _questId;
SmartFox.sfs.sendXtMessage("virtualWorld", "getQuestStatus",
                         params, "json");
}
```

When the wise man tells the player the answer, the daemon will catch that event and update the quest progress.

```
private function onFoundAnswer(e:Event):void {
    _progress++;
    var params:Object = {};
    params.progress = _progress;
    params.questId = _questId;
    SmartFox.sfs.sendXtMessage("virtualWorld", "updateQuestProgress",
                         params, "json");
}
```

When the player tells Tom the answer, the daemon marks the quest as completed in the server.

```
private function onComplete(e:Event):void {
    var params:Object = {};
    params.questId = _questId;
    SmartFox.sfs.sendXtMessage("virtualWorld", "completeQuest",
                         params, "json");
    DaemonManager.instance.unregisterDaemon(_name);
    DaemonManager.instance.completedList.push(_questId);
}
```

In the example, we see that the daemon is useful for checking and holding the status of the quest so that others' logic can determine which state the player is in with the quest.

Introducing achievement

Besides the player triggering quests, there is another type of quest called **Achievement**. Achievements are some default quests which players complete passively. The requirements of achievement can be completed by the players without even noticing them. For example, an achievement may describe the user to stay in the virtual world for 30 minutes. While the players are playing in the virtual world for half an hour, this achievement is automatically marked as completed.

The following graph is an achievement list from the virtual world Habbo. It is a virtual world that focuses on making friends and socializing. Therefore, the achievements are related to the login time and the number of friends in the buddy list.

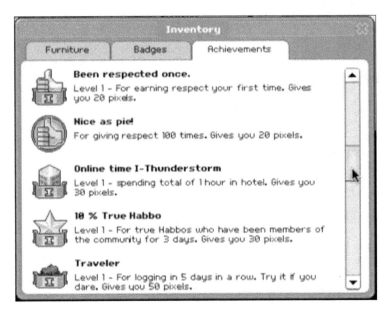

As the achievement quests are completed passively without triggering by players, we need to install the achievement quests as in-progress quests in background in order to keep track of the progress of the achievements. This server-side extension in `virtualworld.as` will be called every time a user logs in to the virtual world. It will then insert a quest entry for that achievement if it does not exist yet.

```
function installAchievementQuests(user) {
    // get the list of achievement quests
    var achievements = [];
    var sql = "SELECT id FROM quests WHERE is_achievement=1";
    var count = getResultArray(sql, achievements);

    for(var i=0;i<count;i++) {
        var q=[];
        /* check if the player already installed the achievement
quests. */
        sql = "SELECT quest_id FROM avatar_quests WHERE avatar_
name='"+user.getName()+"' AND quest_id="+achievements[i].id;
        var exists = getResultArray(sql, q);
        if (exists <= 0) {
```

```
                    sql = "INSERT INTO avatar_quests (quest_id,avatar_
name,status,progress) VALUES('"+achievements[i].id+"','"+user.
getName()+"','1','0')";
                    var success = dbase.executeCommand(sql);
            }
        }
    }
```

We will call the achievement installation functions when a user logs in and joins the virtual world. Therefore, we need to modify the `handleInternalEvent` function in `virtualworld.as`:

```
function handleInternalEvent(e){
    if (e.name == "userJoin"){
            var user = e.user;
            installAchievementQuests(user);
    }
}
```

Let's move to client-side and make an example achievement about making friends. The achievement requires the player to add at least one friend into the buddy list. We make a daemon named `MakingFriendD.as` to check the add buddy event.

```
public function MakingFriendD(stageRef) {
    super(stageRef);
    _name = "MakingFriendD";
    _stage.addEventListener('added_buddy',onAddedBuddy);
}
```

If the player adds another one as buddy, the daemon will catch it and mark the achievement as completed.

```
private function onAddedBuddy(e:SFSEvent):void {
    var params = {};
    params.questId = _questId;
    SmartFox.sfs.sendXtMessage("virtualWorld", "completeQuest",
                                params, "json");
    DaemonManager.instance.unregisterDaemon(_name);
    DaemonManager.instance.completedList.push(_questId);
}
```

In the `InfoPanel.as`, we dispatch the `added_buddy` event when the player clicks the add buddy button to inform the daemon.

```
private function clickAddBuddy(e:MouseEvent):void {
    ...
    dispatchEvent(new Event("added_buddy", true));
}
```

Completing quests

There are several ways to complete a quest. In the previous example, the player completes the quest by talking to the NPC or adding friends. We can complete a quest anywhere and dispatch a complete event to inform the monitoring quest daemon.

Another common method to complete a quest is to hand in an item that the NPC needs. A panel will pop up for the player to hand in some items. The panel is basically the same as the selling item panel that was discussed in the last chapter except that now we are giving a specific item to NPC instead of selling any items. Therefore, the only difference between this panel and the selling panel is that we need to check if the submit item is what NPC needs. The NPC's desired item type is stored in daemon manager as `waitingItemType`. In the following code, players are required to submit a duck item to the NPC:

```
private function handinItem(e:MouseEvent):void {
    var itemList:Array = Myself.instance.itemList;
    var targetItem:ItemData = itemList[19];
    if (targetItem != null)     {
        if (targetItem.type == DaemonManager.instance.
                waitingItemType)
        {
            var params:Object = {};
            params.id = targetItem.itemID;
            SmartFox.sfs.sendXtMessage("virtualWorld",
                    "deleteItem", params, "json");
            removeChild(targetItem);
            itemList[19] = undefined;
            DaemonManager.instance.waitingItemType = undefined;
            dispatchEvent(new Event('complete_duck_
                    shooting',true));

            _controller.closePanel();
        }
    }
}
```

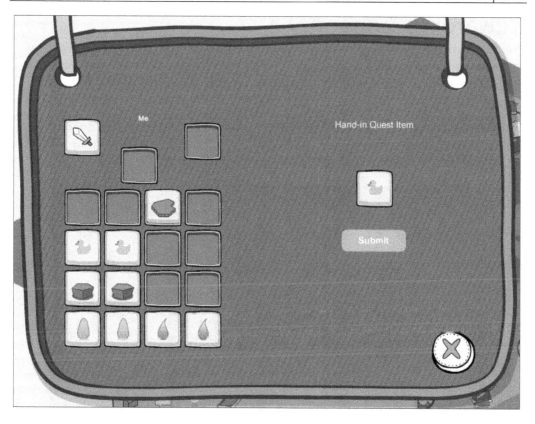

Rewarding the players when finishing the quests

After players complete the quests, what benefit will the players get? Usually players get some rewards after finishing the quests. There are several aspects with which we can reward the players.

Rewarding gold

Rewarding gold is one of the most common ways in online virtual world. Players get the virtual money from finishing the quests and then use the money to equip the avatar with more advanced items for advanced quests.

Rewarding items

We can reward some rare or special items to the players. For easy quests, the items can be common ones that are available all over the virtual world. For advanced quests, the rewarding items can be unique or rare to encourage players to challenge the difficult quests.

In the Fantastic Age virtual world, players can buy stickers and collect a set of special stickers by finishing quests. These stickers are in various forms that players will spend their time collecting set by set in the virtual world.

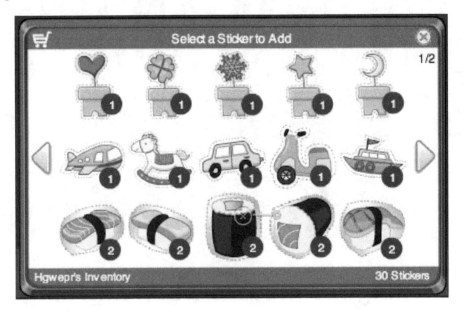

Rewarding avatars advancement or experience

If there is an avatar advancement system in the virtual world, we can reward the players some experience on the avatar. The avatar can have improvement on the attributes after finishing each quest so that the avatar can challenge more advanced quests.

In the Survival Project, a Korean online virtual world, players get experience rewards to advance to a higher level that is able to equip advanced items.

Extending the quests with mini games

In previous quest examples, the quests are completed in the virtual world environment such as talking with NPCs and socializing with friends. However, the forms of quests are not limited to the environments of the virtual world. Quests can be another mini game that players play with the computer or with other players.

We had the hand-in item example that used the duck item. Now we are going to make another quest example that players are required to hunt the duck in the shooting game and collect enough ducks to hand in to the hunter.

In the quest, a hunter NPC said that he needed 50 ducks and asked whether the player can hunt the ducks for him. The score of the duck shooting game will be stored as the progress of the quest. When the number of hunted ducks reaches 50, the player is able to hand over the duck item to the hunter.

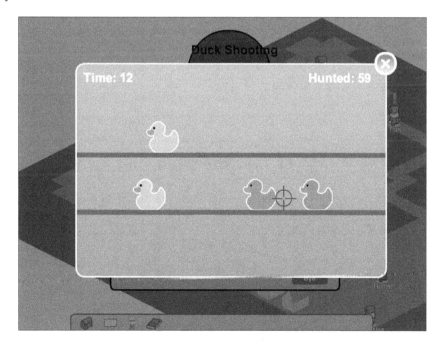

Similar to the Tom's Question quest, we have three conversation options that appear in different criteria. The first option always appears to open the quest-listing panel. The second option will inform the `Panels` class to attach the duck shooting mini games on screen. The third option will inform the `Panels` class to display the hand-in item panel.

The player can play the duck shooting game only after accepting the quest. We can determine if the quest is in-progress by checking the existence of the daemon. The quest daemon exists only when the quest is accepted and not completed.

```
_conversation[4].preRequest = function(){
    var daemon:Daemon = DaemonManager.instance.getDaemonByName
                                        (_daemonName);
    if (daemon == null) return false;
    return true;
}
```

The requirement from the hunter is to collect 50 ducks. The number of hunted ducks stores as the progress of the quest. We check the quest progress from the daemon to see if the player reaches the required numbers and display the option.

```
_conversation[5].preRequest = function(){
    var daemon:Daemon = DaemonManager.instance.getDaemonByName
                                        (_daemonName);
    if (daemon == null) return false;

    var progress:Number = DaemonManager.instance.getDaemonByName
                                        (_daemonName).progress;
    if (progress < 50) return false;
    return true;
}
```

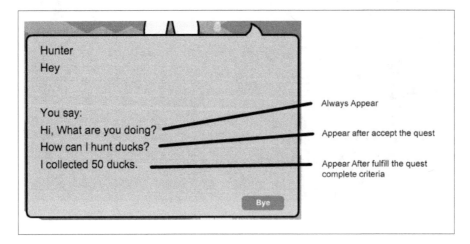

Creating the duck shooting game

The duck shooting game itself is controlled by a class individually. The only communication between the game and the virtual world is the end game score. We will not show the detailed implementation of the game here but we will look inside the essential part that sends the final score to the virtual world.

When initializing the game, we restore the score from the quest progress. Players may not finish the quest immediately after accepting it. They may collect half the number of ducks one day and the other half on the other day. The daemon that we create later is responsible to store the progress on server and restore the progress when the player logs in again.

```
private function init(e:Event):void {
    ...
    var duckShootingD:DuckShootingD = DaemonManager.instance.getDaemon
                                ByName("DuckShootingD");
    if (duckShootingD != null){
        _score = duckShootingD.progress;
    }
    ...
}
```

When the game is over, we dispatch the event to inform the daemon. It gets the final score from the game and will store it into the quest progress.

```
private function gameOver(e:Event):void {
    ...
    dispatchEvent(new Event("duck_shooting_ended",true));

    ...
}
```

Implementing the duck shooting quest daemon

The daemon mainly tracks two events. One is the end of the shooting game and the other is the completion after submitting the duck item to the hunter.

```
public function DuckShootingD(stageRef) {
    super(stageRef);

    _name = "DuckShootingD";
    _stage.addEventListener('duck_shooting_
                        ended',onEndedDuckShooting);
```

```
    _stage.addEventListener('complete_duck_shooting',
                            onCompletedDuckShooting);

    SmartFox.sfs.addEventListener(SFSEvent.onExtensionResponse,
                                  onExtensionResponse);
    var params = {};
    params.questId = _questId;
    SmartFox.sfs.sendXtMessage("virtualWorld", "getQuestStatus",
                               params, "json");
}
```

When the quest daemon is first initialized, it will create a duck item in the inventory of the avatar. This item will be submitted to the hunter NPC later after collecting 50 ducks.

```
public override function onAccept():void {
    var params:Object = {};
    params.type = 1006;
    SmartFox.sfs.sendXtMessage("virtualWorld", "createItem", params,
                               "json");
}
```

The daemon will update the quest progress from the game score after the game ends.

```
private function onEndedDuckShooting(e:Event):void {
    _progress = e.target.score;
    var params:Object = {};
    params.progress = _progress;
    params.questId = _questId;
    SmartFox.sfs.sendXtMessage("virtualWorld", "updateQuestProgress",
                               params, "json");
}
```

When the player collected 50 ducks and submits it to the hunter NPC, the daemon will mark the quest as completed and remove itself from the monitoring list.

```
private function onCompletedDuckShooting(e:Event):void {
    var params:Object = {};
    params.questId = _questId;
    SmartFox.sfs.sendXtMessage("virtualWorld", "completeQuest",
                               params, "json");
    DaemonManager.instance.unregisterDaemon(_name);
    DaemonManager.instance.completedList.push(_questId);
}
```

Making the quest system better

Quests can be more interesting if designed well; we have implemented several technical techniques of implementing different forms of quests. We will discuss several tricks to enhance the quests.

Avoiding linear quests

We discussed the Quest Chain that a quest is enabled only when the players finish another required quest. We should avoid designing all the quests in linear as the players are required to finish them one after the other. The quest chain should not be the only choice for the players to take.

Image a case where there are two friends playing in the virtual world together. The quests are all chained linearly. In the beginning, they start from the first quest and finish several quests together along the quest chain. On the other week, friend A is studying for an examination and stays away from the computer. Friend B, on the other hand, logged into the virtual world and finishes several quests. The problem now is friend A finished the exam and wants to play together with friend B together and he finds that their progress in the quests is not synchronized. They cannot play on the quests unless friend B waits for friend A to finish those quests that he finished in advance. This problem will be worse when several friends want to play together instead of two.

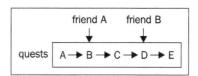

To avoid this problem, we should design our quests in a way that not all quests are chained together. Instead of chaining all quests, we provide some individual quests. Assume that friend A played quest A and friend B is in-progress of quest C. When they log in the virtual world together, they can play quest D or E together without worrying about the progress synchronize issue.

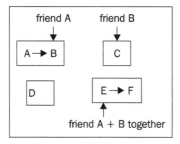

Indicating the availability of quests

We can add an indicator to help players to spot the available quests in the virtual world. The indicator can indicate several states of the quests such as the available quests, in-progress quests, upcoming quests, and completed quests.

We will put an indicator on the head of every NPC that contains quests. We need an extension function to get the number of quests from a given NPC.

```
function hgetAvailableQuestCountFromHolder(cmd, param, user, fromRoom)
{
    var res = new Object();
    res.cmd = cmd;
    var holder = param.holder;
    res.holder = holder;

    var questList = [];
    var sql = "SELECT * FROM quests WHERE holder='"+holder+"'";
    var resultCount = getResultArray(sql, questList);
    res.count = resultCount;

    sendResponseBack(res, user);
}
```

While we create the NPCs in the `World.as` class, we call the server to get the number of quests that NPC carries.

```
for each(var user:User in userList){
...
    /* check if we need to show the indicator of the avatar */
    var isNPC:Boolean = user.getVariable('isNPC');
    if (isNPC){
            var params:Object = {};
            params.holder = user.getName();
            SmartFox.sfs.sendXtMessage("virtualWorld",
"getAvailableQuestCountFromHolder", params, "json");
    }
...
}
```

If the number of quests is not zero, we put an indicator on its head.

```
private function onExtensionResponse(e:SFSEvent):void{
    var cmd:String = e.params.dataObj.cmd;
    var data:Object = e.params.dataObj;
```

```
if (cmd=='getAvailableQuestCountFromHolder')    {
    if(data.count > 0){
            _avatarList[data.holder].indicator.visible = true;
    }
}
}
```

Summary

Designing quests is like telling a story in a virtual world. The virtual world is an interactive environment. Therefore, we have to avoid designing quests that bind the players too much. We have discussed different presenting methods of quests and how we can integrate the quests into the virtual world. The quests are like a guide that guides the players to explore the virtual world step-by-step. The more interesting the quests are, the more players will like to stay in the virtual world.

In the next chapter, we are going to see how we can improve the interaction between the players by implementing socialized features and integrating an existing social network.

12
Social Community

Social networking has been a hot trend on the Internet recently. People want to know what their friends are doing on Internet now and their behaviors will influence their friends. For example, when several friends are doing one thing in the social network, their friends will have a higher chance to follow their behaviors. When they are playing one social networking game, the chances of their friends joining the same game becomes high.

We can enhance our virtual world by adding social network community. We will use the social networking features from existing social network services and use these services to help spread the virtual worlds to potential players.

In this chapter, we are going to integrate several key features of Facebook and Twitter. We will also learn how to use the API provided by those social networking services to put and fetch resources with them.

The benefit of using social network features in virtual world

The main purpose of the social networking services is connecting friends together. We can benefit from it by letting players and friends form their community inside the virtual world. Friends can share news of the virtual world to other friends that are inside or outside the virtual world. The news sharing mechanism increases the exposure of the virtual world and attracts more friends to join.

Players can easily interact with others with SmartFoxServer. By further integrating the social network services, they can socialize inside the virtual world in almost real-time.

The complicated data flow

Our virtual world connects to socket server to interact with server and other players in real time. After integrating other social network services into our virtual world, the data flow between the Flash client-side virtual world and several server-side services becomes complicated. We need to be careful while designing and developing the virtual world and not to confuse different server-side services and the socket server. The following figure shows the data flow of the virtual world:

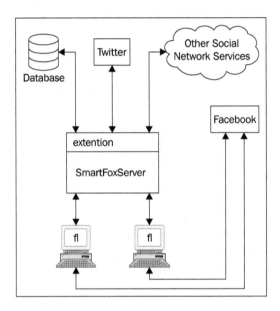

Integrating Facebook platform

Facebook provides a whole set of frameworks for third-party developers to access the Facebook social resources such as friend's data, albums, and events.

There are three ways to integrate the Facebook platform. We can put the virtual world as an application in Facebook, as an external application, or as a desktop application.

When setting up the virtual world as an application inside Facebook, users can log into the virtual world within the Facebook website. The users do not need to leave the Facebook website when transiting to the virtual world from browsing friends photos or news.

With the external website application setup, the players go to the virtual world website instead of the Facebook website. We can authorize a user's Facebook account by logging in with **Facebook connect**. We can then make use of the social features from Facebook in the virtual world.

The desktop application setup will be useful if we deliver our virtual world as a desktop application and need to use the Facebook social services. As we are building a web-based online virtual world, we will not discuss this in detail.

Setting up Flash Facebook API

There are several Facebook API libraries for Flash. We will use the official one from Adobe in these examples.

The Adobe Facebook API is free for download at following address:

`http://code.google.com/p/facebook-actionscript-api/`

We can download the compiled SWC file and zipped source file from the Google Code or check out the latest version of the source through SVN.

As we will not modify this library now, we are going to use the SWC file. Once the SWC file is downloaded, we need to locate it in the Flash document.

The setting can be found in the `File | Publish Setting | Script: ActionScript 3.0 Settings | Library Path`.

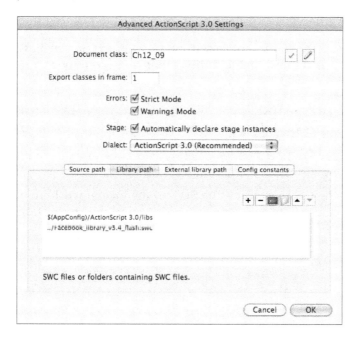

Registering the virtual world in Facebook

In order to access the Facebook API, we need to register the application in Facebook Developer application and obtain a unique API and secret key.

The Facebook Developer app is located at `http://facebook.com/developers`.

We will set up a new app for our virtual world now.

1. Add Facebook Developer app into the Facebook account.
2. Click on the **Set Up New Application** button.
3. Fill in the **Application Name** and read the terms.
4. The application is set up and the API keys are generated.

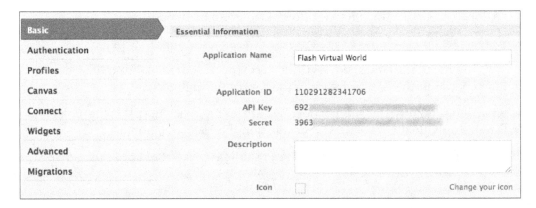

Next we need to set the Canvas page setting. Canvas setting sets how our application appears in Facebook. Three notable settings that we need to be aware of in this setting page are:

- The **Canvas Page URL** is the URL that points to our application.
- The **Canvas Callback URL** is the URL of hosting the application.
- The **Render Method** decides whether Facebook embeds our application inside the page or uses an iFrame to load it.

We need to host the web pages and the SWF of the virtual world in our hosting. The canvas callback URL tells Facebook where to find the application files.

Putting the virtual world as a Facebook application

Facebook provides two rendering methods of Facebook application. They are **FBML** (**Facebook Markup Language**) and iFrame. The main difference between them is that the application is either embedded in the Facebook web page as FBML or rendered by iFrame. These are two different methods and their data flow architecture is totally different.

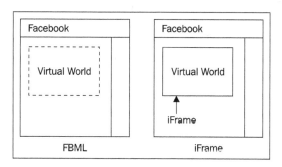

Using FBML rendering

The Facebook is in charge of fetching the web page from the canvas callback URL and embedding it into the Facebook web page. It parses the Facebook Markup Language and converts it into HTML.

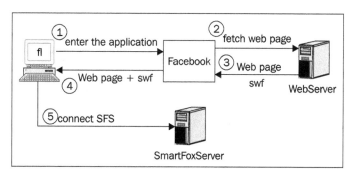

```
<fb:swf
swfbgcolor="ffffff"
imgstyle="border-width:3px; border-color:white;"
swfsrc='http://flashtut.net/virtualworld/ch12_02a.swf'
width='768' height='600' />
```

As the page that loaded the SWF file of virtual world is now fetched from Facebook, we cannot use relative path to load the data in the SWF. We load the virtual world data by using the full path.

```
public function IsometricMapData() {
    …
    _xmlLoader.load(new URLRequest('http://flashtut.net/virtualworld/
    data/buildingData.xml'));
}
```

When embedding the Flash SWF document in FBML rendering mode, it will automatically pass the Facebook session information into the SWF document for Flash to use the session to communicate with Facebook. In the constructor, we can get the Facebook session via loaderInfo.

```
public function Ch12_02() {
    if(loaderInfo.parameters.fb_sig_added == true){
        var session:FacebookSessionUtil=new
FacebookSessionUtil(loaderInfo.parameters.fb_sig_api_
key,null,loaderInfo);
        var fbook:Facebook=session.facebook;
        session.verifySession();
    }else{
            navigateToURL(new URLRequest("http://www.facebook.com/login.
php?api_key="+loaderInfo.parameters.fb_sig_api_key),"_top");
    }
    ...
}
```

The following screenshot shows how the Flash virtual world is integrated into the Facebook page:

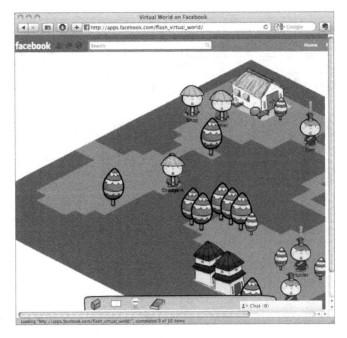

Using iFrame rendering inside Facebook

While using iFrame rendering, Facebook is not responsible to fetch the web pages for us anymore. The Facebook canvas provides us with an iFrame and the browser fetches the web pages inside it. The following graph shows the relationship among the client's computer, Facebook, web server, and the socket server.

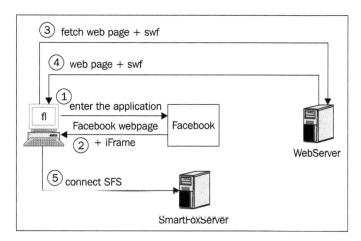

In iFrame rendering, Facebook passes the Facebook session information into iFrame by appending it in the URL query string. Facebook will not process our Flash embedding inside the iFrame page. Therefore, we need to pass the Facebook session from query string into the Flash virtual world ourselves.

```
<body>
    <script type="text/javascript">

        //define your flashVars from the URL GET string
        var flashVars = {};
        var strHref = window.location.href;
        if ( strHref.indexOf("?") > -1 ) {
            var strQueryString = strHref.substr(strHref.
                                            indexOf("?")+1);
            var aQueryString = strQueryString.split("&");
            for ( var iParam = 0; iParam < aQueryString.length;
                                                    iParam++ ) {
                var aParam = aQueryString[iParam].split("=");
                flashVars[aParam[0]] = aParam[1];
            }
        }
    //create your instance of your SWF
        swfobject.embedSWF("ch12_02.swf", "virtualworld", "760",
                "600", "10.0.0", "expressInstall.swf", flashVars);
    </script>
```

```
        <div id="virtualworld"></div>

</body>
```

Authorizing a Facebook account

The user session information is passed to Flash via `flashvars` parameters.

```
if (loaderInfo.parameters.fb_sig_added == undefined) {
    // do nothing when the flash is compiled from Flash IDE
}
else if(loaderInfo.parameters.fb_sig_added == true){
    var session:FacebookSessionUtil=new FacebookSessionUtil(loaderInfo.
parameters.fb_sig_api_key,null,loaderInfo);
    _fb=session.Facebook;
    session.addEventListener(FacebookEvent.CONNECT,onConnect);
    session.verifySession();
}else{
    navigateToURL(new URLRequest("http://www.Facebook.com/login.
php?api_key="+loaderInfo.parameters.fb_sig_api_key),"_top");
}
```

In our first example, we try to simply put the Flash virtual world inside the Facebook platform. Therefore, we leave the `onConnect` function as a placeholder.

```
private function onConnect(e:FacebookEvent):void {
    if(e.success){
        trace("Connected Facebook");
    }
    else{
        trace("Failed to connect to Facebook");
    }
}
```

Getting the profile name and picture from Facebook

We are going to fetch the basic profile information and display it as login name and the profile information panel.

After the connection between Flash and Facebook is established, we fetch the square profile picture and the name from Facebook.

```
private function onConnect(e:FacebookEvent):void {
    if(e.success){
            var fbcall:FacebookCall=_fb.post(new GetInfo([_
fb.uid],[GetInfoFieldValues.PIC_SQUARE,GetInfoFieldValues.NAME]));
            fbcall.addEventListener(FacebookEvent.COMPLETE, onGetInfo);
    }
}
```

The Adobe Facebook API will trace every Facebook request for debug use. We can take a look at the Restful URL request of the `users.getInfo` command.

```
http://api.Facebook.com/restserver.php
?uids=100001017913437
&api_key=3fe38aa87a48b6416458afa3daee40d5
&method=users.getInfo
&sig=46b367dd97079edf462d5790e661cad7
```

```
&session_key=2.
tH8YdlQiDZvPn4Dd0o7Zjg__.3600.1271516400-100001017913437
&fields=pic_square,name
&ss=true&v=1.0
&call_id=12715119668660
```

While posting an unfamiliar Facebook call, we should take a look at the Facebook
Developer Wiki. For example, we can get the whole document of the parameters and
result of the `users.getInfo` command on `http://wiki.developers.Facebook.`
`com/index.php/Users.getInfo`. It contains detailed description on the command
and the input/output of the API function to let us know how to use it.

The parameters in the URL match the document of the command from the Facebook
Developer Wiki. The fields contain what we want to get from Facebook. They are
`pic_square` and `name`.

Facebook returns the result in XML format:

```
<?xml version="1.0" encoding="UTF-8"?>
<users_getInfo_response xmlns="http://api.Facebook.com/1.0/"
xmlns:xsi="http://www.w3.org/2001/XMLSchema-instance"
xsi:schemaLocation="http://api.Facebook.com/1.0/ http://api.Facebook.
com/1.0/Facebook.xsd" list="true">
  <user>
    <name>Steven Mak</name>
    <uid>100001017913437</uid>
    <pic_square>http://profile.ak.fbcdn.net/hprofile-ak-sf2p/hs273.snc
3/23222_100001017913437_530_q.jpg</pic_square>
  </user>
</users_getInfo_response>
```

The Facebook client API will parse the returning XML result and pack it into an
ActionScript object for us to use. We fill the returning name in the username text
field of the login box. We will store the profile picture for later use.

```
private function onGetInfo(e:FacebookEvent):void {
    // remove the event listener after completed the request.
    e.target.removeEventListener(FacebookEvent.COMPLETE, onGetInfo);
    if(e.success){
          var user:FacebookUser = (e.data as GetInfoData).
userCollection.getItemAt(0) as FacebookUser;
```

```
        loginBox.nameInput.text = user.name;
        Myself.instance.profilePic = user.pic_square;
    }
}
```

 As we will have different event handlers to listen to the
FacebookEvent.COMPLETE event for different purposes,
we need to remove the event listener after completing the
Facebook request.

The URL of the profile picture is stored in user variables so that every client in the
same room can get the profile picture of the user and display it.

```
    params.profilePic = Myself.instance.profilePic;
```

In the player's information panel, we will use Loader to load the profile picture and
display it in the panel.

```
var profilePic:String = targetUser.getVariable('profilePic');
if (profilePic != undefined || profilePic != '') {
    _loader = new Loader();
    _loader.contentLoaderInfo.addEventListener(Event.COMPLETE,
                                        profilePicLoaded);
    _loader.load(new URLRequest(profilePic));
}
private function profilePicLoaded(e:Event):void {
    this.profile_pic.addChild(_loader);
}
```

Getting friends list from Facebook

We implemented the buddy list by using the SmartFoxServer's buddy feature in a
previous chapter. Users add those buddies when they meet each other inside the
virtual world.

Thanks to the integration of the Facebook, we can get the friends list of the players and add them into the buddy list automatically. We create two tabs in the buddy list panel, one tab of the original buddy list and the other tab for the friends list from Facebook.

Similar to the `getInfo` command, we create a new `FacebookCall` to call the friend list.

```
var fbcall:FacebookCall = FacebookClient.fb.post(new GetFriends());
fbcall.addEventListener(FacebookEvent.COMPLETE, onFriendsLoad);

FacebookClient.fb.post(fbcall);
```

The friend list returns the user IDs of the friends and we need to fetch the name from the user IDs.

```
private function onFriendsLoad(e:FacebookEvent):void {
    e.target.removeEventListener(FacebookEvent.COMPLETE,
onFriendsLoad);
    if (e.success){
        var friends:Array = (e.data as GetFriendsData).friends.source;

        var uids:Array = [];
        for (var i:uint=0;i<friends.length;i++) {
            uids.push(friends[i].uid);
        }
        var fbcall:GetInfo = new GetInfo(uids, [GetInfoFieldValues.
                                        NAME]);
        fbcall.addEventListener(FacebookEvent.COMPLETE,
                                onFriendsGetInfo);
```

```
        FacebookClient.fb.post(fbcall);
    }
}
```

After fetching the friends' name, we store them into an array for the rendering
function to display them.

```
private function onFriendsGetInfo(e:FacebookEvent):void {
    e.target.removeEventListener(FacebookEvent.COMPLETE,
                                 onFriendsGetInfo);
    if (e.success){
        _fbFriends =(e.data as GetInfoData).userCollection.
                                              toArray();
    }
}
```

The displayBuddyRows originally displays the buddies' information in the buddy
list. We now use the same method to display the Facebook friend list.

```
private function displayBuddyRows(source.String):void {
    /* remove all existing elements in the buddy list area */
    while(_buddyRows.numChildren>0) {
        _buddyRows.removeChildAt(0);
    }

    if (source == 'buddy')      {
        /* original buddy list code */
    }
    else if (source == 'friend_list') {
        this.scrollbar.maxScrollPosition = _fbFriends.length-6;
        for(var i=0;i<_fbFriends.length;i++) {
            var row = new BuddyRow();
            _buddyRows.addChild(row);
            row.txtName.text = _fbFriends[i].name;

            row.y = i*row.height;
            _buddyRowHeight = row.height;

        }
    }
}
```

Facebook provides us with the online status of a Facebook user. We can query
the online status of the friends by using **Facebook Query Language**. The FQL is
something similar to the SQL that we can use to construct a query string to fetch
resources from Facebook.

The Facebook developers page contains the full usage guide of FQL:
http://developers.facebook.com/docs/reference/fql/.

The following FQL gets the list of online friends:

```
SELECT uid FROM user WHERE
online_presence IN ('active', 'idle')
AND uid IN (
SELECT uid2 FROM friend WHERE uid1 = user_id
);
```

We extend our previous example to further query the list of online friends from Facebook.

```
private function onFriendsGetInfo(e:FacebookEvent):void {
    e.target.removeEventListener(FacebookEvent.COMPLETE,
onFriendsGetInfo);
    if (e.success){
        _fbFriends =(e.data as GetInfoData).userCollection.
                                        toArray();


        /* load the online list */
        var fql:String = "SELECT uid FROM user WHERE online_presence
IN ('active', 'idle') AND uid IN ( SELECT uid2 FROM friend WHERE uid1
= "+ FacebookClient.fb.uid +")";
        var fbcall:FqlQuery = new FqlQuery(fql);
        fbcall.addEventListener(FacebookEvent.COMPLETE,
                                    onGotOnlineList);
        FacebookClient.fb.post(fbcall);
    }
}
```

As we are fetching data from Facebook by using FQL, the schema of the result XML varies depending on the query. We will get the data by accessing the XML directly and save the user ID of the online friends into array.

```
private function onGotOnlineList(e:FacebookEvent):void {
    e.target.removeEventListener(FacebookEvent.COMPLETE,
                                onGotOnlineList);
    if (e.success){
        var results : XML = new XML( e.data.rawResult );
        namespace fb = "http://api.Facebook.com/1.0/";
        use namespace fb;
        var friends = new XMLList( results..user );
        for each (var friend in friends) {
            _fbOnlineFriends.push(friend.uid);
        }
```

```
        }
    updateList();
}
```

In the friend list rendering function, we check each friend to see if it exists in the online list and set the online status bubble to green.

```
private function displayBuddyRows(source:String):void {
/* remove all existing elements in the buddy list area */
    while(_buddyRows.numChildren>0) {
        _buddyRows.removeChildAt(0);
    }

    if (source == 'buddy') {
        /* original buddy list code */
    }
    else if (source == 'friend_list') {
        this.scrollbar.maxScrollPosition = _fbFriends.length-6;
        for(var i=0;i<_fbFriends.length;i++) {
            /* show friend list code */

            /* if this is in the online list, we show it as
                                            online */
            for each(var friendId in _fbOnlineFriends) {
                if (_fbFriends[i].uid == friendId) {
                    row.stateBubble.gotoAndStop(2);
                    break;
                }
            }
        }
    }
}
```

Update the Facebook status

Facebook status is a place where we can share what is in our mind or what we are doing. People like to know what their friends are doing or thinking lately. We have implemented something similar in our buddy list system so that players can share a line of their latest status. We can extend that field to Facebook status.

In order to update the Facebook status via the API, we need to grant an extra permission from the players.

We grant the permission of using the user info and friends data when the user joins the virtual world in Facebook for the first time. However, that permission does not allow the application to publish further information. We need to grant an extended permission. There are several extended permissions where we can ask the users to authorize the application to perform. Most of the extended permissions are related to automatically content posting and reading via API such as status, news, and photo albums. A detailed document of the available extended permission can be found from the Facebook Developer Wiki.

```
http://wiki.developers.Facebook.com/index.php/Extended_permissions
```

We first check if the application has the permission to update the status.

```
/* check if the app has permission to post status update */
var fbcall = new HasAppPermission(HasAppPermissionValues.STATUS_
                                  UPDATE);
fbcall.addEventListener(FacebookEvent.COMPLETE,
                        onGotHasAppPermission);
_fb.post(fbcall);
```

A window asking for the permission will pop up.

```
private function onGotHasAppPermission(e:FacebookEvent):void {
    e.target.removeEventListener(FacebookEvent.COMPLETE,
                                 onGotHasAppPermission);
    if (!e.data.value) {
            /* grant required permission for the application to perform
further actions in Facebook */
            _fb.grantExtendedPermission(ExtendedPermissionValues.STATUS_
                                        UPDATE);
    }
}
```

☐ **Allow status updates from Virtual World?**

Virtual World will be able to update your Facebook status on an ongoing basis.

You will be able to change this setting from the Edit applications page.

[Allow status updates] or Leave application

When players close the profile information panel, we send the emotion message to Facebook status.

```
private function clickCloseBtn(e:MouseEvent):void {
    if (_username == SmartFox.sfs.myUserName) {
            /* original set buddy emotion code */

            /* Set the emotion message to the Facebook status */
            var fbcall:SetStatus = new SetStatus(this.
    txtInputEmotionMessage.text,false,true,FacebookClient.fb.uid);
            fbcall.addEventListener(FacebookEvent.COMPLETE,
                                    onSetStatus);
            FacebookClient.fb.post(fbcall);

    }
    parent.removeChild(this);
}
```

Refresh the Facebook page and then we can verify that the Facebook status is successfully being set to the emotional message from the virtual world.

Steven Mak is playing in the Flash virtual world inside Facebook now.

2 seconds ago via Virtual World · Comment · Like

Sending news feed to Facebook

News feed in Facebook shows what friends are doing. Any actions from friends will become news feed in Facebook. It can be a friend updated the album, comment on other friends, playing a game in Facebook, or anything. We can make use of news feed to let players share their latest information inside the virtual world. For example, we can let players post news when they finish a quest.

In order to publish news feed via API, we need the `publish_stream` permission. The permission of publishing stream is a super set of the update status permission we just used. Therefore, granting the permission of the publishing stream will also allow us to update the status.

```
_fb.grantExtendedPermission("publish_stream");
```

We will pop up a dialog when we finish a quest. The dialog asks the players whether they want to publish this news or not. Players can also leave comments on the news.

```
private function onComplete(e:FacebookEvent):void {
    /* code to send extension to server */

    /* Let player publish the story */
    var dialog = new social.NewsFeedDialog();
    _stage.addChild(dialog);
}
```

When players click on the **Post** button, we pack the news feed and comments, and publish the post via Facebook API. We can post a rich content news feed by providing images or even videos in the attachment parameters.

```
private function onClickedPost(e:MouseEvent):void {
    var attachment:Object = {
            'caption': '{*actor*} finish the quest in Flash Virtual
                                                    World',
            'description': 'A world that let you and your friends
explore in real time',
            'media': [{ 'type': 'image', 'src': 'http://flashtut.net/
virtualworld/attachment.jpg', 'href': 'http://apps.Facebook.com/flash_
virtual_world/'}]
            };

    var fbcall:PublishPost = new PublishPost(txtComment.
                                    text,attachment);
    FacebookClient.fb.post(fbcall);

    parent.removeChild(this);
}
```

When players choose to skip the posting, we just close the dialog without doing anything.

```
private function onClickedClose(e:MouseEvent):void {
    parent.removeChild(this);
}
```

After posting the news feed, the news and the comment appear on the user's Facebook wall. Other friends can also read this message from the Facebook page and they can join the virtual world by clicking the virtual world image.

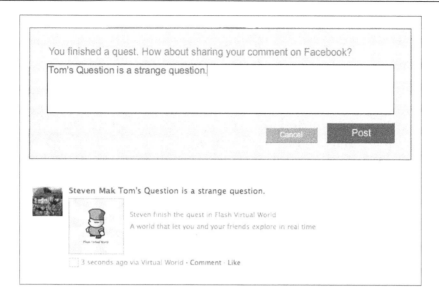

Reading news feed into the virtual world

Inside an online social community, users want to know what their friends are doing. News feed is one of the sources that friends can share what they did recently or what they think is interesting. The news feed is displayed on the front page of the Facebook account by default. We can fetch the news feed from the API and display them inside the Flash virtual world. We will further filter the news feed to only display friends' news feed which is related to the Flash virtual world application.

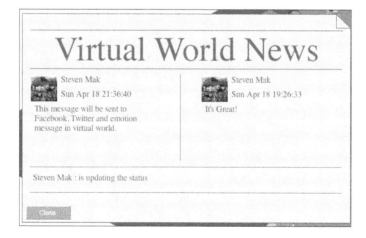

In order to fetch the news feed from the API, we need to grant another permission from the user.

```
_fb.grantExtendedPermission("read_stream");
```

We will use the GetStream class to fetch the news feed stream. There is a parameter to filter the fetching result. We can pass the app_ApplicationID to filter the result with the specific application only. Here my application ID of the Flash virtual world is 10910600246265, and the filter parameter is app_10910600246265. You should have another application ID when creating your own Facebook application.

```
private function readNewsFeed():void {
    var fbcall:GetStream = new GetStream(FacebookClient.fb.uid,null,
                            null,null,30,'app_109106002462653');
    fbcall.addEventListener(FacebookEvent.COMPLETE, onGotNewsFeed);
    FacebookClient.fb.post(fbcall);
}
```

The result data is in GetStreamData structure. We can get the news feed content from stories and related users information from profiles. According to our newspaper layout, we will display the actor's profile picture of the news feed and also the dates and content from the latest two news feed. Then we display the headline of the third news feed.

```
private function onGotNewsFeed(e:FacebookEvent):void {
    e.target.removeEventListener(FacebookEvent.COMPLETE,
                            onGotNewsFeed);
    var i:int = 1;
    if (e.success){
        var data:Array = (e.data as GetStreamData).stories.
                            toArray();
        var profiles = (e.data as GetStreamData).profiles;
        for each(var streamData:StreamData in data)     {
            var profile = profiles.findItemByProperty('id',stream
                            Data.actor_id);

            if (i <= 2){
                this['txtName'+i].text = profile.name;
                this['txtDate'+i].text = streamData.updated_
                                    time;
                this['txtContent'+i].text = streamData.
                                    message;
                if (profile.pic_square != undefined &&
                    profile.pic_square != '')
                {
                    this['_loader'+i] = new Loader();
```

```
            //this['_loader'+i].contentLoaderInfo.addEventListener(Event.
                                      COMPLETE, profilePicLoaded);
      this['_loader'+i].load(new URLRequest(profile.pic_square));
      this['profilePic'+i].addChild(this['_loader'+i]);
                    }
              }else{
      this['txtContent3'].text = profile.name + " : " + streamData.
   message;
                  }

                  i++;
            }
      }
}
```

Capture a screenshot and share to a Facebook album

Letting players capture screenshot of the Flash virtual world can further increase the exposure of the virtual world.

Facebook requires every application to grant permission from users in order to upload photos. We had granted the permission publish_stream from users in the news feed example. The publish_stream also includes the permission of uploading photos and videos so that we do not need to grant extra permission again in this example.

The Flash player environment limits the file access. We cannot save the encoded JPEG directly into the filesystem from the Flash player in the browser. Instead, we will directly post the encoded JPG binary data to Facebook by the UploadPhoto command. We format our name to the current time so that the filenames will not be conflicted with each other.

```
   private function uploadScreenshot(e:MouseEvent) {
      var jpgSource:BitmapData = new BitmapData (stage.width, stage.
   height);
      jpgSource.draw(stage);
      var jpgEncoder:JPGEncoder = new JPGEncoder(90);
      var jpgStream:ByteArray = jpgEncoder.encode(jpgSource);

      _fb.post(new UploadPhoto(jpgStream, null, 'Flash Virtual World : '
   + new Date().getTime(),null)) as UploadPhoto;
   }
```

We can verify the snapshot feature by clicking the snapshot button and refresh the Facebook Photos page to see if the current virtual world screen is uploaded to the Facebook album.

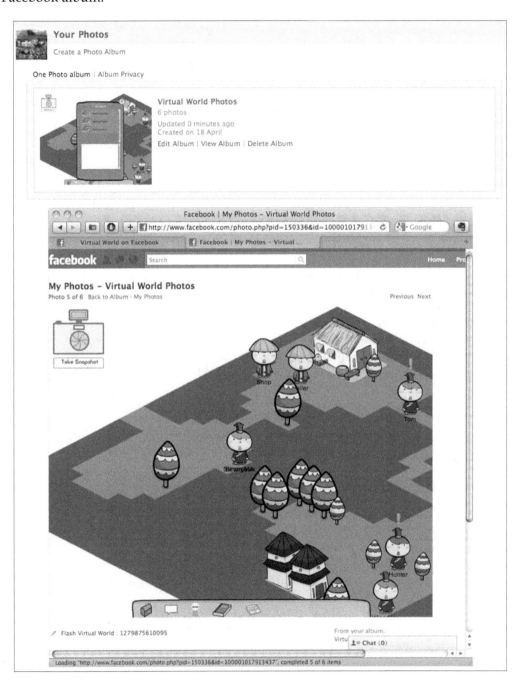

Integrating the Twitter platform

Twitter is a simple yet popular social network service that asks a simple question, "What are you doing?" Friends and followers will then have their conversation related to this topic.

We are going to demonstrate another approach of communicating with the social networking API. We will use the extension approach with the help of Java extension.

We need to set up the Twitter API by:

1. Download the `jTwitter.jar` class from `http://www.winterwell.com/software/jtwitter.php`.

2. Place the `jTwitter.jar` file in `SmartFoxServer Installation Directory | Server` folder.

3. Edit the `start.sh` file in the `Server` folder to add `jtwitter.jar` into the classpath.

Publish latest virtual world news in Twitter

We are getting back to the emotion message that we used for updating the Facebook status. We are not trying to post the same emotion message to Twitter. Unlike the Adobe Facebook API, Twitter sets a more restrictive access from Flash player. Therefore, we are going to use the server-side extension and the Java Twitter API to access the Twitter social network service.

```
/* send the emotion message to Twitter, if there exists  */
if (TwitterClient.isUsingTwitter) {
    var params = {};
    params.login = TwitterClient.twitter.login;
    params.password = TwitterClient.twitter.password;
    params.message = this.txtInputEmotionMessage.text;
    SmartFox.sfs.sendXtMessage("virtualWorld", "updateTwitterStatus",
                              params, "json");
}
```

In the server-side extension, we access the Java Twitter client by using the advanced extension technique of accessing Java class inside the ActionScript extension. We connect Twitter in server-side by providing the player's login name, password, and the message to be sent.

```
function hupdateTwitterStatus(cmd, param, user, fromRoom) {
    var res = {};
    res.cmd = cmd;
```

```
var twitter = new Packages.winterwell.jtwitter.Twitter(param.
                                        login,param.password);
twitter.setStatus(param.message);

sendResponseBack(res, user);
}
```

If the code works correctly, the same emotion message will be posted to both the Facebook platform and Twitter.

Choosing the right social network service

There are so many social network sites existing now on the Internet. We need to pick the right one to integrate with. Every social network service has its own characteristics. Choosing the right one to match the features and the characteristics enhances the effect. For example, if the virtual world focuses on friendship then Facebook will be a suitable one; if making funny screenshots is part of the virtual world, letting players share their screenshots on Facebook album and Flickr will be good; if the virtual world links real location in the game play, integrating the Four Square, a location-based social network service will be fun.

Summary

Social network services are so hot now on the Internet that people's behaviors are influenced by their friends on social networks. Integrating the Flash virtual world with social networking features can help to spread the virtual world. News and screenshots of the virtual world will spread from one friend to other friends and increase the exposure.

There are too many social networking services to cover all of them. We just discussed several key features of Facebook and Twitter. As almost all social network services provide API for third-party developers, similar techniques can be applied to integrating the Flash virtual world into other social networks.

We have discussed and created a very basic Flash virtual world in the previous chapters. In the next chapter, we will discuss the deployment and maintenance of the virtual world. We will also have a brief introduction on how we can extend our virtual world into other platforms that SmartFoxServer supports.

13
Deploying and Maintaining Flash Virtual World

We have built a Flash virtual world throughout the book. We are getting close to deploying the virtual world in production environment. There are some other topics that are useful after creating the entire virtual world.

What is the next step. We will see how to scale the virtual world to meet the high loading requirement. We will also compare different hosting solutions to host the socket server.

After several months of effort put into the virtual world, we want to find out how we can earn money by operating the virtual world. We will discuss several sources of making money from the virtual world.

Hosting the virtual world

After creating the Flash virtual world, our next issue will be finding a server to host it. As it requires the process execution of the socket server and the use of socket binding, we cannot host SmartFoxServer in the normal web hosting plan. We have two options of hosting. We can either host on hosting that is designed to support SmartFoxServer or hosting that allows us to execute a socket server process.

Hosting that supports SmartFoxServer

Shockwave Server hosting (http://www.shockwaveserver.com/) is the hosting partner of SmartFox that provides hosting that has the SmartFoxServer ready for running. The benefit of using it is that we almost do not need to set up anything to plug in the virtual world code and run on the hosting.

Hosting SmartFoxServer in dedicated server

We can also apply for the hosting of dedicated server or **Virtual Private Server (VPS)** hosting. Renting dedicated server or VPS means we have full control of the server that can run anything under the hosting agreement. We can set up the Java Runtime Environment and SmartFoxServer ourselves and configure the port in firewall to get it to work. VPS and dedicated server usually charge from 10 dollars to several hundred dollars depending on the server setting. SmartFoxServer uses around 600 MB-800 MB RAM and I would suggest using the dedicated server hosting that comes with around 1GB RAM or more.

Media Temple (http://mediatemple.net/webhosting/dv/) provides virtual dedicated hosting where users can switch between the $50, $100, and $150 plan at anytime to adapt the usage of the SmartFoxServer.

The Planet (http://www.theplanet.com/) hosting provides dedicated server hosting so that users can choose one of their server configurations and rent the server for several hundred dollars per month.

Another approach is to put our own physical server in the data center. It will be around several hundred per month. The benefit of using our own server is that we can take control of everything, including the hardware configuration. However, it requires more advanced server hosting techniques.

Some data center provides the Apple Mac mini server hosting service. Hosting such as Mac Mini collocation (http://www.macminicolo.net/) and Mac Mini World (http://www.macminiworld.net/) lets users rent a Mac Mini in their data center or ship their own Mac Mini to the data center. The staff will then set up the Mac Mini for the users to remote control them. Beacuse SmartFoxServer can host in Mac OS, it is a nice solution for hosting the server.

Hosting SmartFoxServer in cloud service

Cloud service is a kind of Internet-based computing service that is flexible and scalable at a reasonable price. In contrast to the dedicated server, we are not renting a physical machine. We rent the computing service from the cloud service provider. We can then launch an instance and host the virtual world.

The benefit of the cloud computing service is the flexibility to start/stop the hosting and scale up or down at any time. The cloud service provides charge only on the up time of the instance. That means we can launch the SmartFoxServer for several hours for testing in development and we only pay for that several hours instead of a whole month. After deploying the server in production, we can choose from charge per minute or charge per month.

Rackspace Cloud (`http://www.rackspacecloud.com/`) and Amazon Elastic Compute Cloud (`http://aws.amazon.com/ec2/`) are two cloud service providers. They both provide similar pricing and features.

There is a preconfigured Amazon Machine Image with SmartFoxServer Pro set up in Ubuntu OS. We can use this image in the Amazon Elastic Compute Cloud.

Comparing the hosting solution

The three approaches come with their own advantages and different requirements on administrating the hosting. The following table compares the three hosting solutiona:

	Shockwave hosting	VPS/Dedicated server	Cloud computing
Setup fee	$900 - $2600	Mostly Free	Mostly Free
Cost monthly	$80 - $110	$10 - $500	$20 $600
Long term contract	1 year required	Mostly no	Mostly no
Pay monthly	Yes	Yes	Yes (optional)
Pay on demand	No	No	Yes
SmartFoxServer installation	Pre-installed	DIY	DIY
Hosting administration difficulty	Low	Medium	High

Scaling up the virtual world

After deploying the virtual world, the user base will keep growing. When the virtual world spreads and gets popular, the increasing traffic and large amount of simultaneous player connections may push the limit of the server capacity. Hence, we will need to scale up the backend infrastructure at that time.

When scaling up the backend with multiple server instances, we need to set up some load balancing mechanisms. We may either create parallel instances of the virtual world or extend the virtual world with clustering technology.

The article *Building MMO Virtual Worlds* from SmartFoxServer documentation provides a comprehensive guide to scale up the SmartFoxServer-based virtual worlds (`http://smartfoxserver.com/docs/docPages/articles/build_mmo_p2.htm`).

Earning money from the virtual world

Creating a virtual world often means putting money into development for months or years. We need to earn from the virtual world after deployment in production to cover the cost. There are several common ways to earn money from the virtual world.

Google AdSense

Google AdSense is the advertising system for web publishers. **AdSense for Content** will display advertising on the website of the virtual world. We earn money when the players visit the virtual world website and click on the advertisement.

In-game advertisement

Instead of advertising on the website, we can put ads inside the game. It can be a billboard on some advertisement painting on the wall of the buildings. It can also be a virtual item. Imagine that drinking a Coke can recharge the health point quicker than drinking water. Then we find a Coke company to pay some advertising fee to put their logo on the item.

The following screenshot shows the Sony BMG in-game advertisement from Second Life:

Monthly subscription

We can charge the players monthly for playing in the virtual world. Normally the virtual world would let players try the virtual world free for a certain time and then limit the features until the players subscribe to the monthly plan to unlock all features.

We can use the Paypal subscription or ClickBank Recurring Billing to charge the players monthly.

Point-based subscription

The mechanism of point-based subscript is like the pre-paid SIM card. Players buy a card that contains points. The points reduce while the players play in the virtual world. The advantage of point-based compared to the monthly subscription is that players pay more to play more and pay less to play less. It is not bounded by a time period. It is the players' freedom to pay the playing time in the virtual world.

MyCard (`http://mall.fujiya-mit.com/index.php?app=goods&id=7`) is a point-based card system and the buyer can refill their account with the value inside the card and convert the point into virtual currency. The virtual currency can then be used in several virtual worlds and online services including the virtual items inside Facebook.

Selling virtual items and virtual currency

The biggest earning business model currently in the online game industry is selling virtual items.

Many online games and virtual worlds now provide free game play without any subscription. The low cost entry points attract players playing in the virtual world and then the company charges the players for buying advanced virtual items. People are willing to pay for virtual clothes to decorate their avatars inside the virtual world. The following screenshot from WeRule for iPhone, virtual items shop requires players to pay virtual gold, which can trade with real money, to build extra buildings:

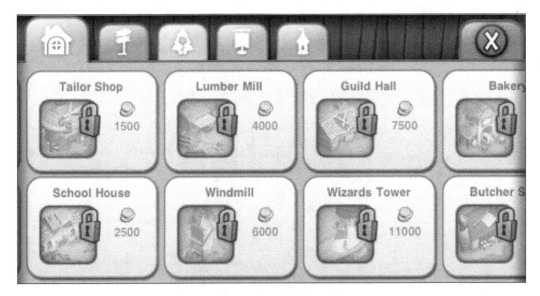

Operating the virtual world

Operating the virtual world decides the success and failure after development. A good developed product without good promotion will not sell well. On the other hand, a normal quality product with a good promotion and operation will sell enough to earn money.

Tracking the cost of maintaining a Flash virtual world

There are several costs that we need to know while running the Flash virtual world. Some of the costs charge us monthly while some are one-off payment. We need to calculate carefully if we have a health business model to maintain the Flash virtual world without losing our money.

Paying the hosting fee

The hosting fee for socket server is usually much expensive than normal web hosting. The costs depend on the number of players. If there are few players, a virtual private server for around $50 a month may be enough. If there are thousands of players in the virtual world, we may need some high profile server that would cost several hundred monthly. This expense will keep summing up and we will need to rent more machines for clustering the servers for even more players.

Therefore, it is important to establish an earning business model so that we can earn more while many players are playing. Otherwise, the whole business fails, as earnings from the virtual world cannot cover the monthly hosting fee.

Licensing the Socket server

We introduced several Socket servers for Flash in an earlier chapter. The SmartFoxServer, Electro Server, or Flash Media Server charge for the license. Take SmartFoxServer as an example—it costs around 200 Euro to 2000 Euro per license. We also need to multiply this cost by the number of servers when scaling up.

Hiring customer service

Usually, we need to hire some game master for providing customer service. The customer service will be in charge of replying to the players' e-mails or forum posts. They will also be the moderator in the virtual world to provide some basic maintenance such as kicking an abnormal user's connection and helping players inside the virtual world. The cost depends on the normal industry hourly rate of different countries, and this is a cost that will be charged monthly.

Losing players

Normally, the number of players is proportional to the money we earn from the virtual world. Losing players means we will be earning less money. There are several points that often cause the dramatic loss of players. We need to be aware of these aspects.

Losing players at sign up process

The first barrier for the players is the process from knowing the virtual world to completing the sign up. Players may encounter different types of problems while signing up for an account such as losing the activation confirmation e-mail, not passing the robot checking code, or leaving due to loss of patience for filling out a large sign up form.

We may have some usability tests before launching the virtual world to find out some problems but often the big issues appear after launch.

We will discuss the analysis method that will help us to find out the drop-off point of a process in the next section. We can then use the analysis result to know where to improve the sign up process.

Losing players at a certain level

While leveling may not be perfect during the designing stage, players will encounter an abnormal barrier at a certain level plus the constant failure on certain quests may discourage the players a lot and this can cause them to leave the virtual world. In the next section, we will discuss some logging and data mining methods to keep track of players' behavior to improve the leveling and prevent this problem.

Losing players after updates

Usually we need to keep updating the virtual world to make it fresh. While we are modifying the virtual world, some new settings may make existing players uncomfortable. And it will finally lead to the loss of existing players who are not satisfied with the new policy.

We should roll out the update gradually at a smooth pace. Changing the setting dramatically cannot make players adapt the new policy or updates and may discourage them from continuing to play in the virtual world.

Losing players due to the low quality

The ultimate reason for losing players is due to a low quality of the virtual world. It can be low quality of the user interface design, low quality of the game play design, or low quality of anything in the virtual world.

In this case, we may need to do a survey of the players to know what they think. We may also need to read from Internet to track any comments from the virtual world. After knowing the problems, we need to fix them, improve them, and then market hard to promote the updated version or even rebrand the virtual world to sell again.

Product lining

While losing players is sometimes unpreventable, we can try to keep the players with the help another virtual world. Instead of operating one and only one virtual world, we can try putting effort into making several virtual worlds with different themes and game plays. Different virtual worlds may target different types of customers.

Let's take a look at the Shanda Interactive Entertainment Limited, one of the world's leading online interactive media companies in China. They are currently operating 15 massive multiplayer online games and 15 others casual game platforms. The wide range of virtual world products helps to transfer losing players from one virtual world into the other. And finally, these players are all paying money to the same company.

Analyzing players actions on a virtual world

We are not free after deploying the virtual world in the market. When players are playing in the virtual world, they will generate a lot of useful data to help us improve the virtual world.

Tracking players actions with funnel analysis

Funnel analysis is an analysis method on some predefined flows. The flow can be a sign up process of a new player, the training process for newbie, the progress of quests, or the buying process of the virtual item. There are many steps in each flow. Players may fail or give up the whole process during each step. Funnel analysis provides information such as the conversion rate and where the players give up the process most of the time.

Mix Panel (http://mixpanel.com) is one of the funnel analysis tools; we can use their API at the track point inside the virtual world to track those data to Mix Panel. It will output the metrics and provide a useful graph to illustrate where the drop-off happens.

The following graph illustrates a sample of funnel analysis on the sign-up process. There is a drop-off from filling the sign up form to robot checking steps. The rate drop of 40 percent may imply that we have done something wrong in the **Robot Checking** step. May be if the checking is too harsh then even human cannot recognize the code and pass the checking. Or maybe it fails to load the checking image sometimes. Our further action is to recheck the step and find out the reason for the low completion rate of that step.

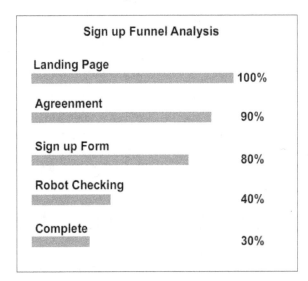

Data mining

Players' actions generate a lot of useful data. Funnel analysis will track the success rate of the flows. We also need to log others data from the actions for data mining to mine useful information to improve our virtual world.

Gathering useful information

What data is useful for data mining? We have mentioned the players' actions. Besides that, we can also analyze the frequency and content of players seeking help from the game master. If there is a similar question that is raised by players repeatedly, it is most likely there is something not good enough there.

We can also track the buying record of virtual items or any other payment. Usually we want to know how frequently players are paying on the items and where they buy the virtual items if they sell in more then one place.

Another data that we often want to get is how many items or how much money has been generated by the system. We need a track of this data because it is generated from system without much trade-off and it will easily make the virtual world unbalanced after running for months.

Logging the data

There are two types of loggings. We can log the data by events that are triggered by action or we can log the data at every certain time.

When there is event-driven logging, we can set the event on actions that we are interested in. The event will be triggered when players do the actions and we can then log them into our database.

We can either log the raw data into database such as:

Makzan bought a magic scroll at zone A with 50 dollars.

Or we can log the increment of an acuminated amount of the action, such as:

Amount of magic scroll at Zone A sold at 50 dollars: 132.

With raw data, we will need to analyze later to get the statistic data. On the other hand, the accumulated amount is already the statistic data.

With the logging that executes at every certain time, we can log statistic data that is not related to the player's action. For example, we may want to know how the players distribute in the virtual world. We can sum the players' count in different areas of the virtual world every hour. Then we will get to know how they distribute at different times. We can further sum the players' count into different level segments to see how at different levels players behave differently. If we find that there is an area that we designed for high-level players but the result is that only few high-level players go to that area, we know that something is wrong.

Both logging methods are useful so we should use both in the virtual world. However, there is trade-off for logging the data. The logging process itself requires the server computing power. It will be especially expensive if we log the data to the database every time. We can log the data in RAM in server-side and save them to the database at daily maintenance time.

After collecting the data, we can use a data-mining tool to help us analyze the data. Weka (`http://www.cs.waikato.ac.nz/ml/weka`) is an open source one among those data mini software.

While game designers are designing the game, they often assume that players will act in certain manner. However, the players will always do something unpredictable in reality. That's why we need to do data mining, to know how our players behave in the virtual world. It helps us know which quests are too difficult or which items are worthless for the players.

Rapid development with OpenSpace

We introduced the virtual world environment and the movement of the avatars in the beginning of the book. It is good for us to learn the fundamentals of the implementation methods and the design decision. However, when we look at the existing virtual world in detail, they are all using similar avatar movement and isometric perspective. These parts of implementation actually can be reused in different virtual world projects. We can boost up the development speed by applying some environment and movement engines to the project.

OpenSpace (`http://www.openspace-engine.com/`) is an isometric engine that's developed by the same company of SmartFoxServer and can fully be integrated into it.

OpenSpace comes with all basic features that an isometric engine should have such as view port panning, zooming, and 8-direction avatar's movement. Besides the basic features, there are several advanced features from this engine.

Editing with advanced map editor

The OpenSpace comes with an advanced map editor with which we can define the perspective of the isometric world and create objects and environment. We can configure the isometric world to work in 4-direction or 8-direction movement.

Moreover, we can edit the map in runtime. Other players will receive an event notification to reload the map after the moderator edits the map in runtime.

Raising the avatars from the flat platform

One notable feature from OpenSpace is the support of the tile elevation. The tile elevation enables us to extend the virtual world from isometric X/Y coordination to certain Z direction that gives the height to the world. The path finding function from OpenSpace also takes the elevation into calculation to provide fast and correct paths.

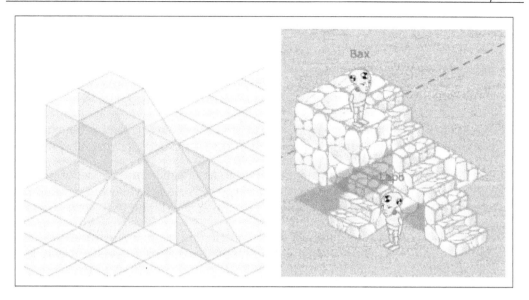

Creating custom tile events

Thanks to the custom tile behavior system, we can dispatch custom events on special tiles and control how the players' avatars interact with these tiles. For example, we can dispatch an event to animate the door opening effect while the avatar steps on the tile that is in front of the door.

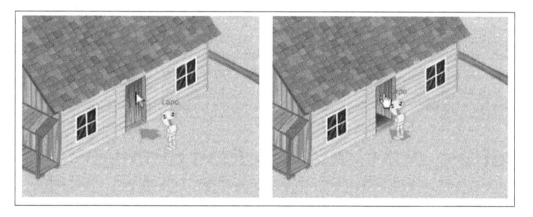

OpenSpace comes with a lot more handy features that greatly help in creating the Flash virtual world. It is worth giving it a try and even more considerably while using it along with the SmartFoxServer.

Updating and patching the virtual world

Flash virtual world is a kind of online service. The characteristic of online service is that the update is very easy so that we can keep updating the Flash virtual world with new features and bug fixes. When we are operating the virtual world, we get valuable data from players and know where to improve the virtual world.

We should keep developing the virtual world after deploying it. This will include bug fixes, improvement patches, and content updates such as quests or new area.

The World of Warcraft was originally designed to have a maximum 60 levels for the game characters and 300 quests. After operating the World of Warcraft for years with patches and expansions, there are now a maximum 85 levels and over 8000 quests.

Players want fresh new things when they are playing in the virtual world. Without updates and patches, a virtual world will soon be forgotten by players and may lead to a failure result.

Keeping an eye on the virtual world industry

There is a Chinese idiom from The Art of War saying:

> *"If you know both yourself and your enemy, you can win a hundred battles without a single loss."*

The online game and virtual world industry is changing every day. Many new online virtual worlds are released every month and old ones are being forgotten. Some virtual worlds can last for ten years while some close shortly after release. As a virtual world designer, we need to keep track of the latest industry news and know how the trend is going in order to create a world that lasts long.

Putting our virtual world in mobile

Mobile gaming is a big trend recently. Adobe has been working on putting full feature Flash player into mobile devices. Smartphone that runs android can use the Flash player 10.1. This makes it possible to extend our virtual world into any android mobile device. However, usually we cannot give users a good experience by directly playing the Flash games in mobile phone without any optimization. There are several limitations that we need to consider for running Flash in mobile devices.

Small screen size

The screen size of the mobile devices is usually very small compared to the desktop. It may range from 480x320 to 800x600. We cannot simply scale down everything to fit the screen size. All elements should be of a reasonable size so that they are recognizeable and can be touched. If the buttons are so small that the players can't touch them correctly, it will be useless.

Low RAM

RAM in mobile devices is often very low. We need to make sure we do not allocate a large block of RAM because it may make the system unstable or even crash.

Relatively slow CPU

The CPU in mobile is designed to run in low speed and consume less power for longer battery usage. We should avoid heavy loading of the CPU when designing the mobile version.

Limited network bandwidth

Flash virtual world establishes a connection with the socket server. The network bandwidth of the mobile network is an issue if the players does not have the unlimited data plan. We should at least warn the players of the high usage of the data plan network bandwidth on mobile phones.

Benefit of porting virtual world into mobile

Smart phone is becoming a new gaming platform. Porting the virtual world into mobile devices can encourage players to interact with friends inside the virtual world while they are on bus or sitting in café. The seamless integration of both mobile and desktop versions can help keeping players return to the virtual world.

Extending the virtual world to other platforms

SmartFoxServer is a real time socket server that was designed for Flash originally. After years of improvement from the SmartFoxServer team, it has become a generic socket server that can be used on different platforms. They now provide support on Java, .Net, Objective-C, and JavaScript. It is possible to build up similar real-time virtual worlds in Google Android, iPhone, and iPad platform. We can download the APIs from SmartFoxServer's API Central web page (`http://smartfoxserver.com/labs/API/`).

Apple iOS

With Objective-C client API, we can extend the virtual world to Apple iOS platform, which does not support Flash. Apple iOS platform has a large user base and has the ability of playing the virtual world on this platform, meaning we can reach a lot more potential players and generate more revenue from it.

.Net and Unity

Unity (http://unity3d.com/) is a 3D game engine that is free for publishing web-based 3D games. It also comes with paid version for deploying 3D games into other iPhone and Nintendo Wii. Unity uses the .Net networking library that is supported by SmartFoxServer. It means that we can create the online virtual world in Unity and interact with players in real-time by the SmartFoxServer. The ability of deploying the 3D virtual world in web browser and iPhone also means we can reach a large number of potential customers.

Java and Android

While we just discussed that we can put our Flash virtual world into Android's Flash player, we may also want to build the native Android virtual world with Java. The main difference with using Java in Android over Flash is that we can access the hardware on the device such as the tilt sensor and camera that can be used to enhance the game play experience in the virtual world.

Ajax

SmartFoxServer supports the JavaScript and HTML socket connection via the BlueBox HTTP tunneling techniques. BlueBox is an add-on module that tunnels all traffic between SmartFoxServer and clients into HTTP protocol.

There are some limitations to using JavaScript and HTML to connect SmartFoxServer due to the web browsers' settings. However, it will be useful sometimes when we want to deliver some kind of real-time interaction without requiring the Flash player. For example, we can implement a real-time notification and chatting system on the websites while the players are browsing for game information instead of playing in the Flash virtual world. It enables the users to keep connected to their buddies and friends inside the virtual world without loading Flash.

Summary

We have introduced the SmartFoxServer and developed the virtual world from the basic avatar movements to the inventory and quests system. We also discussed how the virtual world integrates with existing social network services to help players form their social community.

In this chapter, we discussed how to improve the virtual world from players' behavior by logging and data mining. We also glanced at the possibility of scaling the SmartFoxServer into clustering. We also compared different hosting solutions and their advantages.

Learning how to design and implement the Flash virtual world is just the beginning of the journey. The techniques from this book are the entry ticket to the virtual world industry. Traditional online virtual world has been hot for years but Flash and Flash in mobile is still relatively new. Running multiplayer virtual world in light-weight client such as Flash player and mobile devices is a coming trend after the traditional online games.

There are lots of possibilities to interact with multiplayer in real time. The imagination is unlimited and it will be my pleasure to see your virtual world launching.

Index

C

casual game design
  versus MMOG 29
ChatBox class 270
chat bubble
  displaying 254, 255
  scaling 255, 256
ChatBubble class 256
checkPortal function 209
choiceMessages, property name 294
choices, property name 294
Classname.getInstance() 163
Classname.instance 163
CLOSE_WAIT state 284
client-server network
  polling 15-17
  socket-based connection 17, 18
cloud computing 363
cloud service
  SmartFoxServer, hosting 362, 363
Club Penguin 30
collecting items
  quests, getting from 307
color_area 149
ColorTransform class 149
communication methods
  buddy list, implementing 256, 257
  by public messages 250
  by sending group messages 250
  by sending private messages 250
  by sending public messages 250
  chat bubble, displaying 254, 255
  chat bubble, scaling 255, 256
  communicatin,g, in real-time voice 250
  public chat channel 252, 253
completedList, property name 316
completeQuest command 313
complete_tom_question event 320
conditional branching 299
configuration file
  administration panel access to IP addresses,
    limiting 70, 71
  administrator login, setting 70
  administrator password, setting 70
  bots connections, blocking 70
  default names, assigning to users 73

idle user logouts, timers setting for 69
information separator, defining in raw
    protocol 72
IP addresses, binding to server 69
policy load data setting, from machines in
    other domains 69
port, listening for connections 69
room numbers in zone, limiting 73
room variables with room list requests,
    getting 74
server, configuring 68
structure 67, 68
user account, broadcasting 73
zone access, limiting 73
zone, configuring 72
zone information, displaying 71
zone moderators, setting 74
zone, naming 73
config.xml
  about 67
  new zone, creating 183
cooperative whiteboard
  creating 93-99
  testing 99
create block 238
createNPC server-side API call 281
create_time field 225
CustomizationPanel class 153

D

Daemon class, properties/functions
  name 315
  onAccept 315
  onRemove 315
  progress 315
  run 315
  status 315
daemons
  quest daemons, running 316-318
  running, for quest 312-315
daemons, property name 316
data flow, virtual world 336
data mining
  about 370
  logging, types 371
  useful information, gathering 370

hosting fee, paying 367
players, losing 368
players, losing after updates 368
players, losing at certain level 368
players, losing at sign up process 368
players, losing due to low quality 369
product lining 369
socket server, licensing 367
voice communication, problems
logging problem 251
message filtering problem 251
number of users, limitation 251
revisit problem 251
VPS/Dedicated server 363

W

waitingItemType 324
walkByPath function 167
WalkingAvatar class 166-170, 178-181, 212
walking function 181
walkPath array 166
walkTo function 168
walkTo method 170
WAMP
installing, on Windows 55
weapon item 220
Windows
JDK, installing 45
SmartFoxServer Pro, installing 49
SmartFoxServer, running 50
WAMP, installing 55
world
creating 160
scrolling 180
walking, by mouse click 178, 179

World class 161, 170, 209
world to explore
World of Warcraft
about 32, 33
URL 9

X

XML
about 38, 39
using 196

Z

z-index 199
zone
configuring 72
default names, assigning to users 73
logging into 91-93
moderators, setting 74
naming 73
new zone, creating in config.xml 183
room numbers, limiting 73
user account, broadcasting 73
zoneName parameter 282
Zone tag 256
z-order
about 199
rendering, for l-shaped buildings 201
rendering, for rectangle buildings 202
rendering, for square buildings 203
sorting, loop created 203, 204

**Thank you for buying
Flash Multiplayer Virtual Worlds**

About Packt Publishing

Packt, pronounced 'packed', published its first book "*Mastering phpMyAdmin for Effective MySQL Management*" in April 2004 and subsequently continued to specialize in publishing highly focused books on specific technologies and solutions.

Our books and publications share the experiences of your fellow IT professionals in adapting and customizing today's systems, applications, and frameworks. Our solution based books give you the knowledge and power to customize the software and technologies you're using to get the job done. Packt books are more specific and less general than the IT books you have seen in the past. Our unique business model allows us to bring you more focused information, giving you more of what you need to know, and less of what you don't.

Packt is a modern, yet unique publishing company, which focuses on producing quality, cutting-edge books for communities of developers, administrators, and newbies alike. For more information, please visit our website: www.packtpub.com.

Writing for Packt

We welcome all inquiries from people who are interested in authoring. Book proposals should be sent to author@packtpub.com. If your book idea is still at an early stage and you would like to discuss it first before writing a formal book proposal, contact us; one of our commissioning editors will get in touch with you.

We're not just looking for published authors; if you have strong technical skills but no writing experience, our experienced editors can help you develop a writing career, or simply get some additional reward for your expertise.

Flash 10 Multiplayer Game Essentials

ISBN: 978-1-847196-60-6   Paperback: 336 pages

Create exciting real-time multiplayer games using Flash

1. A complete end-to-end guide for creating fully featured multiplayer games

2. The author's experience in the gaming industry enables him to share insights on multiplayer game development

3. Walk-though several real-time multiplayer game implementations

WordPress and Flash 10x Cookbook

ISBN: 978-1-847198-82-2   Paperback: 268 pages

Over 50 simple but incredibly effective recipes to take control of dynamic Flash content in Wordpress

1. Learn how to make your WordPress blog or website stand out with Flash

2. Embed, encode, and distribute your video content in your Wordpress site or blog

3. Build your own .swf files using various plugins

4. Develop your own Flash audio player using audio and podcasting plugins

Please check **www.PacktPub.com** for information on our titles